June 26 - 98   To the Prince Family
Hope you enjoy - We found it
informative + know the Author -
Kindest Regards
Rita & Gil

DOWNTOWN SPOKANE IMAGES,

1930 - 1949

Looking north on Howard Street, 1941. *(Eastern Washington State Historical Society, Spokane, Washington, L85-143.164)*

DOWNTOWN SPOKANE IMAGES,

1930-1949

CAROLYN HAGE NUNEMAKER

Graphic design and lay-out by Jan Nunemaker

Printed by National Color Graphics, Spokane, Washington

DOWNTOWN SPOKANE IMAGES, 1930-1949

CONTENTS

ACKNOWLEDGEMENTS

Nancy Gale Compau, Historian in the Northwest Room of the Spokane Public Library, deserves special recognition. She gave me ideas, assistance, and encouragement from my beginning research to the final draft. She took on the task of editing the manuscript, spending hours of her own time. Without her this book would not be what it is, and I will always be grateful to her.

I also acknowledge assistance from the following people: Laura Arksey, Curator of Special Collections, retired, Eastern Washington State Historical Society; Karen DeSeve, Curator of Special Collections, Eastern Washington State Historical Society; Sharon Prendergast, Special Collections Assistant, Ralph E. and Helen Higgins Foley Center, Gonzaga University; Staff of the Spokane Public Library; Inland Empire Railway Historical Society; and many people who have generously given their time, stories, knowledge, and pictures. Many photographs, especially those by Charles Libby, Wallace Gamble and other photographers helped my memory and provided me with information.

I also thank the following family members: John Nunemaker, Ingrid Holmlund, Marianna Stensager, Gene Stensager, Jan Nunemaker, Lars Olsson, Steve Walker, Kristine Walker, Blake Walker, and Karina Walker.

INDIVIDUALS INTERVIEWED, 1992 to 1997

Ed Antosyn, former Chief Engineer at KFIO, and former Broadcast Engineer at KREM and at KNEW

Robert Armstrong, longtime Spokane musician

Frank Bates, General Manager, American Linen Supply Company

Darlene Pappas Compton, daughter of one of the owners of George's Coney Island

Jim Delegans, Jr., renovator of the old City Hall

Don Eagle, musician at the Garden Ballroom and at KGA and KHQ

Lou Farline, Assistant Superintendent of Construction, Trentwood Plant; employee, Mead Plant, 1941 to end of WWII

Sophia Gerkensmeyer, Davenport Candy Factory employee; interviewed through her niece, Carol Measel

Gerald Hartley, musician at KHQ and son of Fred Hartley, musician at The Davenport and at KHQ

Shirley Curtis Hawkins, vocalist at KGA

Jim Haynes, retired Spokane policeman

Gilbert Heggemeier, recruit at Farragut, and later on permanent duty there

Carole Cooke Jones, daughter of the owners of Cooke's Nut Shop

Harry Jones, former Vice President of the Old National Bank

John Luppert, musician at the Italian Gardens, Davenport Hotel

Edith Meeker, longtime Spokane resident

Robert Peters, former owner of Peters and Sons

Jim Read, retired Spokane policeman

John Reed, longtime employee of The Davenport Hotel

Earl Rogers, Glen Dow Academy of Hair Design, retired

Eleanor Anderson Schafer, clerk at Wraight's dime store

Betty Schnabel, Secretary for Army Air Force officer, WWII

Michael Smith, Manager of The Met Theater, 1997

Don and Lillian Sperry, longtime Spokane residents

Damien Thompson, employee for Fox Theater

Norm Thue, musician at Liberty and Orpheum theaters, and at KHQ and KFPY radio stations

Lee Tillotson, Member, Inland Empire Railway Historical Society

Della Travo, owner of the Aster, Outside-Inn, and Travo's

Helen Turner, longtime Spokane resident

Steve Walker, renovator of Carnegie Library

Jim Wallrabinstein, Member, American Theater Organ Society

John Warn, former shoe store owner

Sue Nikotich Weipert, Usherette at the Fox theater

James M. White, Usher at the Orpheum theater

Arthur Zepp, musician at The Davenport Hotel, and Music Director at KHQ and KFPY radio stations

HOW THIS BOOK
CAME INTO BEING

Our Spokane roots are deep. Both my parents, and my sister and I were born and raised here. My mother was born in a house that still exists on Thirteenth Avenue. Near the east end of Spokane Falls Boulevard there was a house in which my father was born, but it is now gone.

In 1889, my grandparents on my father's side, immigrants from Norway, came as a young couple to Spokane. They arrived immediately after the Spokane Fire because they thought there would be work in Spokane and, sure enough, my grandfather found work as a carpenter. He worked at that for several years. Later he became a policeman and was on the Spokane police force from 1903 until 1924, when he retired. We still have his "keystone cop" police helmet, his long, fitted, and gold buttoned jacket, a handcuff—an old style single cuff with an extension for the policeman to hold—and two of his police badges. He was a city jailer during part of that time.

Around 1903, my grandparents on my mother's side arrived in Spokane from Missouri, via a few years in Ritzville. This grandfather was a minister, and early in my mother's life he was assigned to churches in several different communities near Spokane. So my mother, while born in Spokane, lived in such places as Deep Creek, and Harrison, Idaho, until they returned to Spokane permanently when she was eight years old.

My father was in the army in World War I, and within a few days of arriving at the Front in France, was wounded by shrapnel and suffered some hearing loss from exploding shells. Returning to Spokane after the war, he studied accounting at Kinman Business University where he met my mother.

I was born at the old St. Luke's Hospital on the west side of Spokane and grew up in the Gonzaga neighborhood. My schooling was in the public schools—Stevens Elementary and Rogers High School.

Most Spokanites spent a lot of time downtown in those days, but I believe I spent more time there than most people. The reasons were many and ranged from kindergarten to working in my father's office. The public schools had no kindergartens in the 1930s so I went to a musical kindergarten in the Norfolk Building. I took piano and violin lessons in the Radio Central Building and later in the Norfolk Building and played in a number of piano and violin recitals in the YWCA Building and the Radio Central Building.

My father's accounting practice was located in the Mohawk Building. My mother worked with him part of the time and they worked long hours at certain times of the year. At those times, particularly after my sister was married and away, I would go downtown after school and stay in the office with them, sometimes into the evening. During the income tax season and at the time of other tax deadlines, we frequently had dinner in one of the restaurants downtown.

Sometimes I went for a walk and bought a good-sized bag of popcorn for a nickel at the window of a restaurant that was near the Orpheum theater. Often I'd run errands or go to the dime stores. The majority of our shopping for clothes, shoes and other necessities was downtown. On Saturdays an aunt often took my sister and me to a movie and afterwards to dinner in a downtown restaurant.

During my elementary school years, I attended summer music classes at Lewis and Clark High School, walking along Howard Street to and from the bus on Riverside Avenue. During one or two summers I went to day camp at the YWCA when it was located on Main and Monroe facing the Lincoln statue. While I was in high school, I was in a number of music groups that frequently performed downtown. These performances would take place in The Davenport Hotel, in the Masonic Temple, at Kiwanis or Chamber of Commerce lunches.

In high school, I played violin in the Spokane Philharmonic Orchestra, and in the Junior Symphony (now the Spokane Youth Symphony) in 1949, the year it was organized, and was its first Concertmaster. These groups rehearsed and performed in the American Legion Hall, in the Armory when large choral groups were involved, in the Post theater, in the KXLY Studio in the Symons Building, and in the Masonic Temple. My senior piano recital was in the auditorium of the Norfolk Building.

Years later I have realized that the time I spent in the downtown area in those days made me grow to love it and the memories of it. It now seems such a precious time and place that I felt the need to try to recapture it for myself and for others, and also to recall what life was like in those days. Some of this is based on research, some on memory.

Some memories come from my sister, her husband, and from my husband, who remember some things that I do not. Interviews with other people, many by telephone, added personal recollections. It is hoped that these personal memories will help readers recall their own downtown.

Memory may have played some tricks, but we have done our best to remember it faithfully. Occasionally it was difficult for people to recall the time period in which something occurred, but it was often possible to check this. In any case, most of what is here is within the 1930s and 1940s. Some of the writing from those days seems quaint today. In the following pages, many quotations from newspapers are used simply to add the flavor of that time through the language. Even the ads often used a different style.

For those of us who knew our old downtown, to imagine returning to it is a sentimental journey that is warm, sweet, and tender. For those who cannot remember this time in Spokane, perhaps these pages will bring it to life.

INTRODUCTION

To anyone who lived through the '30s and '40s, the two things that stand out most significantly from that time are the Great Depression and World War II. It is striking to recall the high and low extremes in the economy during that twenty year period. The effects of the Depression lasted until the economic boom of World War II. The postwar period was precarious because there weren't enough jobs for all the returning veterans, but the needs of veterans and their new families—housing, schooling, civilian clothing, cars, housewares, and baby supplies—helped create jobs and a period of prosperity.

THE DEPRESSION IN SPOKANE

The Depression in the early '30s affected most of Spokane's population in some way. During this time, one out of four Spokane workers was without a job, including many who headed families.[1] Though some families lived comfortably through the depression in Spokane, I personally knew of people who suffered from malnutrition, though they kept this to themselves until years later. For a family with limited or no income it was a time of extreme anxiety. Even if the breadwinner had a job or was able to keep a business going, there was nagging fear that it might be lost.

Edith Meeker, longtime Spokane resident, recalls two incidents that illustrate what it was like for those who had low paying jobs or were unemployed. Mrs. Meeker worked at one of the newspapers in the '30s. A family man who helped distribute newspapers to the downtown newsboys was having trouble making it financially. His wife came to the newspaper office and complained to Mrs. Meeker: "I can't buy milk for my babies on $5 a week!"

Mrs. Meeker also remembers an article at the time that told about a group of men who were lined up waiting for a chance to work. A man fainted and other men looked through his things trying to identify him. They found that he had brought only potato peelings to eat in his lunchbox.

In 1933, there were 132 candidates for the paid job of City Commissioner, probably an indication that the Depression was especially grim then.[2] Want-ads in *The Spokesman-Review* from 1929 through 1939 seem to show that 1933 and 1934 were the lowest times in Spokane. Almost no "help wanted" advertisements are found in these two years while many ads under "Labor for Necessities" offer work in exchange for food, fuel, wood, clothes, and housing. Even vegetables were asked for in one ad. The newspaper accepted ads free of charge under the heading of "Unemployment Relief" and the tone of many of these ads is desperate. Some examples are: "Man with family will do any kind of work..." or "Family man needs work immediately..." or "Young man, well educated: Can do hard work, wife: 2 children..." and another, "Machinist and auto mechanic will do anything for groceries or clothing."

Food being essential, some workers kept jobs because much of the local economy was centered in agriculture. Though construction projects fell drastically from 1930 to 1932, building construction did not come to a complete halt. Buildings constructed include the Sears-Roebuck Building, the Spokane Civic Building/Chamber of Commerce headquarters in 1930; the Fox theater, the Spokane and Eastern Trust Building, and Kress Dime Store Building in 1931; additions and modernizing of breweries at the end of prohibition in 1933; the Rookery Building and the Pratt Furniture Building in 1934. Other buildings outside the downtown area were a new Masonic Temple in Hillyard and True's Oil Company offices on Hamilton Street in 1930, and Rogers High School in 1931 after an affirmative school bond vote in 1930.[3]

The Depression may have been somewhat shorter here than in other parts of the country. The economic problems started in the east and spread west. When the Depression began to subside in the east, people in the west gained confidence, knowing that it was coming to an end. Business people here gradually began making investments in the future, hiring employees, and expanding their businesses in other ways.

A personal story of the experiences of a well-known musician suggests that Spokane was slowly beginning to climb out of the Depression by the end of 1934. Arthur Zepp drove to Spokane from Chicago in his Model-A Ford in October, 1934. He recalls: "It was difficult to find work in Chicago as the Depression there was very severe." Zepp had heard from his brother-in-law, who lived in Spokane, that things were better in this part of the country. His intention was to check out Spokane, then Seattle, and Portland.

Zepp arrived in Spokane first, liked it, and decided to stay. He had tried selling pianos in Chicago, but almost nobody had money for such an expensive instrument; he also worked in a grocery store. After he arrived in Spokane, he found that jobs were easier to get here, and by January, 1935, Zepp was working at Welch's Market, located at W. 708-10 Main, across from The Crescent. "I was astonished to see people come into the store and buy as many as a dozen oranges and other food in large quantities. People in Chicago had not been spending money so freely."

GOVERNMENT AID IN SPOKANE

As unemployment figures rose, the federal government began instituting programs to help. The kind of aid we now call welfare was then referred to as being "on relief." The numbers of people receiving such aid climbed each year to a peak of 9,346 in 1937.[4] By 1939, the number dropped to half of that; this was out of a Spokane population of about 122,000.[5]

WPA

With the election of Franklin D. Roosevelt, the government began its New Deal programs. The WPA, or Works Progress Administration, was one of the federally funded government agencies that offered jobs for the unemployed. Many people in Spokane County found work through the agency. The central office for the WPA was first in an old school building, but later moved to the former Federal Land Bank Building on the southeast corner of Third and Monroe. This building became the headquarters for all WPA projects in eastern Washington.

In its early days, the WPA employed 1,100 family men, each man working a two-day shift per week.[6] From 1935 through 1938, WPA projects in Spokane County totaled nearly $9 million and included the creation of scenic High Drive, Rutter Parkway along the Little Spokane, and work on the Sunset and Inland Empire highways, the city paying for 25% of the latter project.[7] By 1940, a hundred miles of city streets had been leveled and graded, WPA hand labor had dug most of the sewers on the south side, and twenty miles of water mains had been installed.[8] Felts Field was leveled, repairs were made on school buildings, and school desks were resurfaced.[9] Men worked on a new grandstand at Playfair and installed a sprinkler system and planted grass at Fort Wright.[10]

Another federally sponsored program, the Civilian Conservation Corps (CCC) employed young workers who were brought in from all over the country to build roadways along both sides of the Spokane River in the Downriver area; they built countless campgrounds, picnic areas, and roads throughout the region. Working in the WPA headquarters, three hundred women workers made dresses, children's clothes, work shirts, blankets, and "comforts" from worn-out CCC shirts and trousers.[11]

A large and significant federal program in the area was the construction, begun in 1933, of Coulee Dam; it would provide inexpensive electricity and irrigate the Columbia Basin. One of the most important projects of the Twentieth Century, it provided jobs for thousands of people and was a major factor in helping the area economically beginning in 1933. Spokane proudly called itself the gateway to the Grand Coulee Dam, "Greatest Man-Made Structure in the World." Many men lived and worked at the Coulee Dam site during the week, coming back to Spokane and their families on weekends. Clearing the land alone provided work for 4,000 WPA workers for over three years.[12]

Not all of the work done by the WPA was physical labor. One valuable task was that of indexing *The Spokesman-Review* newspaper from 1887 to 1920. Another WPA project was the Spokane Art Center which opened in 1938 at N. 106 Monroe. This center offered free classes to both children and adults, with instruction given by talented, trained artists, some of whom were brought here from the East. The center also had a gallery which displayed a wide variety of exhibits of both local and internationally known artists. The exhibits included works of oil paintings, tapestry, sculpture, Indian art, watercolors, mosaics, American design, and photography. Each Wednesday night a talk on one of the arts was given at the center.[13]

Recreational classes taught through WPA were harmonica playing, bicycle riding, drawing, painting, and tap dancing.[14] Tap dancing classes were very popular; 1,250 people of all ages enrolled in 1937.[15] In 1938 and 1939, 18,941 people attended the tap dancing classes![16]

Though it was announced in 1939 that WPA projects would be discontinued, some of the work continued. In 1940, WPA workers did the initial clearing of land for Geiger Field, leveled and graded one hundred miles of city streets, and improved city park drives, tennis courts, and baseball fields.[17] While unemployment decreased steadily in 1940, there were still enough WPA workers that the federal government set up a food stamp program for them.[18]

OTHER WAYS IN WHICH PEOPLE COPED

From major needs such as shelter to the smallest items, people found imaginative ways to get along during the Depression. One family I knew rented their house to another family, moved to a smaller rental house, and in this way felt less financial pressure. Some people raised vegetables and chickens in town if there was enough space in their yards. Although a quart of milk was as low as 8¢ and a loaf of bread 6¢, to afford these basic items some people were innovative with other things, finding ways to "make do." Cardboard, cut to match the inside sole and inserted

in a shoe to cover a hole, saved the cost of shoe repair. Clothes were patched; bags from flour, which was sold in 100 pound cloth sacks, were made into clothing. People ate certain kinds of cereal or bought a particular brand of soap because a cup, plate, or other dish was in the box and a set of the dishes could be collected this way. It was a time of "make do, or do without."

Throughout the Depression, many organizations took part in solving problems. In 1932, the Kiwanis Club opened a Health Center for underprivileged children. Doctors selected 125 boys and girls who needed this care most, but more than 2,000 other children between the ages of eight and twelve were also given care.[19] By October that same year, there were soup lines near downtown Spokane for hungry people. The Salvation Army, Volunteers of America, and Sacred Heart Hospital all fed a number of unemployed people daily.[20] The Junior League of Spokane collected clothing and bedding that year for emergency relief.[21]

In 1932, the city closed its Manito Park Zoo to save an annual cost of $3,000.[22] Over 380 street lights were not lighted at night for an additional savings.[23] City employees, teachers, and plumbers all made voluntary reductions in their salaries.[24]

Transients often came to our back door asking for a meal during these years. This happened all over town, but we happened to live across Mission Park from the Great Northern tracks. The men found it easy to jump off the train in that area because the trains slowed as they neared downtown. Sometimes these men would do a little yard work in exchange for food, but most of the time my parents simply gave them a plateful of whatever we were having or some leftovers. They ate their meal in the yard. It was rumored that houses at which people were fed were marked in some way.

Shortly after the beginning of the Depression, transients began finding shelter in the old Schade Brewery, at 538 E. Trent, which had been abandoned because of Prohibition.

Several charities began feeding men and furnishing cots for sleeping there. The operation was later controlled somewhat by the city health department.[25] The building was dubbed "Hotel DeGink," gink being a slang term for an odd man or boy. The operation was discontinued when Prohibition was repealed and the Golden Age Brewery began brewing beer in the building. With this shelter gone, another was needed, so in 1934,

Men form a soup line in the snow at the transient quarters of Hotel DeGink. *(Eastern Washington State Historical Society, Spokane, Washington, L93-18.62*

a federal transient hotel service started at N. 210 Bernard, providing lodging, medical care, food, and a tailor, presumably to mend clothes.

Though there had been few working mothers until this time, many of them were forced to work to try to ease family financial problems. In 1935, nursery schools were opened at Emerson and Arlington Elementary schools to care for the children of working mothers.[26]

Dr. David Cowen and his crew of dentists would trade just about anything for dental work during the Depression. People would line up with items such as garden vegetables, chickens, firewood, or home canned foods, and wait their turn to exchange them for time in a dentist's chair.[27]

BANKS: SOME SOLVENT, SOME FAILING

Almost half of Spokane's banks closed between 1929 and the mid- '30s. Of 20 banks listed in the Polk City Directory in 1929, only 14 were listed in 1930. Still another was gone by 1931. The First National Bank of Seattle took over the Spokane and Eastern Trust Company Bank in 1935.[28] The Farmers and Mechanics Bank closed

on November 23, 1931. The years 1933 through 1937 show eleven and sometimes twelve banks.

The Exchange National Bank, (located on the northwest corner of Howard and Riverside) closed January 18, 1929. Its failure apparently stimulated D.W. Twohy, chairman of the board of the Old National Bank and Union Trust Company, to lead in the purchase of the Exchange and other banks; mergers with First National Trust and Savings Bank of Spokane and twenty other banks in eastern Washington and northern Idaho were accomplished. These purchases and mergers, transpiring before the stock market crash, formed the Old National Corporation. The year 1929 had been one of great progress for the Old National Bank.[29]

Spokane saw no immediate financial problems in 1929 or 1930; but 1931 was a difficult year for all banks in the country. By 1932, the Old National and other Spokane banks were at the lowest point since World War I.[30]

Mable Wahlstrom worked at Spokane Savings at W. 713 Sprague when it failed: "One of the directors of the bank, Alex Turnbill...stood on the balcony of the beautiful bank that isn't any more and announced that they would be getting their money. [Later, the amount] went down to $200, then $150, then $100, so everybody could get something. Then $50...Those were horrible days...People were panicking, naturally, and the workers were panicky, too...It's surprising what people will tell you across the counter thinking it was your fault that the bank failed...I remember the lines were just long in front of every bank in town as far as that goes."[31]

Margaret Westmore: "American Bank...do any of you remember it, you Scandinavians? It was the first bank to close here in Spokane. If you were Scandinavian your money was in that bank...That was the first one; it was kitty-corner from the Davenport Hotel. We all got our money back, but the American Bank was hard hit."[32]

Harry Jones, formerly with the Old National Bank and Union Trust Company, began to work there in the '20s as a messenger in the mail department. As the Depression became more critical, some bank employees were fired. One man presented people with pink slips and Jones knew "if we got out the door on Fridays without being stopped by this man, we had a job for another week."

"Many customers withdrew money that was in their checking and savings accounts. In order to supply the money, some of the notes of the Old National Bank were sold to the Spokane Branch of the Federal Reserve Bank," located then in the Auditorium Building, on the northwest corner of Main and Post.

To stabilize the "run" on the banks, Governor Clarence D. Martin issued an edict that all banks in the state of Washington would be closed from midnight March 2, 1933 through March 6. Margaret Westmore's sister was working at the Old National Bank and "she came home one day...she had the longest face...She thought she'd never get back in the bank again. They did open again."[33]

On March 6th, President Roosevelt ordered a "Bank Holiday"—the closure of all banks in the United States. Many banks reopened in about five days with banking continuing as usual. Being short of funds, the Old National Bank was unable to continue regular banking; but they accepted money in "Trust Accounts" with the understanding that the money would be held, but not lent. Money in other accounts was not released.

Meanwhile, negotiations were proceeding with federal authorities to re-open the bank for normal business. After seven months, the Old National and its affiliate banks began regular business again on October 9, 1933, by releasing 40% of original deposits, and retaining 60% until bank loans and other assets were liquidated.

When regular banking was resumed that day, the bank was prepared to distribute a large amount of cash. Stacks of currency over a foot high in all denominations were ready at each teller's cage. Some customers, seeing the piles of money, were reassured and left the bank without withdrawing their deposits. Much to the surprise of bank employees, by the end of the day, there were still stacks of cash left. More deposits had been made than money withdrawn. Jones said, "As time went on, the Old National Bank prospered. By the late '30s, 100% of the money, plus interest, was returned to the depositors."[34]

THE DEPRESSION SUBSIDES

By the end of the '30s the Depression was declining. Spokane's Chamber of Commerce successfully promoted increased military spending here, which aided the local economy. The beginning of World War II in 1941 gave a further boost to Spokane's economy. A study made at Washington State College showed: "Department store sales, bank debits, postal receipts and man-hours of employment were all considerably higher [in Spokane] in 1943 than in 1940. The most rapid increase occurred in 1942...Total employment in Spokane County increased from 59,093 in March 1940 to approximately 76,700 in September 1942, almost 30 percent above the March 1940 level."[35] By 1947, payrolls in Spokane were three times what they had been in 1940.[36]

WAGES THROUGH THIS TWENTY YEAR PERIOD

During the Depression wages were low. Edith Meeker recalls a young girl she knew who supported her family on $11 a week in the early '30s. The minimum wage was first set by Congress at 25¢ an hour in 1938. By the beginning of 1949, it was only 40¢ an hour, but was raised that year to 75¢.

High salaries were made public information by Congress in 1936. Salaries of the president and secretary-treasurer of some Spokane companies and banks were published in *The Spokesman-Review* under the heading of "Big Salaries Drawn by Nine Spokane Men." These ranged from $16,368 per year to a high of $39,166.[37]

John Luppert, when hired as a musician in a band that played in the Italian Gardens of The Davenport Hotel in 1937, was paid "the then princely sum of twenty-five dollars a week...got married on the strength of that salary, and we lived very well on it."[38] In 1942, School District #81 hired John Shaw to be assistant superintendent of schools for $4,800 a year.[39] That same year my husband was paid $120 a month for a summer job making photostat copies for a government agency.

In 1946, my sister Marianna worked as a clerk at Roy Goodman's music store and earned $25 a week, working eight hours a day Monday through Saturday. After a year she was given a raise to $29. Her husband worked there for a short time after the war and was automatically paid more because he was a man. John W. Graham paid 75¢ an hour in 1946 to its warehousemen.[40]

Prices were controlled by the government during the war and early postwar days. The prices of restaurant meals, clothing, and other items that are found in the following pages reflect the difference in prices and wages compared to today.

Bustling sidewalk scenes crowd my memories of downtown Spokane in the mid-'40s. Throughout much of the day, the streets were alive with shoppers, office workers, bankers, shop clerks, waitresses, stock traders from the Spokane Stock Exchange, typists, secretaries, doctors, dentists, nurses, and people hurrying to restaurants, theaters, and busses. People shopped in numerous downtown food markets. They attended radio programs produced in downtown studios. Most of the city's stores and other businesses were in the central area. Nearly every office building was filled.

Howard and Riverside was the hub of life. Here we saw the heaviest traffic, often a crush of people, and many kinds of activity. Walking on a crowded corner there on a warm summer day, I saw a young woman dressed as a majorette coming toward me. She wore a big smile that was enhanced by bright red lipstick. As she threaded her way through the crowd, she passed out individually wrapped pieces of Dentyne Gum, repeating over and over their slogan, "Keeps the teeth white!"

A street photographer from Joyner's drug store stood nearby taking pictures of individuals as they passed. The photographer would snap the picture, then give the person a paper tag on which there was a number. The person could go into Joyner's later, look at the picture, and buy it. The pictures weren't very good, but it got people into the store. The '30s and '40s were the last days that a few horse drawn delivery wagons were seen on the streets of Spokane. I dimly remember seeing at least one on Trent Avenue (Spokane Falls Boulevard) just west of Division, possibly a milk delivery or beer wagon with two horses. Orville Pratt, in his book that chronicles items from newspapers of earlier days, says that in 1942, "the last two horses used in delivering mail to the postoffice were replaced by motor trucks."[1]

It was a time when we heard the sounds of the "newsboys," often grown men, each on his way to "his own" corner. As they waved the latest edition of *The Spokesman-Review*, the *Spokane Daily Chronicle*, or *The Spokane Press* (the *Press* was a daily afternoon paper that was in business from 1902 to 1939) we would hear the "boys" call out the day's headlines: "EIGHT PERSONS ARE BURNED BY CAVALCADE FIREWORKS." "READ ALL a-BOUT it!"[2] Often if there was unusual news, the papers would put out an "extra," an additional edition to the regular ones. Then they would call: "EXTRA! EXTRA!"

Early in this period when radio was quite new, newspapers were still the main source of news. Newsboys were occasionally still coming into the neighborhoods—sometimes even in the middle of the night—hollering the headlines. My sister remembers their coming to our neighborhood once when she was very small. It would have been in the '30s.

Red, white, and blue banners were strung on lines high across the streets on patriotic holidays. On special occasions, usually parade days, street flags on wooden poles were inserted in holes near the edges of the curbs.

These were the last days when we saw Civil War soldiers marching or riding in parades. The parades would begin with many units of military men, mostly from Fort Wright. It was quiet except for the distinctive and unforgettable sound of the marchers' shoes on the street as we stood watching. Then came veterans, first a large group that had been in World War I. Following these came veterans from the Spanish American War. Finally there came a few old soldiers who had served in the Civil War. I remember seeing these old soldiers one Armistice Day (now known as Veterans Day), though I was only six or seven years old.

Newspapers from that time tell about the

Pictures of my parents taken in front of the Kuhn Building by Joyner's street photographer. My mother is hatless as she often was when she had been working.

Armistice Day parades in 1938 and 1939, some seventy-three years after the Civil War had ended. In 1938: "under the Stars and Stripes that reached from one end of the parade to the other, with 1000 flags massed in one block[!], the history of America was symbolized from the Civil War to the World war. But two Civil war veterans braved the frosty morning, C.W. Corwin, 95...and C.A. Whaley, 91..."; and in 1939: "The five Spokane survivors of the Civil war rode in cars...But the Spanish war veterans still marched, bent and graying men, who laid down their arms 40 years ago."[3]

These were days the first traffic lights appeared in Spokane. In January 1930, three of the new lights had been in place for only two months. They were all on Riverside—one at Howard, one at Washington, and the other at Post.[4] Lights at

twelve more intersections were installed downtown later that year.[5] In the entire city there were only twenty-six traffic lights in 1935.[6]

A highpitched jangling bell rang for several seconds when the light was about to change color. It would ring again as the light actually did change. Only red and green lights were used for most of this time; a few amber lights came into use late in the period.

In winter, excess steam rose from manholes in the streets as heat moved from the Central Heating Plant to nearly every building in the city's center. There were no one way streets downtown. The first days of downtown's parking meters were in the early '40s. They were installed late in 1941, and first used early in 1942.[7]

These were the days when policemen walked a "beat." In the daytime the policemen would usually be working alone, but if it was during the graveyard shift, and in skid row, they worked in pairs. We might see a paddy wagon going by; this was a police van that was used to haul people to jail.[8]

Looking west on Main Avenue from Wall Street. Photographed in 1931, traffic lights have not yet been installed here. A newsboy crosses the street in the foreground. Note street railway tracks and people wearing hats. *(Eastern Washington State Historical Society, Spokane, Washington, L87-1.76-31)*

Young men on bicycles rode out to deliver telegrams from Western Union. They wore dark uniforms, and hats with a military style brim. Telegrams were used more extensively than long distance telephones, and were hand delivered. People often assumed when receiving a telegram that it brought bad news. Perhaps to dispel this image, Western Union conceived the idea of the "singing telegram" in 1933. The telegraph delivery boys came most often from the main telegraph office on the north side of Sprague, at West 808, where there were racks to accommodate the numerous bicycles. From 1935 through 1945 there were six to eight downtown locations of Western Union.

We saw some odd vehicles downtown in those days. We might see a tall, white, rectangular delivery truck that made almost no sound. It was one of the electric trucks of the Spokane Toilet Supply, delivering linens and towels to businesses. It was almost eerily quiet except for the sound of its large drive chain. Like a giant bicycle chain, it made a quiet purring sound along with a clicking of the links as they passed over the sprocket. We were so accustomed to seeing these vehicles that we paid little attention to them. A fleet of 15 to 20 of the trucks was used, according to Frank Bates, General Manager of American Linen Supply Company, successor of the Spokane Toilet Supply.

Though it was a rare sight, we might also see the erect figure of Mrs. Agnes McDonald in her shiny black 1916 Rauch and Lang electric car driving through the streets. She appeared to be

A truck from the Spokane Toilet Supply with old fashioned solid tires and thick wooden spokes. Soiled linens were thrown in the cargo rack on top and carried back to the company. *(Eastern Washington State Historical Society, Spokane, Washington, Detail of photo L85-258)*

tall as she sat in her black hat in this imposingly high automobile. She seemed to be maneuvering the control stick from the back seat, as the driver's seat was toward the rear of the car. This elevated, rectangular automobile, with its three large side windows and center side doors, each with a hanging shiny silver handle, was shaped more like a stagecoach than the cars of today. During World War II, because of gas rationing, Mrs. McDonald had a number of offers from people who wanted to buy the car.[9] In 1952, Mrs. McDonald gave the car to the Cheney Cowles Museum, W. 2316 First Avenue, where it is on display.

The first days of neon signs downtown were in the early '30s, as the initial neon sign in Spokane had been installed at the RKO-Orpheum theater in 1929.[10] Neon would be commonly used by the end of the '40s.

We saw many lighted signs at night. Not only was there color from neon signs in such stores as Joyner's, Owen Specialty Shop, and Leed's Shoes, but often the name was surrounded by lighted bulbs. Many theater marquees had resplendent flashing white bulbs, like glistening diamonds.

From Main between Post and Lincoln we could look over the roof tops and see a lighted "Reddy Kilowatt," a stick figure that was a symbol of electricity, running happily across the top of the Washington Water Power Building. Several red neon "Reddys" lit up in sequence, giving the appearance that he was running. Reddy's arms, legs, and body resembled streaks of lightning. He had a round head, a friendly smiling face, a socket for an ear, and a lightbulb for a nose.

A sign on the southwest corner of Riverside and Wall said, "Dr. David Cowen, Peerless, Painless Dentist." A neon sign on the south side of Riverside near Howard was that of Binyon Optometrists. It was a huge pair of rimless glasses, the stylish glasses of the '30s.

High above the streets was a sign that few of us knew about. Painted on the roof of the Old National Bank Building was a huge arrow that pointed northeast, along with the words "SPOKANE AIR PORT" in large block letters. The arrow was aimed at Felts Field, our airport until post war days.[11] Imagine planes flying so low over the city center that pilots could see this sign.

Other signs were painted on the bricks of the backs and sides of some of the buildings. A rectangular block on the east side of the Ziegler Building showed a profile of a bald man with a dark fringe of hair and a trimmed dark beard. Above this picture was: "Henry George, 5¢ Cigar." If the idea of a five-cent cigar didn't lure you, surely the picture of this bald man would do it. On the west side of the Norfolk Building was a sign that featured a large grand piano, and proclaimed, "Hoffman Bros. Music Company, Home of the Kimball." Painted on the Bon Marche in the late '40s was a sign that covered nearly the entire building: "Let's Visit the Bon Marche at Main and Howard, Spokane's smart new store."

We could watch boots and shoes being made at White's Shoe Shop (White's Boots), located on the northeast corner at Main and Stevens. A series of windows on both the front and side of the building allowed passersby to see craftsmen working on this well-known footwear. The company had begun business at this location about 1920.

Window gazing was also common through the immense windows of the Chronicle Building on the northeast corner of Sprague and Monroe. Here we watched the presses printing the *Chronicle* and *Spokesman-Review*. People overseeing the area worked matter-of-factly while those of us who were outside shook our heads in disbelief as the huge machines raced at tremendous speeds to print, cut, fold and stack the papers.

Next to the Spokesman-Review Building on Riverside stood a wood carved figure on the sidewalk. It was in front of a cigar store called "The Chief," but the place was known as "the Poor Man's Press club" by newspaper workers, as it was a hangout for newspaper men. Standing at the entrance of the shop was a life-sized, painted wooden Indian in brightly colored full headdress. The figure's right hand was above its eyes, seemingly shielding them from the sun. In the other hand it held a package of tea and a packet of cigars. This large carving was reportedly wearing authentic Iroquois war regalia. Over 100 years old in 1948, it had come from New York in the 1890s when it was 50 years old.[12]

Deliveries were made to many stores through freight elevators that hid under metal covers in the sidewalks. The closed square of metal made a slight rattle when we walked on it. Why it didn't collapse from our weight is a mystery. Basements in these stores extended under the sidewalks out to the streets. Light was provided through small square glass bricks of a purplish color that were in large rectangular areas in the sidewalk.

In the early '30s, we would still see streetcars. After the street railways were gone, we could see their tracks throughout the downtown area for a long time, but they were gradually covered over or dug up. Bus styles changed through this period, going from rather short busses to much longer ones. I particularly remember those from the late '40s that were silver-colored and had a red stripe painted just below the window level.

Spokane was a railroad center with five major lines going in and out of town. The lines were: 1)The Chicago, Milwaukee, St. Paul and Pacific Railroad Company, commonly called The Milwaukee Road; 2)The Great Northern Railway; 3)The Northern Pacific Railway Company; 4)The Union Pacific Railroad; and 5)Spokane, Portland and Seattle Railway Company, or the S.P. and S. There were also the Spokane International Railway, or the S.I., which went to Canada, and various smaller lines that went to regional places, such as south to the Palouse area.

Downtown was defined on the north and south by its elevated tracks. We could look north on Stevens, Howard, and Wall Streets and see huge lighted block letters above the streets on the elevated tracks that read: "UNION STATION," and below this, varying a little on each street: "The Milwaukee Road," "Union Pacific," or: "S.I.R.R."

In 1930, sixty-eight passenger trains and about the same number of freight trains went through Spokane every day.[13] Along Trent Avenue we would see a hustle and bustle of freight delivery and of passengers coming and going, and we would hear the sounds of trains on the elevated tracks just to the north. Perhaps we would hear the rhythmic "kabunk, kabunk, kabunk" of the wheels on the track, or hear the whistle of a train. A train could be slowly coming into the station, and we might hear the wheezing sound of the steam being released.

These were the days when many things came to us via the railroads. One of my early memories is of seeing Franklin Delano Roosevelt on the observation platform at the end of a train at the Great Northern Depot. This was probably on October 2, 1937, when he came through Spokane after a visit to Coulee Dam.

When I was about five years old, I was taken to the tracks near the station of either the Great Northern or the Union Pacific. We saw an immense preserved whale in a freight car. We walked into the car and went all the way around this mammoth creature. Its huge red-hued mouth was open so wide that I believe I could have stood inside of it. We were told that it could not swallow anything even as large as an orange, though it seemed as though it could easily have swallowed me!

A number of warehouses were positioned along the north side of Trent near Division for convenient unloading, as most of our freight came by railroad. Trains brought us circuses with all their trappings—immense circus tents with trapezes and high wires at the top of the tents, brightly painted collapsible bleacher seats, the three rings for the show, working elephants that helped set up the "big top," sideshows, and the combined smells of cotton candy, popcorn and sawdust. Sometimes caged animals, elephants, and clowns would parade through the downtown streets before going to the circus grounds.

A hum of activity took place underneath the elevated tracks on the north side of downtown in the '40s during the day. In this sheltered area young men hurried to park cars for people who were shopping or doing business downtown. The Crescent, and perhaps some other stores, paid for part of the parking time if one had the ticket from the parking area stamped at the store.

A yearly "Sportsmen's Show" focusing on hunting and fishing was held under the tracks in the '30s. A few regional animals were displayed in cages, and fish from nearby lakes were in tanks. Other highlights were there to lure viewers. An ad in *The Spokesman-Review*, May 14, 1937, states:

"See 5 Ferocious African Lions in an amazing performance at the *SPORTSMEN'S SHOW*, under Union Station viaduct, Spokane-May 17-23, 10 A.M. to 11 P.M., Children 10¢, Adults 15¢. The show of 100 striking features." My sister Marianna remembers that at one of these shows (the weather must have been cool) there was a life-sized cow on display that had been molded from butter. The Sportsmen's Show was discontinued in 1939.[14]

Trains left the north side of downtown to go west by means of two trestles. Trains leaving the Union Station went on a huge trestle that crossed over the main falls, then over the Monroe Street bridge. Trains going west from the Great Northern Depot crossed over Monroe Street just north of the bridge.

Several northbound downtown streets went under the elevated tracks, across what, at this writing, is Riverfront Park. On Howard, two bridges crossed the river, first to what was called Havermale Island, then across the north channel of the river to Crystal Island, named for the Crystal Laundry which was on the island for many years.[15] Crystal Island was renamed Canada Island during the time of EXPO. These two bridges are now footbridges. Wall Street turned just north of the tracks, then went diagonally northwest joining Post, where the two streets shared a bridge to cross the river.

Immediately north of the railroad viaduct on Washington Street, the street split into two parts, giving a choice of two bridges. A high bridge climbed steeply on the right, while a low bridge stayed just above river level on the left. Each bridge went over the south channel of the river to Havermale Island. The high east bridge went over the river, over the roof of the Great Northern Depot, then over the tracks and down to the island. When driving on this bridge, we heard a sort of kerplunking, clattering rattle, as the surface of the bridge was of somewhat loose wooden planks. The low bridge went over the river to the entrance of the Great Northern Depot. The bridges were necessarily narrow as they had originated from a single 75 foot wide street.[16]

An intercity bus station, extending from Howard to Wall Streets, was on the south side of Trent. This proximity to the railways made it easy to transfer from bus to train and vice versa. On the east end of the building was a passenger waiting area and ticket office; at the west end, across from what was then our City Hall, was a covered waiting area for busses. A new bus station was built in the West 1100 block between Sprague and First Avenues in 1949.

Downtown Spokane was becoming run-down in some places, usually close to the railroads. An indistinct, invisible line separated the core of Spokane into two areas. One had first rate and high class stores and businesses; the other was shabby, seeming dirty and inferior to the rest of the center of town. Tired looking cafes, seedy barber shops, cheap hotels and flop houses, hidden houses of prostitution, empty storefronts, taverns with signs in the windows that read: "Booths for Ladies" (Washington State had a law that women could not sit at a bar), were along much of the south side of Trent, on parts of Main, and on the east end of Riverside near Division. Transients, especially during the Depression, were common in the area. Men without jobs "rode the rods" or "the rails" traveling from place to place. They would jump off the trains downtown and spend their time on the streets.

It was not uncommon to see drunk people in these parts of town. My mother often parked our car under the elevated train tracks and would walk quickly through the area to get to the better part of town. On one particular day, Mother, who seldom had an alcoholic drink, was walking on Howard from Trent when she caught her foot on a raised place in the sidewalk, taking a bad fall. As she picked herself up, she heard a man who stood nearby remark: "Too much drink! Too much drink!"

My father, who had an accounting business, had a client who owned two hotels. One was in a respectable part of town, the other on Main, east of Washington. It began to seem doubtful that the one on Main was actually in the hotel business when it looked on the books as if individual rooms were rented out more than once on any given date. Occasionally my father had to go to this "hotel" to leave or pick up some books. Though still unsure, my parents thought it was amusing when, several times, my father left my mother waiting in the car for him while he went inside. One day my dad was surprised to find another of his clients there, a man who was the owner of a large cab company. This client looked startled when he saw my dad and exclaimed, "Why, Al! What are *you* doing here?"

2

STORES, SHOPS, AND MARKETS

What intriguing names some of the stores of the '30s and '40s had. Imagine shopping at *The Whitehouse*, or at *The Palace*. It sounds as though you had your choice of a president's or a king's residence. Early in the period, you could have shopped at *The City of Paris*. The word "box" was popular in names for stores, including *The Hat Box* from the early '30s, *The Music Box* from the late '40s, and *The Jewel Box*, which was downtown for the entire period. One charming name was *The Blue Bird Shop*, which did not sell blue birds, or birds of any color, but gifts.

Shopping in those days meant being outdoors a lot, as skywalks were an unimaginable thing of the future. The Christmas shopping season did not begin until after Thanksgiving, and then crowds would be heavy on the streets. A feeling of nostalgia would run through us as we hurried in the biting cold from store to store. On nearly every corner there were Salvation Army bell ringers, their distant sounds adding to the sweet excitement and anticipation of the holidays. Observing other shoppers, we found that most people were quite "dressed up." When women went downtown in those days, they wore dresses, coats if the weather was cold, high heeled-shoes, gloves, and usually hats. The hats, shoes, and gloves often had matching colors.

Service in the stores included amenities unheard of in later times. While trying on kid gloves, a woman would sit at a counter and put her elbow on a tiny pillow while the clerk painstakingly worked the glove onto her hand. When looking at hats, the woman sat in front of a mirror and the saleswoman brought the hats to her, stood behind her, and carefully placed and pressed the hats onto her head. Sometimes the hats were of the customer's choice; some were selected by the clerk from those on display or from the stock room. A person felt quite pampered while shopping, as salespeople in the majority of stores were very attentive.

Cash registers were not uniformly found throughout stores in the '30s. In my early memories there are stores in which baskets carried money for change from clerks to offices. Moving on wires that ran back and forth across the ceiling, the baskets went to balcony offices or to other floors through holes in the ceilings. This device, used in many early stores, had a "clickety-clickety-click" sound as the baskets swung in the air overhead. By the late '30s or early '40s these were gone. They were replaced by small brass containers that went through pneumatic tubes (larger versions were later used in drive-in banks) to carry money and change back and forth. These were used in *The Crescent* and in *Montgomery Ward*, and I believe also in *The Palace* and at *Graham's*. Toward the end of the '40s, some stores' customers began to use a "Charga-Plate," a small metal plate on which were the holder's name and address in raised letters. When charging, the plate was put on a clamping device, a handle lowered down, and the name was transferred to a charge slip.

Up-to-date elevators at that time were quite different from those of today. Sometimes there were glass doors and windows on elevators. Nearly all elevators had operators. I can think of only one elevator that was self-operated, and it was not downtown. Often the operator wore a leather glove on the hand that operated the handle of the round control. When the elevator arrived at a floor, the operator would call out information such as, "Third floor! Going up," or "Toy department. Furniture." Sometimes the "car" had to be adjusted to the floor several times before the door could be opened, as it could be difficult to make the elevator and the floor line up evenly. The ability to get it right the first time depended on the skill of the operator. Less experienced operators sometimes found it necessary

STORES, SHOPS, & MARKETS

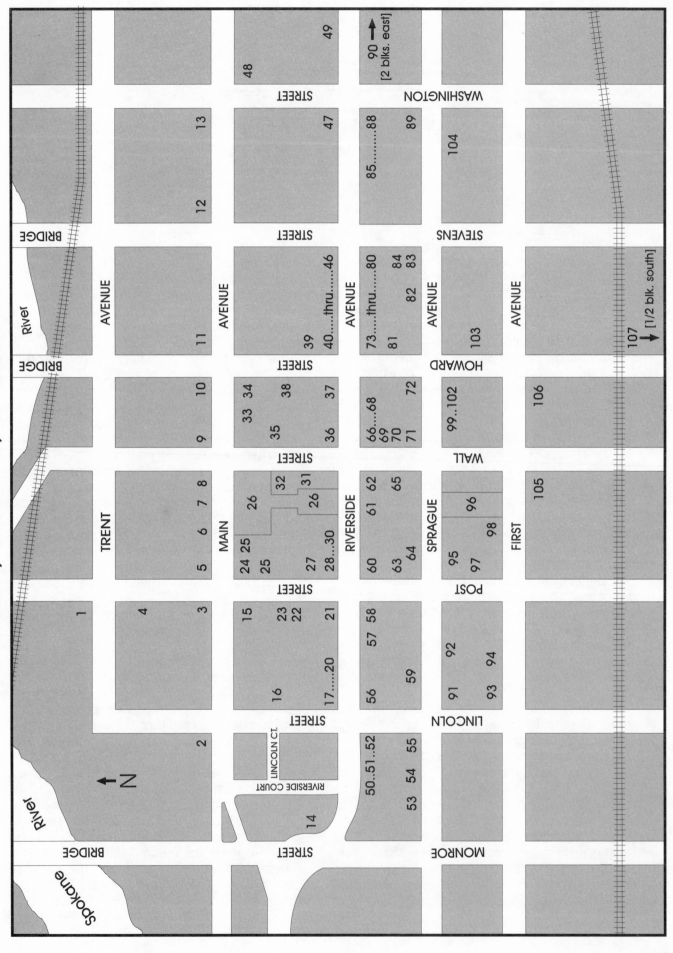

During this twenty year period, many changes occurred. Businesses came and went. There were many more stores, shops, and markets than are listed below.

DEPARTMENT STORES
10. Culbertson's, Closed, 1930
13. Kemp and Hebert, Closed, 1942
81. The Whitehouse (west end of block), Closed 1933
10. The Bon Marche, Opened 1947
26. The Crescent
1. Montgomery Ward
5. The Palace
21. J.C. Penney
2. Sears Roebuck

DIME STORES
6. Kress
36. J.J. Newberry
61. Woolworth
9. Wraight's

DRUG STORES
78. Bates Drug
84. Hart & Dilatush
52. Joyner's/Howard's Pharmacy/ Fisher Pharmacy
73. Joyner's/Densow's
62. Owl Drug Store in '30s
24. Owl Drug Store in '40s
37. Payless, to about 1943
3. Payless, after 1943
85. Whitlock's
99. Wylie-Carlson

FLORISTS
65. Eugene's, after earlier location on Riverside
87. Peters and Sons, early location
56. Peters and Sons, later location
34. Schlosser's Flowers, (in the Central Market)
102. Spokane Florist Company

GIFTS
93. Blue Bird Shop
69. Carolyn's Gift Shop
97. Mayfair Gift Shop

MEN'S HATS
29. Hat Freeman's in '30s
23. Hat Freeman's in '40s
39. John's Hat Shop
82. As above, operating simultaneously

WOMEN'S HATS
74. Adair Hat Shop
68. Reed's
71. The Vogue

JEWELERS
30. Ben Cohn Jeweler
77. Dodson
94. The Jewel Box
70. Sartori

MANUFACTURING
55. The Hat Box, early '30s
12. White's Shoe Shop (White's Boots)

MARKETS
106. Kroll Market, early '30s
22. Burger's Public Market, early '30s
104. Burgan's Store No. 20, early '30s
7. Welch's Market, early '30s, A&K Market, Burgan's Market, Johnston the Coffee Man
34. Central Market
19. Riverside Food Shop
48. Washington Market
15. Westlake Market, to 1947, then Main and Post Market
101. Rowles
35. Wall Street Market
90. Pacific Market, to 1935, Inland Meats, to '70s

MEN'S WEAR
11. Brooks Clothiers
44. Dundee Smart Clothes
33. Dundee (later location)
80. Emry's
72. Fogelquist's
100. Fogelquist's, late location
46. Thomas and Gassman

MEN'S AND WOMEN'S WEAR
92. Davenport Sport Shop
45. Curtis Style Shop
57. Eastern Outfitting Company
25. The Wonder, Inc.

MISCELLANEOUS
16. Browne-Johnston
88. Washington Electric
53. Indian Art Shop
49. Jensen-King-Byrd/Jensen-Byrd
96. John W. Graham
14. Mower & Flynne, to 1938
52. Mower & Flynne, after 1938
95. Spokane Trunk and Grip
105. Tull and Gibbs

MUSIC STORES
50. Ruth Sampson Music, pre-1947

54. Ruth Sampson Ayers, after 1947
51. Roy Goodman Music
50. Russ Bailey's, main location; (Bailey-Mann Music, and Bailey's House of Music),3 other locations, 700 and 800 blocks, Sprague
55. Guertin and Ross Music
20. Hoffman Brothers Music (second floor)
107. Hollenback Piano Company
87. The Music Box

SHOE STORES, ADULT
76. Fashion Bootery
28. Feltman and Curme
67. Model Boot Company, Hill's Model Boot Co., Hill's Shoe Store
80. Jake Hill Shoe Store, 1930
8. Saad Brothers
60. Schulein's
79. Warn and Warn

SHOE STORES, CHILDREN
64. Berg's Shoes, early '40s
59. Berg's Shoes, later '40s
86. Buster Brown Shoes

SPORTING GOODS
38. John T. Little
89. Ware-Cochran & Coultas
47. Blazier's Sporting Goods
103. Bill Hatch Sporting Goods
98. Simchuk's Sporting Goods
4. Spokane Cycle
83. Spokane Sporting Goods

WOMEN'S WEAR
32. Alexander's
31. Fred Benioff Fur Shop
63. Fred Benioff, second location
66. Bernard's
43. The City of Paris
75. Grayson's
91. Haddad's
27. Lubin's
41. McBride's
40. Mode O'Day
18. Owen Specialty Shop (also sold children's clothing)
37. Porter's Self-Service Apparel, 1946 to 1949
44. Rusan's
31. Sassy Shop (also sold children's clothing)
58. Savon's
17. The Woman's Exchange and Gown Shop
62. Zukor's, in 40's

DEPARTMENT STORES

There were three large stores in downtown Spokane at the beginning of this period that did not survive to the end of the '40s. They were *Culbertson's, Kemp and Hebert*, and *The Whitehouse.*

Culbertson's department store was an old and established business that had begun as a grocery store in 1904 in a different location, but had been located on the northwest corner of Howard and Main for many years by the '30s. The building now houses part of the Bon Marche. In the '20s, the business expanded by constructing the nine story building on the southwest corner of Howard and Trent (Spokane Falls Boulevard), including the alley crossway between the old and new buildings. The cost of this expansion, combined with the Depression, caused the store to fail.[1] Helen Turner, who has lived in Spokane all of her life, has said that Culbertson's was a lovely first class store. She recalls that it had "a marvelous tea room on the seventh floor with a pleasant view, and tables with linen cloths and napkins." She remembers that it had a Scandinavian cook, excellent food, and elegant style shows. The Culbertsons had a son who worked as a floor walker who always wore a carnation in his lapel. Culbertson's closed near the end of 1930 at which time it advertised daily in the local papers about "the Greatest Sale in the history of the Inland Empire. We feel that the golden opportunities the Store has provided...and the thousands of dollars in Savings are deeply appreciated by the people, who are more than ever desirous of buying to their very best advantage!"

Kemp and Hebert was located on the northwest corner of Main and Washington. The structure is now called the Liberty Building. Built in 1909, this department store was in business until 1941. It carried merchandise that was a little less expensive, more of an economy quality of goods than those of Culbertson's. An ad from the summer of 1930 told of women's voile dresses "that would regularly sell up to as high as $4.95," on sale for $1.39. Several people have mentioned to me that they had an excellent women's hat department. During the Christmas season, the atrium held a very tall decorated tree.[2]

The Whitehouse was located on Howard and Riverside on the southeast corner. The department store extended through the block to Sprague. There were entrances to the store on each of the three streets, though there were

Women working in the "tube room," the terminating point of the pneumatic exchange system, Montgomery Ward, 1929. *(Eastern Washington State Historical Society, Spokane, Washington, L87-1.40986-29)*

to tell the riders, "Step up, please," or Step down, please." Later elevator models would adjust to a floor if it were stopped relatively close. Doors were opened manually by the operator. Some elevators had a single door while others had double doors.

The large number of stores, shops, and markets downtown during the 1930s and 1940s illustrates the importance of the central core of Spokane at the time. The majority of businesses were downtown. In addition, in 1949, there were 61 barber shops and 43 beauty shops in an area roughly bounded by Trent, Second Avenue, Division, and Monroe. There were just under 30 confectionery and ice cream places and 18 to 21 photographic studios. (Incidentally, when being photographed, we were accustomed to having someone look closely at us and make notes on colors of our hair, eyes, clothing, and jewelry, as some of the larger black and white portraits would be hand tinted.)

other small shops on the street level, especially Howard. This business began operating before the turn of the century under the name White House, but changed its name before 1900 to the Whitehouse Co., Inc.[3] My mother remembered especially the fine fabrics that could be purchased in the Whitehouse. The store advertised that it sold Women's Ready to Wear, Millinery, Men's Furnishings, and Dry Goods. The Whitehouse is last listed in the Polk City Directory in 1933.

The Bon Marche arrived in September, 1947. At the time, I thought that it had come from "the big city, Seattle," as there was a Bon there. It is true it was from the big city. It was part of a chain that was owned by Allied Stores of New York City.[4] On opening day, my high school girl friends and I went to see it. In the busy elevators, all of the operators were female and redheads. This might be considered discriminatory now, but then it was considered clever. The *Spokane Daily Chronicle*, September 5, 1947, reported that more than 40,000 people visited the store on opening day, while *The Spokesman-Review* the next day gave a figure of more than 75,000. The new store was on the corner of Main and Howard. Next to the Bon on the west side was a two story building which housed Wraight's, which will be discussed later. The Bon would build the Bon Marche Building and expand to this area in about 1956.

When the Bon had been opened almost two months, the store's manager, Frank Hill, was asked what the fastest moving item had been up to that time. "In a store where we carry thousands of different items, it is hard to determine...[but] of course our Sparkle Plenty dolls have proved quite a sensation." Sparkle Plenty was the daughter of two ungainly characters in the Dick Tracy comic strip, B.O. Plenty, and his wife, Gravel Gertie. Hill also mentioned the apple pies that were baked in the second floor restaurant, commenting, "I'll be willing to bet that we've sold more units—more cuts—of apple pie down in the Palouse room than we've sold of any other single item."[5]

One recollection of mine is of standing with my friends and looking with astonishment into the large corner window at Main and Howard, probably in 1948 or '49. In it were mannequins dressed in an old fashioned style that was returning. They wore white cotton "Gibson girl" blouses, midcalf length colorful cotton skirts, and eyelet petticoats that extended beyond the skirts by about 1 1/2 inches. During all of our relatively short lives we had worn skirts that came to the middle of the knees. One of my mother's friends commented at the time, "I'm not *ready* for long skirts again!" At first we couldn't imagine wearing these long styles. But soon we were all wearing what was called "the *new* look." Short skirts came about because it was patriotic during World War II to conserve fabric; after the war, fashion returned to longer, fuller skirts.

It seemed that The Crescent and the Palace were the two established stores that would be in downtown Spokane forever. Indeed, **The Crescent** would operate for ninety-nine years, though in its last few years it would go by another name. One of the earliest memories I have of The Crescent is of a dress that was purchased for me there when I was three or four years old. I was very proud of this red plaid dress with white collar that had a label named for the most famous Hollywood child star of all time—"my Shirley Temple dress."

Another very early memory of The Crescent is of seeing the Colleen Moore Doll House in the store's Auditorium in 1937. The Doll House, called "a priceless gem of beauty," and "the most superb miniature castle in the world," was traveling around the country with its owner, former movie star, Colleen Moore. Worth nearly $500,000 at that time, it sat on a rock and was 9 feet square and 13 feet high so that it was necessary to stand on an elevated platform to see inside. As described in *The Spokesman-Review*, the medieval style castle included: Eleven rooms and a total of 2,000 items of furnishings; a great hallway, with black onyx floor, vaulted ceiling, painted domes and golden pillars; its own water system; a diamond and pearl chandelier lighted with bulbs the size of a grain of wheat; one of the "bedchambers" in bronze, with a golden mesh screen, a ceiling in gold fresco, and a collection of miniature swords and cannons in solid gold; another bedroom with tiny cubes of mother of pearl, inlaid with a border of gold.[6] This doll house was a wondrous thing to a five-year-old girl, and I remember my delight and amazement at seeing it. Colleen Moore gave the money raised from the admission (Children, 10¢ and Adults, 25¢) to underprivileged and handicapped children. In Spokane, this money went to St. Joseph's Orphanage, Spokane Children's Home, the Hutton Settlement, the Shriners Hospital, and the Washington Children's Home. The Colleen Moore Doll House has been on display at the Museum of Science and Industry in Chicago since 1949.

Other early memories of The Crescent

The basement lunch counter in The Crescent in 1931, when new. *(Eastern Washington State Historical Society, Spokane, Washington, L85-79.140)*

include watching the life-sized bright red goose advertising Red Goose Shoes that was perpetually bobbing in the children's shoe department in the basement. The basement shoe repair area had the peculiar nicety of a row of boxlike chairs, each with a little swinging door in front, so that feet could be hidden while shoes were taken away to be repaired. The restaurant lunch counter was located at the east end of the basement. Three low horseshoe shaped counters were surrounded by wood swivel chairs with backs. When first completed in 1931, the area was set apart by a railing with coat racks in it. Later, I recall that when not in use, the room could be closed off with dark wooden folding doors, each with a rectangular window of frosted glass. The area always smelled like split pea soup. This lunch counter was near one of the three white marble stairways to the lower level. This stairway was still being used when the store closed.

Another wide stairway to the basement was entered from the first floor, directly north of the famous clock. This set of stairs was eliminated around the end of the '40s. The third stairway led also to all other floors and was located near the Main Street entrance.

The "notions department" was at that time on the first floor. Here we could purchase rib-

bon, thread, elastic, sundries, closet items and magazines. Many items were stored in small built-in drawers of dark wood. This department was located just west of the elevators at what was then the northwest corner of the store. Later The Crescent would expand to the corner of Main and Post, a portion of the store that was reached by going down a few steps. The notions department was separated from the rest of the store by a wall, except at the elevator end. There was an outside entrance to the department on Main Street. At this writing, the words "The Crescent" can still be seen on the outside of the building above where this door was located.

A fountain-lunch was first installed in The Crescent next to the already existing candy shop in 1924.[7] This area remained the same through the '30s. A single counter—there were no booths or tables—ran along the area directly behind the bank of elevators on the first floor.

An entrance to the kitchen was at the west end of the area. Some time later, probably in the '40s, the fountain area was enlarged, and U-shaped counters and tables replaced the single long straight counter. I remember the olive-and-nut sandwiches and delicious Burnt Almond ice cream.

The Crescent Tea Room, on the sixth floor, had a wonderful quiet atmosphere for lunch on

The soda fountain in The Crescent as designed by Gustav A. Pehrson. Duplicate spigots and flavor containers indicate as many as four full soda fountains in this long counter. *(Eastern Washington State Historical Society, Spokane, Washington, L85-79.9)*

The Palace department store, October, 1930. On the left the Auditorium theater advertises above the streetcar. The Palace building houses Nordstrom in the mid '90s. *(Eastern Washington State Historical Society, Spokane, Washington, L87-1.43790-30)*

On the right, the Sears Roebuck building just before it opened in 1930. The area to its left, with "Richlube and Richfield," "Sweeney Used Cars," and "B&M Greasing" seemed almost to disappear in 1966 when a street was put in behind the building. The street crossed this area diagonally and ended at Main and Monroe. The railroad trestle, at left in front of the falls, was torn down around 1973 before EXPO '74. *(Northwest Room, Spokane Public Library)*

busy shopping days. Fashion models in chic apparel would walk from table to table showing styles from the store. As advertised in 1934, "A Parade of Fashions During Luncheon Hour...Regular menus are 35¢, 40¢ and 50¢."

In the fall of 1948, The Crescent installed Spokane's first escalators. My high school girl friends and I excitedly took the bus to town after school to ride them. We were not alone in our excitement. *The Spokesman-Review* reported that thousands of people had come into the store to try them out that first day. "They clutched the handrail, grinned a little bit and then made one brave leap—the thousands of bustling shoppers who tried out the 'newfangled' escalators at The Crescent store yesterday. But the housewives were not alone in their new venture on the first escalators in the Inland Empire. Many a business man stepped gingerly on the first moving step, then grinned broadly over his shoulder at his friends with a genial 'C'mon Joe, nothing to it!' The real swarm took place, however, when school was out. Throngs of bobbysoxers and their boy friends 'took over' the escalators. As timid as the oldsters, they giggled and watched bug-eyed as the steps appeared as if by magic from a slot in the floor. "Kid, are you ready? Let's go together,"

one teen-aged miss giggled to her companion. Together they jumped rather than walked onto the stairs, half expecting to be left behind if they didn't make it."[8] Spokane would not have another escalator until 1951 when the expanded Newberry's installed one.[9]

A common meeting place for people getting together downtown was "under the clock." The store had grown with the city. Opening the morning after the fire of August, 1889, The Crescent grew from two employees at that time to 500 in 1911.[10] The Crescent is a place that many of us still miss. Its customer service was extraordinary.

The Palace department store, earlier located on Riverside, was during these years, on the northeast corner of Main and Post. Kemp and Hebert bought the Palace in 1930. Its main floor had a high ceiling which was surrounded by a mezzanine on which were offices and possibly some sales areas. Many years later, the open mezzanine was walled off from the first floor, and escalators were installed that went directly to the second floor, skipping the mezzanine. The Palace had a not unpleasant, but indefinable smell which I associated with its floor pattern, an immense black and white diagonal checkerboard.

S.H. Kress and Company after dark in 1949. *(Eastern Washington State Historical Society, Spokane, Washington, L87-1.61338-49)*

In a summer ad in 1930, women's crepe and chiffon dresses were shown as: regular $10 to $15, at a sale price of $6.95; a clearance of "California Frocks" for girls was offered at $1.33. In October, 1936, the Palace advertised dress woolen coats for women that had been reduced from $99 to $49. In those days, $99 would have been a very expensive coat. And "Special! NEW Fur Felts, [hats] $3.69. Smart 'just arrived' models with flattering high crowns, clever forward brims and smart little turbans. Feather and grosgrain trim. Plenty of blacks as well as a host of other correct fall colors." The Palace was part of Spokane for over 52 years, closing in 1951.

Penney's has had several locations in downtown Spokane. Through the '30s and '40s it was on the northwest corner of Riverside and Post. In the early '30s, this store had Penney's traditional sign that could be seen in many towns

in America. A long yellow metal sign banded the building just below the second level. In black upper case lettering on this background the sign said J.C. PENNEY COMPANY. After the Palace closed in 1951, Penney's took over the northeast Main and Post corner. It remained there until 1974 when it moved diagonally across the street. In 1992, Penney's left the downtown area for Northtown.

The art deco **Montgomery Ward** Building, built in 1929, was located on the northwest corner of Post and Trent (Spokane Falls Boulevard). This building had unique capabilities of freight deliveries, as it had a private railroad spur which led to the nearby elevated Union Pacific tracks. This spur was on a deck at the second floor level in the back of the store.[11] Though I do not have much memory of "Ward's" interior, I do remember some dark wood paneling on several floors of the store and high ceilings. In 1932, a Montgomery Ward ad in *The Spokesman-Review* offered a number of articles for 88¢. These included hardwood end tables, an electric iron "complete with cord"(!) Boys' Bib Overalls, sizes 6 to 16 years at 3 for 88¢, and 12 yards of Color Fast Print fabric. After renovation, the Montgomery Ward Building became our attractive City Hall in 1982.

The **Sears-Roebuck** Building, built in 1930, was a three-story structure that was located on the northwest corner of Lincoln and Main. Sears and Montgomery Ward, located near each other, both featuring catalog buying and lower priced merchandise, could easily be confused. I do not remember clearly the interior of Sears. The Sears Building became the main library in 1963 and remained our library until it was torn down in 1992. A new library was erected on the site and opened January 22, 1994.

DIME STORES

Dime stores, known also as "five-and-ten-cent stores," were such a part of our lives in those days, that in the early '30s a popular song was entitled, "I Found a Million Dollar Baby in a 5-and-10-Cent Store." Much like variety stores or some drug stores of today, they sold many small and inexpensive items such as bobby pins, razor blades, shoe laces, costume jewelry, ribbons, and cosmetics. There was very little pre-packaging. Identical articles were piled together in little cubicles, made by using rather heavy glass dividers that stood on edge on the counter tops. In addi-

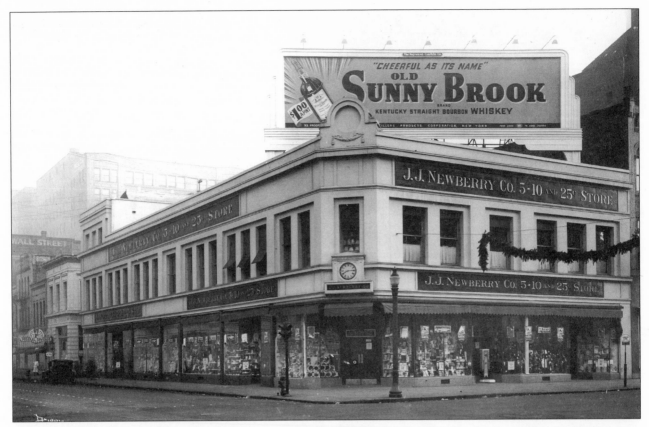

Newberry's dime store in 1939. *(Eastern Wasington State Historical Society, Spokane, Washington, L87-1.17206-39)*

tion, dishes, other kitchen items, oil cloth (used for table cloths), some clothing, fabrics, plants, small aquariums and fish, sheet music, and numerous other things were for sale.

The dime stores did not have self-service in those days. Clerks worked in narrow spaces inside wrap-around counters. Most dime stores had fountain-lunches. With the exception of Kress, floors of the "five and tens" downtown were of narrow gauge hardwood and well-worn.

Kress opened in 1931, on the north side of Main in the middle of the block between Wall and Post.[12] Over its sidewalk was a large, dark marquee, supported by four heavy chains. Inside was a long room that seemed particularly grand because of its two story high ceiling. The room had terrazzo floors and was filled with many counters. At the back, stairs led to a balcony on which additional merchandise was displayed. Stairs at each side of the front led to the lower level. There was a square counter for a fountain-lunch at the far end of this level. In the basement you could buy goldfish at 10¢ apiece and small live turtles that were about two inches long that had their shells

painted in bright colors. We carried them home in small white paper cartons with thin wire handles. In the late '40s, we could purchase a live chameleon with a gold chain around its neck. On the opposite end of the chain was a pin. Some girls around junior high and high school age pinned such chains near their shoulders and "wore" the chameleons like a piece of jewelry.

In 1930, Britt's, a store on the northeast corner of Riverside and Wall, was sold to J.J. Newberry.[13] After mostly interior remodeling, it became **Newberry's**. This Newberry's was nothing like the one of the '50s through '80s in that same location. Two doors, one at the back near the alley, and another diagonal corner door at Riverside and Wall, were the only entrances. Immediately to the left of the corner door, and behind a low counter heaped with music, was an upright piano. There sat a clerk, usually a young woman, who played and sold popular music. Such playing! Wide chords and octaves played the melody and along with it was a "BOOM chuck, BOOM chuck" accompaniment. As a child I thought it would be wonderful to play the piano like that. An added bonus was that you

Interior of Newberry's, 1940. *(Eastern Washington State Historical Society, Spokane, Washington, L87-1.18376-40)*

could hear this music throughout the store as you shopped. Sheet music was sold this way at Payless, and perhaps at Wraight's, but I particularly remember it at Newberry's.

Newberry's was one of several dime stores that had small booths in which you could have pictures taken. The outside of these elongated booths was covered with strips of black and white sample pictures. The inside of the booth was divided, and on one end was a cubicle which you entered by going behind a curtain. A friend could be squeezed into the picture with you if you sat close together on the stool which could be raised or lowered to the right height. You would look into a built-in camera, and a young girl would take a picture of your head and shoulders. An hour or so later you could pick up a vertical or horizontal strip of four pictures. The cost was no more than a quarter,

and may have been only a dime. The picture booths were not automated as they would be later.

Another dime store was **Woolworth's**. Woolworth's was located on the south side of Riverside in the middle of the block between Wall and Post, almost directly across from the entrance to The Crescent. Woolworth's had an L-shaped interior. In 1955, Woolworth closed this store and moved to a new building on the northeast corner of Main and Lincoln. Woolworth also had a store on the south side of Main, west of Washington, from 1916 to 1941.[14]

On the northeast corner of Main and Wall was another five and ten cent store. Owned earlier by the adjoining Culbertson's department store, the business was sold in 1930 to Edward Wraight. In the late '40s, Eleanor Anderson Schafer worked at **Wraight's** after school selling cold meats and cheeses in the delicatessen and

My sister Marianna holds me in pictures from a dime store camera booth.

Woolworth's in 1936. Above the doors was its gold-lettered sign on a dark plum-red background. The Peerless Dentist sign can be seen at the end of the block. *(Eastern Washington State Historical Society, Spokane, Washington, L87-1.8187-36)*

Wraights in 1930. By the '40s its gray sign with black lettering seemed drab. On the far left can be seen the loading area of the old bus depot. No traffic lights aid walkers crossing the streets on this corner yet. *(Eastern Washington State Historical Society, Spokane, Washington, L87-1.43789-30)*

earning 35¢ an hour. It seems to Schafer that the store sold "just about everything." She remembers that it had quite a few canned foods, a bakery, the delicatessen, plants, goldfish, drugs, toys, jewelry, and on the second floor, clothing. In March, 1933, Wraight's opened its "Hollywood Shop," an area in the store that was art deco in design, and reported to have "effective lighting fixtures...richly-colored velour carpets" and a "modernistic tendency." The department featured women's suits, coats, dresses and millinery. "High Grade Apparel At A Saving," a sign in the area said.[15]

Wraight's had a fountain-lunch counter at the north end of the store. Here, as if working in a hole, the waitresses stood on a floor that was at a considerably lower level than that of the customers, making it necessary for them to look up at the customers and reach up to the counter, though customers were seated and they were standing. On a corner of this counter, a winking moon-like face smiled at us from a black, yellow and white lighted sign. The sign said, "Try a hot buttered kist-wich!" The sign had been there for so long that my sister Marianna and I used to wonder if they still served such a thing, and would dare each other to order one. What was it?

Would a waitress say, "A *what*?" Neither of us dared ask, so we'll never know. This fountain-lunch had a particularly long and tempting soda fountain menu. Marianna, who has a sweet tooth, once thought that she would systematically try every item on the menu over a period of time, but she didn't accomplish this dream. Wraight's opened in 1931 and closed in 1949. The building was demolished in 1955 to make way for the second phase of the Bon Marche.

DRUG STORES

In 1930, the Polk City Directory lists 27 downtown drug stores; at this writing, there are but two. **Bates Drug** was located on the south side of the street at W. 507 Riverside. An ad in the *Spokane Daily Chronicle* in 1946 for Bates has toothbrushes for 3¢; 150 sheet rolls of paper towels, 2 for 19¢; a "Giant Size" Colgate toothpaste for 37¢; 100 aspirin for 3¢; and Light Globes for 10¢ each. There was a special close-out of Reynolds Pens, "The Miracle Pen of the Ages" at $6.95. Ballpoint pens were new and had been introduced at $12.50! **Joyner's Original Cut Rate Drug Company**, its full name, had as many as four downtown locations during this period. It had stores on the corner of Riverside and Lincoln in the Empire State Building, on Howard and Riverside on the southeast corner, on South Post, and on Sprague and Washington. Joyner's in the Empire State Building, W. 907 Riverside, had a soda fountain, the only downtown pharmacy I can recall that had one. (In the late '40s this became **Howard Pharmacy**, and then **Fisher Pharmacy**.) Soda fountains were usually found only in neighborhood drug stores. The **Owl Drug** was on the southwest corner Riverside and Wall through the '30s, and on the southeast corner of Main and Post in most of the '40s.

Payless Drug was located for most of the era on the northwest corner of Howard and Riverside. An interior picture taken in 1934 by Charles A. Libby shows signs for sales items: "10¢ —Colgate's Lavender Delicately perfumed soap now—5¢," "10¢ now 5¢ Camay or White King," "Shaving Cream 29¢," and "PRINCE ALBERT 10¢."[16] In this picture, the store looks as if it is set up to be a self-service store even this early in the period. Payless moved to the northwest corner of Main and Post about 1946. Here, a sign on the corner of the store said, "The World's Largest Self Service Drug Store." Other names of downtown drug stores of that era are: **Hart & Dilatush** which was at N. 9 Stevens, **Wylie-Carlson**, then in the 600 block on Sprague, and **Whitlocks**, through that entire period located on the ground floor of the Paulsen Building.

FLORISTS

The number of downtown florists ranged from eleven to fourteen in the '30s and '40s. Four florists were downtown for the entire two decade period—**Eugene's**, **Schlosser & Sons**, **Spokane Florist Company**, and **Peters & Sons**. Florists were also located in several of the markets, and in The Davenport Hotel, The Crescent, and Culbertson's.

GIFT SHOPS, or ART GOODS and BRIC-A-BRAC

Listed in the City Directory under Gift Shops for a good part of this period are **Carolyn's** at 12 N. Wall, and **Mayfair Gift Shop**, at S. 11 Post. Also listed under Gift Shops, but in most years listed under Art Goods and Bric-a-Brac, was **The Blue Bird Shop** in The Davenport Hotel, which featured table linens, crystal, ceramic vases, Spode and other fine china.

HAIR—BARBER AND BEAUTY SHOPS

The symbol of a barber shop was a turning pole with red and white stripes. A blue stripe was added sometime around the early '50s, perhaps as a patriotic gesture after World War II.

Peering into a window of a beauty salon, a person could not see much, because curtains, like those used around hospital beds were discreetly drawn around each "beautician's" station. No one was to know if milady dyed her hair, though the dyes were often unnatural looking solid blacks, blue tints for white hair, or intense henna, a bright reddish-orange. A woman might be having her hair curled with a curling iron, or she might be getting a "finger wave," a method of waving the hair using a lotion, then combing it into place by holding each new wave with a length of the finger. When the hair dried, the waves were in place. In 1931, a shampoo and finger wave were advertised for 75¢ by the Cardinal Beaute Shoppe located in the Norfolk Building.

Permanents, then called "permanent waves," were first given in the early '30s. They used chemicals and heat. The "victim" would sit under a contraption that had many hanging black electrical cords, each with a clamp at the bottom. The device was plugged in and heated, then the clamps were attached to rollers in the hair. Sometimes women were given a wooden stick with which to point at areas of the head that were too hot.[17] In the ad mentioned above, permanent waves were advertised: "Special Croquignole— regular $5, now for $3.50." Croquignole referred to the type of wrapping used. A "ringlette Croquignole" cost $5.00, and a "Spiral Wave," $1.95.

In the mid to late '30s, a new machine appeared. Clamps were put on a small unit for heating, then transferred to the hair. When I was about six years old I had a permanent of this type. The clamps were so heavy that by the time all of them were on, I could not hold my head up. The beautician put her arm under my chin and held my head up until time to take the clamps off. In the early '40s, the so-called "cold wave" arrived whereby permanents were done only with chemicals. Home permanents were introduced in the late '40s.

In the '40s, some women wore "page boys," shoulder length, smooth styles that were rolled under at the ends. Some wore snoods, a revival of a 19th century style. These were heavy nets that gathered the hair into a pouch at the

The interior of the Western Hair Company, 1940, showing a row of machines to which hair was attached for "permanent waves." (*Eastern Washington State Historical Society, Spokane, Washington, L87-1.19219-40*)

back of the head. Pompadours, in which the hair was rolled away from the face and pinned into place, were also popular.

HATS

Men and women wore hats nearly everywhere they went. Several stores specialized in men's hats: **Hat Freeman's**, located near the Liberty theater on Riverside, and **John's Hat Shop**, which had three locations downtown and one on east Sprague. Some hat stores, or milliners, catered to women. In 1930, there were 16 stores downtown that sold women's hats, not counting the department stores. By 1949, there were still 12. These included **Adair Hat Shop** on Riverside next to Joyner's, **Reeds**, at W. 607 Riverside, **Sibyl's Hats**, just around the corner from the Adair Hat Shop, on Howard, and **The Vogue**, a very large hat store on the northeast corner of Sprague and Wall.

JEWELERS

In 1930, the Polk City Directory lists 36 jewelers downtown. By the end of the decade and the Depression there were only 25. Most were at street level. Jewelers that I remember from the period are: **Ben Cohn**, located near the Liberty theater at 722 W. Riverside, **Dodson's**, then on the south side of Riverside at W. 517, **The Jewel Box**, in The Davenport Hotel, **Mandell's Jewelers**, in the Hyde Building, **Nelson Jewelry Company**, at W. 408 Riverside, across from the Paulsen Building, and **Sartori** Jeweler's, at N. 10 Wall, (in the early '30s, **Sartori & Wolff**.)

Mandell's Jewelers opened in 1936. Both the front of the building and the inside show-

Interior of John's Hat Shop at 512 W. Sprague in 1938. *(Eastern Washington State Historical Society, Spokane, Washington, L87-1.13908-38)*

Interior of the Adair Hat Shop, 1940. The sign announces Spring Hats for $2 and up. *(Eastern Washington State Historical Society, Spokane, Washington, L87-1.17690-40)*

An A & K Market at 925 W. First in 1930. *(Eastern Washington State Historical Society, Spokane, Washington, L87-1.42084-30)*

room were said to have been designed "along the lines of the Hollywood type."[18] People were enamored of Hollywood and California in those days. The movie industry represented glamour to those weary of the Great Depression.

Sartori was a lovely little store. A stairway at the back of the customer area led to a small balcony where several jewelers worked. Some of their time was spent on custom made items such as school and club pins that were worn by high school students. Albert Sartori, owner and founder of the store, announced his retirement in 1965, but apparently sold the operation, as it remained in business (part of the time at a similar address on Howard Street) until 1978.[19]

MARKETS

Various aromas, of baking breads and pastries, fresh fruits and vegetables, flowers, fish, and sawdust on the floors beneath butcher blocks, greeted market shoppers. Business men stopped by after work for a special cut of meat, customers walked from downtown apartments, and women came down to shop in the downtown markets. Though each market was a single open area, shoppers moved from one individually operated business to another, stopping at one for a head of lettuce, at another for some canned or packaged food, at another for meat or fish. Bright colored fruits in one area included whole stalks of bananas hanging upside-down from hooks, leading many of us to believe that bananas pointed down as they grew, instead of up. When buying meats or fish, customers dealt directly with a butcher. Pre-packaged items were in the future. A health food counter that served and sold "healthful" foods was sometimes part of the mix of stalls. In some markets there was a lunch counter.

Nine markets were scattered about the downtown area in 1930. This number gradually diminished over time, so that by 1940 there were seven, and by 1949 only four. Several markets

The Central Market in 1946. *(Eastern Washington State Historical Society, Spokane, Washington, L87-1.47054-46)*

The Riverside Food Shop in 1939. To the right of it is the entrance to the Norfolk Building; just beyond the market is the Aster Tea Room sign, then a corner of Owen Specialty Shop's sign, and beyond that, the post office. *(Eastern Washington State Historical Society, Spokane, Washington, L87-1.17242-39)*

The Westlake Market in November, 1930, later called the Main and Post Market. Undoubtedly taken around Armistice Day parade because of the flag on the wooden pole in the sidewalk. *(Eastern Washington State Historical Society, Spokane, Washington, Detail of photo L87-1.43998-30)*

Johnston The Coffee Man's building and truck, opposite the Cresent on Main, 1934. *(Eastern Washington State Historical Society, Spokane, Washington, L87-1.4208-34)*

from the earliest part of this period are not in my memory. One was the **Kroll Market** at 601-21 W. First Avenue. This large market was the location of at least 13 different marketing businesses, some of them competing. Three fruit operations, two meat companies, three restaurants, along with a bakery, a butter and eggs specialist, a creamery, a grocer, and a another seller of groceries and fish did business in the spacious area.

Burger's Public Market was a meat market at 117 N. Post. In 1933, they advertised Short Ribs for 6¢ a pound, Tender Roasts for 8¢, and "fresh dressed fancy Turkeys" for 15¢, 17¢, and 20¢ a pound. The difference in price is not explained. Alongside of Burger's was **Burgan's**, which was then in the food business. It had markets at a number of places, calling its stores by number, such as **Burgan's Store No. 20**, which was at 429 W. Sprague in 1930. Another grocery location was at Burgan's Furniture on north Division, where both furniture and groceries were sold. Still another **Burgan's** shared a spot with one of the **A & K Markets**, at 710 W. Main, just east of Kress. This was a bustling location for markets throughout the period. **Welch's Market** was also at W. 708-10 Main in the early '30s.

Four of the markets were downtown for the entire two decade period, each staying in the same location. They were: 1. **The Central Market**, which was on the southwest corner of

Main and Howard. On the Main street side of the building hung a neon sign that said "SEA FOODS." This was framed by a neon fish which poked its nose toward the street. 2. **The Riverside Food Shop**, located on the street level of the Norfolk Building. Here my sister and I sometimes endured drinking carrot juice at the health food counter on Saturdays before being taken by our aunt to an afternoon movie. 3. **The Washington Market**, which was on the southeast corner of Washington and Main. This was the location of Spokane's last downtown market and in later years would be named Gino's. 4. **The Westlake Market**, on the southwest corner of Main and Post, which became **The Main and Post Market** in 1947.

Johnston The Coffee Man should probably be added as a fifth market that retained its location throughout the period except that in 1930 it was at 710 W. Main, (there's that busy market address again) and by the end of the '30s and through the '40s was at 706 W. Main, just one door

The Pacific Market, 1933, later to be Inland Meats, looking east from Browne toward Division. Note 5¢ hamburger sign on the north side of the street. (*Eastern Washington State Historical Society, Spokane, Washington, Detail of photo L87-1.2124-33*)

east. This business sold tea and freshly roasted coffees. An ad in 1939 for Johnston's coffee stated, "Rooster Brand Coffee, 23¢ the pound," and "Johnston's Union Brand Coffee, Pound...15¢." By this time, Johnston's also sold groceries, and had a lunch counter. By 1949, it shared this active space with a bakery, a natural foods operator, a wholesale and retail meat business, and a fruit company. All the while, other marketing was going on at the adjoining address. Johnston was in the location into the early '50s.

The several **A and K's**, Mike Scaler Fruits and Vegetables in **The Riverside Food Shop**, **Rowles Grocery**, and **The Main and Post Market** often displayed their produce in boxes on the sidewalk "big city style."

The 1949 Polk City Directory lists 13 meat markets and four wholesale meat markets downtown. Meat was wrapped in pink butcher paper, then tied with a string, which the butcher broke off from a huge spool that hung from the ceiling. Incidentally, cottage cheese was purchased from the meat counter and was sold in bulk. The butcher would dig out the amount that the customer wanted and put it in a white container with wire handles. One of many meat wholesalers in the early '30s, the **Pacific Market** was located at 39-41 W. Riverside on the south side of the street in the modified Spanish style stucco building that has several large arched areas over the doors. From 1936 through the '70s, this wholesale house was called **Inland Meats**.

MISCELLANEOUS STORES

"Modernize your kitchen now! Enlist the aid of electricity," **Brown-Johnston**, at N. 118 Lincoln urged in an ad in 1937. Many people were still cooking on wood stoves. A Norge Electric Range was offered for $59.95 with trade-in of "your old fuel stove." An accompanying picture showed a good-sized three burner electric stove on long legs. Another store that specialized in electrical products and service was the **Washington Electric**, on the southwest corner of Riverside and Washington, which featured General Electric products and Zenith radios. These places sold small and large appliances, such as wringer washing machines. In the late '30s, dishwashers, automatic washing machines, and mangles were introduced. A mangle is a machine that is about the size of a small low table. One sits in front of it and feeds flat items such as table cloths and sheets into it. The articles come out of the other side, having been ironed by smoothing and pressing with large hot rollers.

The **Indian Art and Book Shop**, at W. 914 Sprague in the mid-'30s, sold Indian crafts, baskets, and books. My sister Marianna remembers it being called "The Indian Store" when her fifth grade class went there on a field trip.

Jensen-Byrd (until the late '30s, **Jensen-King-Byrd**), had an outlet at 314-324 W. Riverside. It did both wholesale and retail business, selling hardware, large appliances including Easy

John W. Graham & Company, 1943. Nearby are the Bandbox theater, and on its right, Spokane Trunk and Grip. A sailor crosses the street; an old style street light is on the left. KFPY's tower can be seen on the Symons Building in the background. *(Eastern Washington State Historical Society, Spokane, Washington, L95-80.26)*

brand washers and ironers, and kitchen equipment, in a large display room with high ceilings. The glassware display was spectacularly effective. This was in a separate room about ten feet square with mirrored walls; the area was brilliantly lighted and all kinds of glassware were displayed on glass shelves. The double images of sparkling glass and lights were dazzling. As a child, I would try to take a peek into the little room whenever we were in the store. Sometime in the '40s, the retail part of the business was closed.

The **John W. Graham** company was located in the middle of the 700 block on both Sprague and First Avenue, as it stretched through the block from one street to the other. Graham's was started in a tent a few days after the Spo-

kane Fire in 1889. It moved to the Sprague location in 1901.[20] In its five-story and basement store were many spacious areas, but also strange nooks and crannies. Walking toward the back from the Sprague Avenue side, you would find a short narrow stairway. After climbing five or six steps, you would find yourself in a low ceilinged area and at the First Avenue level. Or you could choose to turn and go up an additional bit of stairs to a mezzanine. Because of the odd plan, the elevator had doors that opened to the front and to the back, depending upon the floor. A stranger wandering in might have gotten lost in the peculiar arrangement, but those of us who knew its secrets felt comfortably familiar there. The occasional friendly creak of the floor underfoot simply added to the

Graham's fountain pen department, near the Sprague Avenue entrance, 1945, with clerks Virginia Turnley, Helen Louise Lincoln, Celia Allen, and Ella Calliott. *(Eastern Washington State Historical Society, Spokane, Washington, L83-10.88)*

homey feeling.

In this maze could be found office supplies, a huge book department, engineering supplies, and learning materials—maps, puzzles, textbooks, and workbooks. As a child, I remember the satisfaction of working on special construction paper posters purchased there. On neutral-colored paper were outlines of scenes of stories or faraway places. Detailed drawings of various parts of the scene could be found on other colors of paper that were to be cut out and pasted over the outlines, making a colorful finished poster.

"If it's made of paper, we have it" was Graham's slogan, but there was much, much more. Graham's had an immense toy and game department, a large art department, it sold furniture, large framed pictures and picture frames, cameras, umbrellas, leather purses and billfolds, stationery, fountain pens, and scarves. There was also a large gift shop. The store sold wallpaper and paint, and in the mid-'40s sold Kem-Tone, the first water based house paint.

The basement area of Graham's was a sort of treasure trove. American flags, party favors, crepe paper in every imaginable color, small boxes of gold, silver, red, green and blue stars, children's stickers (you had to lick them in those days), party napkins, paper plates, and doilies. All were displayed on old wooden shelves and counters with wood dividers. Graham's building was torn down in 1973 to create space for the Washington Trust Bank Financial Center. Graham's moved its store to much smaller quarters on the first floor of the southeast corner of Riverside and Stevens, and later sold to J.K. Gill.

Mower & Flynne began business in 1898 in the Dodd Block. In 1938 it moved to the east half of the ground floor of the Empire State Building. Known as "Spokane's linen store," it imported Irish linens, sold dry goods, men's and women's furnishings, and hotel and institution supplies.[21]

Spokane Trunk and Grip was at W. 721 Sprague, next to the entrance of the Radio Central Building and near the Bandbox theater, for the entire period.

For the most part, **Tull and Gibbs** was a furniture store, but it also sold rugs and carpets, linoleums, bedding, draperies, large appliances, table linens, silverware, and dishes. It was located on the southwest corner of First and Wall. At Christmas time in the '30s their corner window seemed alive with delightful animated figures. The earliest one of these that I know of is in my sister's memory and was of a man and his wife with small figures telling the story of "The Elves and the Shoemaker." In a later one that I remember, a full-sized horse pulled a sleigh and trotted in place toward the corner. In the sleigh sat a smiling couple dressed in late 1800s style clothing. They bounced along to the merry music of "Jingle Bells." In other years, we listened to jolly music and saw a comical round-headed Old King Cole who sat smiling in his crown on his throne. He seemed to weave gently in rhythm to music that was being "played" by his fiddlers three. Nearby small dancing figures held the king's pipe and bowl. The two windows that I remember alternated, each returning for several Christmas seasons. How we anticipated walking to that area to see these enchanting figures each year!

On August 23, 1931, Tull and Gibbs advertised its 40th Anniversary Sale in *The Spokesman-Review*. A Dining Room Suite including a large table, five side chairs, a host chair, and "beautifully carved" buffet, all with "French walnut finish" could be purchased for $99. You might select a five-piece breakfast set for $23, or a bedroom suite with full-sized bed, a chest of drawers, and vanity for $75.85. A 54-piece dinner service "with rose pink glassware to harmonize," very popular at the time, sold for $14.95. In December, 1941, Tull and Gibbs advertised scores of fine tables in walnut and mahogany for $8.95. "Only $1 a Month—No Down Payment", the ad said. (It also stated the following: "For Customers Who Have Not Exercised Their $50 Exemption Right Since Sept. 1st." What this meant, we can only guess.) Tull and Gibbs opened in 1891, but closed due to bankruptcy in 1957.[22]

MUSIC STORES

Ruth Sampson's, "opposite the Post Office" as they advertised then, specialized in all kinds of printed music. By 1947, Miss Sampson had married, and the store became **Ruth Sampson Ayers Music Company**. Around that time it moved through the block to a location on the north side of Sprague, almost behind where they had been. The store had an enormous stock, and wonderful service.

Roy Goodman was a music store that sold Baldwin pianos, other instruments, and phonograph records, 78 r.p.m., of course. After a brief time on Sprague across from The Davenport, Roy Goodman moved to a Riverside address near Ruth Sampson's in 1941. In front of the entrance to the store, a large life-sized black and white dog made of a composition material, sat on its haunches. Head cocked to one side, he seemed to be listening to "His Master's Voice." The image of the dog listening to an old "Victrola" was for many years the symbol of the RCA-Victor company. A dog is still used, though it sits by a more modern machine. At Roy Goodman you could take a record into a glass-windowed booth to listen to it. You might not buy, and you might have scratched the record, but it was kept without checking the condition and sold to someone else. This was common practice in record stores.

SHOE STORES AND SHOE SHINES

Several shoe stores in this era used fluoroscopes to view the bones of the feet inside the shoe. This exposed the feet to X-rays or other radiation. The machine was especially common in children's shoe stores. It was amusing to look in the machine, see the bones of your feet, and entertain yourself by wiggling your toes. John Warn, a veteran of the shoe store business in Spokane, says this was largely a gimmick, but that "a salesperson could show a parent a child's foot and say, 'See where the end of his toe is? He has all that room to grow before he'll need new shoes.'" The machines were banned by the government in the early '50s.

Twenty or more shoe dealers were downtown during most of this time, not counting department stores and several shops that sold both clothing and shoes. In 1932, **Berg's Shoe Shop** was established, first carrying shoes for adults and located in the Bandbox theater area, then moving to the Peyton Building, and later to W. 720 Sprague, by then specializing in children's shoes. Another children's shoe store was **Buster Brown Shoes**. Buster Brown shoes had an illustration on the inside of each shoe of a small boy with his dog. **The Model Boot Company**, established well before this period, went by other names as time passed—**Hill's Model Boot Shop**, and **Hill's Shoe Store**. **Schulein's**, which featured the most fashionable and probably the most expensive women's shoes, was on the southeast corner of Riverside and Post.

A number of shoe shine parlors, most tiny hole-in-the-wall places, were in the downtown area. During most of the '30s, there were seventeen shoe shine places. By 1949 the number had dropped to fourteen.

SPORTING GOODS

Through the '30s, perhaps reflecting that these were hard times, the Polk City Directory lists only three places downtown that specialized exclusively in Sporting Goods—**John T. Little**, specialists in fishing tackle, **Robinson Trading Post**, on Second Avenue, and **Ware-Cochran & Coultas**. By the end of the '40s there were fifteen listings. I remember going to **Simchuk's** for ice skates on a cold winter day. The store was packed with children and adults renting and buying them.

The **Spokane Cycle** was at 217 N. Post on the west side of the street between Main and Trent (Spokane Falls Boulevard) and next to Pratt Furniture Company. Bicycles! Tricycles! Wagons! Scooters! Small cars to sit in and pedal or push with your feet. How I wanted one of those cars when I was about four! The smell of real rubber tires permeated the show room. "Balloon tire bikes" were desired by most kids. These wide tires gave a smooth, "cushy" ride. It was exciting to go to the Spokane Cycle.

SMALL SHOPS

The small shops told about here must be limited as there were many. One that is memorable is **Alexander's**, a store of several stories that carried elegant women's clothes. It was located at N. 117 Wall, just south of the Wall Street entrance to The Crescent, and just north of the alley. Alexander's had an attractive interior. Photos taken in 1936 by Charles A. Libby of workrooms in Alexander's show ten people working in its tailoring department and nine working in its fur tailoring department. An ad from 1939 for Alexander's says: "Spokane's Complete Store for Women. Distinction and Quality...at moderate prices...Everything in wearing apparel from crown to sole...A very pleasant atmosphere for shopping...SUITS COATS FURS DRESSES ACCESSORIES FOUNDATIONS MILLINERY BEAUTY SALON."

Alexander's and the Sassy Shop, 1949. *(Eastern Washington State Historical Society, Spokane, Washington, L87-1.60362-49)*

Across the alley and south of Alexander's, the **Fred Benioff** shop, one of a large chain of furriers, opened in 1939. The building had been newly remodeled into the modern International style, and changed from three to four stories. Its second, third, and fourth floors each had horizontal series of sleek glass and glass brick windows which swept around the curved corner of the building. These windows were to give "daylight illumination to bring out the elegance of the furs" according to the owner.[23] Apparently the fur store shared the location with the **Sassy Shop** during at least part of the time, as the Sassy Shop is also listed at this address in 1940. Benioff's moved about 1944 to N. 8 Post, and continued in business there until 1951. The Sassy Shop, which carried women's clothes, maternity dresses, and little girls' dresses, remained in the Wall Street location through the end of the decade. Along with the Marble Bank Building, the two buildings that housed Alexander's and the Sassy Shop were torn down in the early '50s for expansion of The Crescent.

Still another store with fine women's fashions was **Bernard's**, located at that time on the southeast corner of Riverside and Wall. Though

Lubin's Women's Apparel around 1940. Also pictured, Feltman & Curme Shoe Store, Hat Freeman, and Ben Cohn Jeweler at far right. *(Eastern Washington State Historical Society, Spokane, Washington, L85-79.210)*

not a large place, the store made good use of its space with a small curved mezzanine at the back, the access of which was from a curved stairway that swept up one side of the room.

The **Davenport Sport Shop**, located off the lobby of The Davenport Hotel, sold only men's clothing in the early '30s, but by the end of the decade a women's section had been added. This department specialized in sports skirts, sweaters, and blouses in early years, and later in Scottish and Swiss sweaters and knit suits. The men's department sold conservative clothing aimed at businessmen and young professionals.[24] **Haddad's**, also located in The Davenport Hotel, had elegant shoes and clothing for women.

Rusan's, at W. 512 Riverside, was opened in 1940. Its name was derived from the combined names of the married owners, Russell and Ann Walker. "Just Smart Things" was Rusan's slogan. When the store was being designed, it was said that it "planned to follow the lines of smart Hollywood shops...[and would] specialize in ladies' sports apparel the rage in California."[25]

Owen Specialty Shop was located on the north side of Riverside between Post and Lincoln, near the Norfolk Building and the Aster Cafe. This small clothing shop was another place with its own smell, again not unpleasant, and perhaps an odor something like furniture polish. I remember when I was about eight, and the new school year was coming, that I skipped down Riverside with delight and excitement after getting new school dresses at the Owen Specialty Shop. Women, young girls and teenaged girls wore dresses for most occasions; we wore cotton dresses or skirts and blouses to school. In the summer we sometimes wore shorts, or a one piece sunsuit, but we did not usually wear long pants. When World War II came along, women and girls began to wear pants at times, but never to school or for anything but casual events.

Some other nice stores for women were **Grayson's**, **McBride's**, **Savon's**, and **Zukor's**. Among less pricey stores was **Lubin's**, which had window displays at the second floor level on the northeast corner of Riverside and Post and all along this level on both streets, though its entrance was mid-block on Post. Another less expensive store, **Mode O' Day**, was on the northeast corner of Howard and Riverside for most of this period, and sold inexpensive women's "housedresses," the everyday wear for women in the '30s and '40s. Imagine! These dresses had to be ironed! **Porter's Self-Service Apparel**, selling women's clothing, opened on the north-

west corner of Howard and Riverside in the summer of 1946, soon after Payless Drug moved from that property. Porter's moved to the southwest corner of Main and Howard in late 1949 or 1950. Along with the opening of the Bon Marche, Porter's move was seen as bringing revitalization to Main Street—much of it was rundown and shabby—and adding an important district of retail sales to downtown.[26]

A shop that was located in the Golden Gate Building at W. 824 Riverside advertised: "We Buy, Sell and Exchange High Grade Used Merchandise, Specializing in Gowns, Antiques, and Jewelry." It was called the Woman's Exchange, though its full name was **The Woman's Exchange and Gown Shop**. Remembering its name brought back some funny memories. Though at the time I had no idea where it was or exactly what it did, we used to hear my dad tease my mother if she did something he didn't particularly like. He would say: "You'd better be careful or I'm going to have to take you down to the Woman's Exchange!"

3

BUILDINGS

Spokane has a rich heritage of elegant buildings in a number of architectural styles. Many are handsomely decorated with ornate elements that can be missed unless a person makes a point of studying them. It would be nearly impossible to create some of the elaborate detailing today, or find craftsmen who could do it. If we could find these artisans, the cost for the work would be enormous.

Sometime around the decade of the '50s, "improvements" were taking place in many buildings. Store fronts were modernized in ways that were not in keeping with the styles of the buildings. Not only exteriors, but interiors of some buildings were changed. Ceilings were lowered, and decorative detailing was hidden or destroyed. Ornate chandeliers went out, recessed lighting came in. Today, this sort of remodeling seems insensitive, but styles at the time dictated a smooth and streamlined look.

A number of significant buildings that were part of Spokane's downtown in the '30s and '40s are gone. Interest in preservation of older buildings did not come into focus until the late '70s. Until then, buildings were often demolished without public notice and with little protest. Replacing buildings with new construction was considered a sign of progress. Even with the gradually developing interest in our architectural legacy, some charming buildings were swept away when condemned to the wrecking ball. In preparation for EXPO '74, entire blocks were destroyed along Spokane Falls Boulevard with no regard for the value of some individual buildings.

OFFICE BUILDINGS AND BANKS

The **Auditorium Building** of red brick and white granite, stood on the northwest corner of Main and Post. It was designed by Ger-

man trained Hermann Preusse, Spokane's first schooled architect. Under construction at the time of the Spokane Fire in 1889, the Auditorium Building escaped the flames and was completed in 1890.[1] A grandiose five story landmark, its massive stone exterior, large arched entries, and solid shape are elements of its Richardsonian Romanesque style. The main tower, one of several, was topped by an inverted funnel shaped dome, and atop this was a gilded statue of Thalia, the Muse of comedy. She wore a crown of roses and myrtle and held a golden lyre in her hand.

The building housed a theater, a variety of businesses through the years and also some apartments. Living quarters were commonly included in upper floors of office buildings constructed during the 1890s. In 1930, the Polk City Directory lists tenants as: two banks, one of which was was the Northwestern and Pacific Hypotheekbank which owned the building, two architects, six music teachers, three dressmakers, a hemstitcher, and a number of individuals who lived in the building. In 1933, the owners made plans to remodel it into a modern department store, but, unable to find a tenant, demolished the building in 1934.[2]

When the building was razed, there were reports of putting the golden statue someplace in town, possibly in a park. After several years it was reported that the statue had been lost. When it was found, the statue had been sawed in half, ending ideas of erecting it.[3] The corner on which the Auditorium Building stood was empty for several years after the building was demolished.[4] (Information about the theater will be found in the chapter on theaters.)

The **Crescent Block**, which took its name from the shape of the front of the building, was located next to the Review Building on Riverside. It was Romanesque in style, three stories tall, of off-white brick and had a wood frame. The Cres-

BUILDINGS

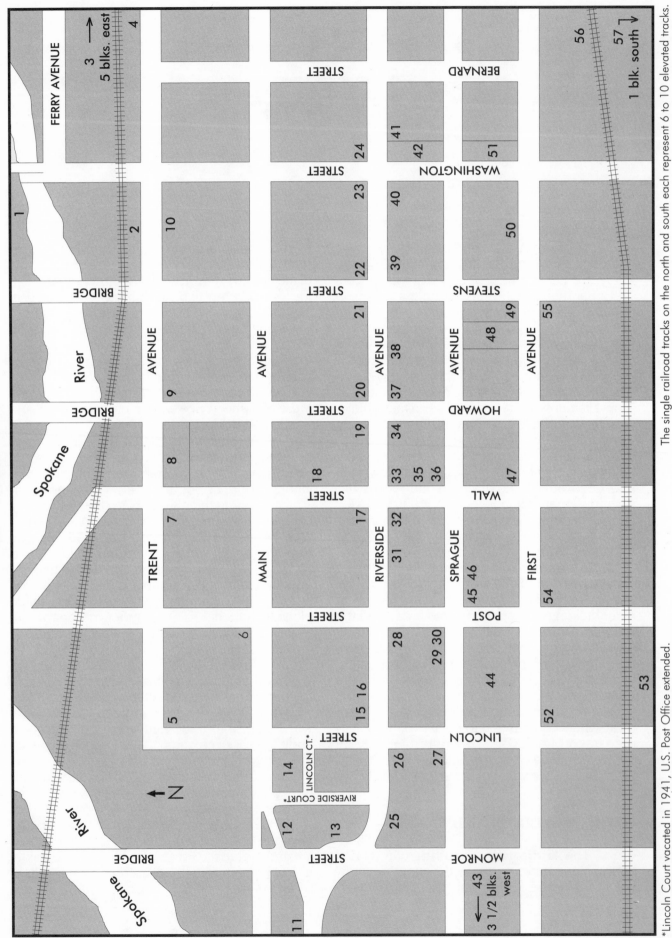

*Lincoln Court vacated in 1941, U.S. Post Office extended.
*Riverside Court vacated in 1966, Federal Building constructed.

The single railroad tracks on the north and south each represent 6 to 10 elevated tracks.
Another series of tracks was north of the Great Northern Depot, No 1 above.

The following list includes buildings that are discussed in this chapter and buildings that existed in the '30s and '40s that have been demolished. Dates of construction and demolition are given with those not dealt with in this chapter.

OFFICE BUILDINGS AND BANKS
6. Auditorium Building
25. Crescent Block
13. Dodd Block
21. Eagle Block (1890-1953)
26. Empire State Building (Great Western Building)
19. Exchange Building
28. Falls City Building (1890-1967)
15. Golden Gate Building (1892-1962)
51. Hutton Building (Built 1907, three stories added 1910)
33. Hyde Block
18. Hypotheekbank; also, First Federal Savings and Loan
32. Jamieson (Zukor) Building
14. Arthur D. Jones Building (entire block)
31. Kuhn Building
42. Lindelle Block
17. Marble Bank Building (First National Bank)
24. Metals Building (American Legion Building)
38. Mohawk Building (Built 1890, interior burned 1915 and rebuilt)
41. Nichols Building
16. Norfolk Building
22. Old National Bank; also Federal Reserve Bank
39. Paulsen Building
40. Paulsen Medical and Dental Building
27. Perry Block
45. Radio Central Building (Standard Stock Exchange Building)
37. Rookery Building (old and new)
34. Spokane and Eastern Trust Company Building
23. Temple Court Building (1890-1962)
36. Title Building (1890-1979)
46. Washington Trust Bank
30. Whitten Block (Built 1889)
20. Ziegler Block

RAILROAD DEPOTS
1. Great Northern
4. Milwaukee Freight Office
56. Northern Pacific
2. Union Station

HOTELS
9. Coeur d'Alene
44. Davenport (entire block)
54. Dessert (Desert)
55. Spokane
48. Ridpath, old
49. St. Nicholas (YWCA location, 1919-1938; then Ridpath Annex)
47. Victoria

OTHER BUILDINGS
8. Bus Depot, Intercity
53. Central Heating Plant
7. City Hall
10. OK Coffee House
50. Fire Station No. 1
11. Masonic Temple
35. Sartori Building
5. Washington Water Power Company Building
52. YMCA Building
12. Spokane Amateur Athletic Club, 1904-1930; Spokane Athletic Club, 1930-1933; YWCA, 1938-1966
29. Western Union, main office

FRINGE AREA
57. Armory
43. Carnegie Library
3. Golden Age Brewery

The Auditorium Building. Its main tower was at the corner of Main and Post, adding a sixth and seventh level there. *(Eastern Washington State Historical Society, Spokane, Washington, L93-18.48)*

The Review Building, and to the left of it, the Crescent Block. *(Eastern Washington State Historical Society, Spokane, Washington, L93-34.60)*

cent Block, one of the few buildings that escaped the Fire of 1889, was the first home of the Crescent Store, which opened, as scheduled, the day after the fire. Though the store was named after the building, it stayed in this location for about a year, then made two more moves before settling in its final Riverside location in 1899.[5]

Through the '30s and '40s, a number of hotel rooms or apartments were in upper floors of the Crescent Block. Small stores were at the street level. The building was razed in 1982 along with two other buildings, at which time the Review added an extension of its building in the area. Color, vertical lines, and arches were matched with that of the lovely old landmark Review Building with its French Renaissance tower.

The **Dodd Block**, built in 1890, was a three story brick building located across Riverside Avenue from the Review Building.[6] Especially interesting because of its shape, the street side of the building had a sweeping double curve, a sort of elongated backward "S" shape. The sidewalk followed the same pattern. Eclectic in style, with Victorian, Early Commercial and Romanesque Revival elements, the building had interesting decorative brickwork, round arched windows, and both strong horizontal and vertical divisions. The Dodd Block was demolished in 1966, the Federal Building (United States Court House) was built on the site in 1967, and the shape of Riverside was changed to a smooth, rounded curve. At the same time, Riverside Court, a very narrow street that was on the west side of the post office between Riverside and Main, was vacated.

The **Empire State Building**, renamed the **Great Western Building** in 1961, was Spokane's first steel frame construction.[7] The building sits on the southwest corner of Riverside and Lincoln. The old-fashioned style elevators were still in it in the '30s and '40s, one of several buildings that had them. It is said that these were the fastest elevators west of Chicago when the building was constructed in 1900.[8] This type of elevator had giant metal cages for elevator cars. In some buildings the cars were a fili-

The Dodd Block, with the Spokane Club in the background to the left. (*Eastern Washington State Historical Society, Spokane, Washington, L86-219.137*)

gree of iron or brass, sometimes they were painted black or white. The elevators were situated in large open areas that were surrounded by balconies, stairs, and walkways. Everyone could see in and out of this type of elevator as it moved, and could see the "works" of the elevator—hanging loops of cable, pulleys, ropes and counter-weights.

It seemed almost daring to ride these open elevators. Most elevators were enclosed by the '30s/'40s era. I remember the thrill of using the ones in the Empire State Building and at least one other cage elevator downtown. Robert Hyslop recalls in *Spokane's Building Blocks* that the elevators in the Empire State Building made a ringing sound that was a characteristic part of the atmosphere there. At this writing, a remnant

of one of the elevators in the Empire State Building can be seen at the second floor and at higher levels. Here one will find an atrium that fills the center of the building. A cage for the shaft of one elevator is still in the atrium, but the elevator and mechanism are gone. The interior of the building is intricately decorated with antique marble, bronze, steel, and ironwork.

The **Exchange Building**, once the Exchange Bank, (built as First National Bank), was on the northwest corner of Howard and Riverside. It was built in 1890, replacing a building that had been lost in the Spokane Fire. The new building was mainly of red brick, but the first floor was of large red sandstone.[9] Elements of Richardsonian Romanesque style are evident with its arches and its heavy, solid look, while its decorated brickwork

The Exchange Building, 1935. A Libby studio sign shows to the left of the entrance. John T. Little Sporting Goods is to the right of the building, and Jack Burt's Flower Shop to the left. *(Eastern Washington State Historical Society, Spokane, Washington, L94-36.53)*

Riverside Avenue looking east, 1931. On the right, the Jamieson Building and beyond it and across Wall Street, the Hyde Building. *(Eastern Washington State Historical Society, Spokane, Washington, Detail of photo L87-1.76-31)*

The Hypotheek Bank. *(Eastern Washington State Historical Society, Spokane, Washington, L87-1.18599-40)*

is Victorian. Pictures of the Exchange Building look strangely modern in the 1990s, as similar large arched windows and tiled hip roofs are being used in contemporary buildings. When the building was to be demolished in 1949, an article in *The Spokesman-Review* stated that it was "considered by most architects to be one of the worst eyesores in the city."[10]

The **Hyde Block**, built in 1890, was a six-story brick building on the southeast corner of Riverside and Wall.[11] Its handsome exterior had strong vertical lines, arched windows at the top, and elaborate detailing in granite, sandstone, and terra cotta.[12] The interior of the building had little ornamentation. Simple wooden posts and railings without adornment guarded its stairways.[13]

The Hyde Block was one of a series of buildings along the south side of Riverside that remained until the late '70s. From the Paulsen Buildings to the Spokesman-Review Building there was little change. An exception was the construction, in 1945, of the building containing Peters and Sons Florist. The Hyde Building was

torn down in 1979 to make way for the SeaFirst Bank Building.

After the Auditorium Building was demolished, the **Hypotheekbank** Building (Northwestern and Pacific Hypotheekbank—Hypotheek is a Dutch word for mortgage) was located on the east side of Wall between Riverside and Main, just north of the alley. The little building, built around 1891, was earlier called the Merrick Block, and in 1949, the **First Federal Savings & Loan Association**. The Hypotheekbank was the major Dutch mortgage company that had owned much of the downtown area in the 1890s. The building was enlarged several times during the '30s and '40s, including one addition of three floors to its already existing two.[14] The Hypotheekbank moved to the Great Western Building around 1954. The business closed in 1971.

The **Jamieson (Zukor) Building**, a six-story red brick structure on the southwest corner of Riverside and Wall was a mix of Richardsonian Romanesque and Early Commercial styles. Designed by Hermann Preusse, the building's elegant brickwork patterns were a major feature of the

The Arthur D. Jones building. *(Eastern Washington State Historical Society, Spokane, Washington, L87-1.9122-36)*

exterior. Metal panels set into the bricks on each side of the building showed that one street was Riverside, and the other Mill Street, an early name for Wall Street. Dr. David Cowen had his large dental practice on the second and third floors of this building for many years.

Zukor's, a clothing store for women, was on the corner from 1937 through the early '70s. Benjamin Zukor, the owner of the store, bought the building. During that period it was called the Zukor Building. On March 2, 1980, a fire destroyed the building along with a major tenant on the first floor, B. Dalton Books.[15] The area was vacant for about 14 years, after which the entire east end of the block was cleared and the Spokane Transit Authority Building was constructed on the site.

The two story **Arthur D. Jones Building** is described by Robert Hyslop as "a little glass jewel box, with show windows around all four sides."[16] This small building was located on its own small block bounded by Main, Lincoln, Riverside Court, and Lincoln Court, the last two now vacated. It was built in 1911 for the Arthur D. Jones realty company. The little building was torn down in 1940, and the Federal Building (Post Office) was extended to Main Avenue in 1941, the new addition matching the original Federal Building's Beaux Arts Classic/Second Renaissance Revival style.

The **Kuhn Building**, a five story granite

and brick building that was located across from The Crescent on Riverside, was actually two coordinated Romanesque Revival style buildings. Both were built in 1890, and were originally called the Van Valkenburg and the Holland Buildings. The two shared an entrance, a granite arch. In the semicircle of the arch, ornamental iron was used in geometric patterns. Twisted pieces in the center formed a pattern of sunburst rays. This later supported a huge brass plate that said Kuhn Building.[17] The Kuhn Building was demolished in 1989 and the Spokane Transit Authority Building was constructed on the site.

The four story **Lindelle Block**, on Washington between Riverside and Sprague, and the five story **Nichols Building**, next door on Riverside, had many similarites. Both buildings were built in 1890 and demolished in 1963.[18] Designed by the Reid Brothers of San Francisco, and in the same style, the buildings had many windows above the second level because of deep courts.

The **Marble Bank Building**, on the northwest corner of Riverside and Wall, was a gem. Hyslop calls it a "twelve carat diamond set in the center of Spokane's belt buckle." Built in 1892 for A. M. Cannon's Bank of Spokane Falls, which failed, it housed a series of different banks in earlier years. In 1929, the bank then in the building changed its name to **First National**, which was the name by which we knew this building in the '30s and '40s. This lovely classic style

The arched doorway of the Kuhn Building. *(Eastern Washington State Historical Society, Spokane, Washington, Detail of photo L87-1.81844-55)*

building was of veined gray polished marble. Symbolic of power, it had four life-sized stone lions guarding two of the building's entrances. Those of us who knew the building as children have especially fond memories of the lions.

By the late '40s, the bank was using all of its space and additional space in The Crescent's second story. With pressure from The Crescent, the bank moved in 1953; The Crescent then demolished the building and constructed an addition.[19]

Several owners and names are involved in the history of the **Metals Building**, located on the northeast corner of Riverside and Washington. Built in 1900 for the Spokane Club, it was used by the Chamber of Commerce from 1910 to 1931, then was purchased by some mining interests and renamed the Metals Building. It was called the **Assemblee Building** for a brief period in the '30s.[20] Purchased by the American Legion Post No. 9 in the late '40s, it was renamed the **American Legion Building**.[21]

The Lindelle Building at Riverside and Washington, and the taller Nichols Building on the left. *(Eastern Washington State Historical Society, Spokane, Washington, L94-36.173*

The Marble Bank Building, 1940. (Eastern Washington State Historical Society, Spokane, Washington, Detail of L87-1.19149-40)

In the '30s, this building had a different roofline. A six story building with even higher attic windows, the elaborately embellished upper floor and hip roof were removed after a fire in 1939. Of French Renaissance Revival style, the building lost many of its distinctive elements in the fire.

The five story **Norfolk Building**, constructed in 1912, was located in the middle of the 800 block on the north side of Riverside.[22] By the '40s, the building was not especially distinctive. It seemed antiquated, with dark hallways and unnecessarily large areas near the elevator. Hoffman Brothers Music Company, with sales of instruments, took up much of the second floor. Nearly all of the rest of building was occupied with teaching studios. If you were a music, dance, or drama student in those years, it is likely that you took lessons in the Norfolk Building. The 1937 Polk City Directory lists 22 music teachers, 8 dance studios, 3 drama coaches, a violin maker, an elocution teacher, the National Institute of Music and Arts, a booking agent, the Eddy School of Public Speaking and Dramatic Art—Miniature Theater,

The Metals Building. Its ornate roof was destroyed by fire in 1939. (Eastern Washington State Historical Society, Spokane, Washington, Detail of photo L94-36.114)

Part of the interior of the Old National Bank, showing a large skylight that was in the center of the ceiling. *(Eastern Washington State Historical Society, Spokane, Washington, L87-1.15742x-19)*

a beauty salon, a photography studio, and an office for the Fairmount Cemetery.

Walking around on the upper floors of the building, one heard at times a lone clarinet or soprano, at other times, a cacophony of sound—a tenor here, a violin there, several pianos, perhaps a trumpet—all combining to make a dissonance that is not altogether unpleasant to those involved in music. The building had a recital hall on the third floor with a wonderful Steinway grand piano on a small stage. The Norfolk Building was razed in 1962, and the Lincoln Building was constructed on the site.

The U.S. Bank, formerly the **Old National Bank**, located on the northeast corner of Riverside and Stevens, is an excellent example of the Chicago School of architecture. The interior of the banking area was very different from what it is today. Most striking was the green

marble throughout the public areas on columns, stairs, and edges of the floor around the tellers' cages. Some was white marble veined with green, some was dark green marble veined with white.

Inside the main entrance, one faced a grand and spacious central area. Rows of columns on either side led the eye to the other end of the long open area. Tellers' cages were at the left, and desk areas on the right. The tall marble columns, which supported the higher of two mezzanines, had Ionic capitals.

Rectangular iron grill work in geometric patterns was used below railings at the edges of the mezzanines. Double pilasters separated each rectangle at the top level. The ceilings were beautifully decorated with square recessed areas that had lovely geometric designs.[23]

The **Federal Reserve Bank** of San Francisco moved its local headquarters from the Auditorium Building to the Old National Bank in late 1933 or early 1934. The Federal Reserve Bank took 17,000 square feet of space on three floors of the bank and on the 15th floor. A new door was cut into the Stevens Street side of the building, walls were built to separate the two banks, and the existing decor matched.[24] The Old National Bank did not lose much of its spacious lobby area and, for the most part, the interior of the bank did not change again through the '40s.[25]

The **Paulsen Building**, on the southeast corner of Riverside and Stevens, was built in 1908. In those days, the elevators in the building were unique, at least in Spokane. Centered under each elevator was a piston that was at least as long as the building is tall that went deep into the ground. The piston pushed the elevator hydraulically to lift it. The piston could be viewed from outside the elevators, as they had glass doors. When the elevator started and stopped, there was hissing and wheezing. The elevators were in the building well into the '40s.

The **Paulsen Medical and Dental Building**, on the southwest corner of Riverside and Washington, was new at the beginning of the '30s/'40s period, having been started in 1928, and completed in 1930.[26] The architect was Gustav Pehrson. The exterior of the newer building is especially interesting in its detailed designs on the first few levels, which include figureheads, geometric and floral patterns. I remember that the elevators in the building seemed very fast and there were red light bulbs that lit up near an elevator when it was arriving, rather than the arrows there today. A similar sounding "ping" can be heard now when an elevator arrives at a floor.

The **Perry Block** was a three story wood frame building that was on the northwest corner of Lincoln and Sprague.[27] To my knowledge, it was the only building with a wood exterior in the downtown area during the '30s and '40s. The top two stories were razed in 1949, and the ground floor remodeled, covering the wood exterior. The building was torn down in 1976.

The **Radio Central Building**, first called the Eilers Building for the Eilers Music Company, a seven story brick building on the southeast corner of Sprague and Post, was built in 1911. Its entrance was on the Sprague Avenue side of the building. In 1929, because of the stock exchange on the second floor, it was renamed the **Standard Stock Exchange Building**. By 1935, it was the home of both KGA and KHQ radio stations, so was renamed the Radio Central Building. A

The Radio Central Building, ca. 1928 before the radio tower was on the building. (Eastern Washington State Historical Society, Spokane, Washington, L94-9.246)

large radio transmission tower was on top of the building.

On the floors below the radio stations were a variety of offices, a few music studios, and a small recital hall. The Radio Central Building was torn down in 1971 and replaced by the Washington Trust Financial Center.[28] As a child, I would stand staring out of a fifth floor window looking at the Spanish Mission architecture of the east end of The Davenport Hotel while waiting for my piano lesson to begin.

The **old Rookery Building** stood on the southeast corner of Howard and Riverside where the newer Rookery Building stands today. Hyslop's *Spokane's Building Blocks* says that the old Rookery was actually "a conglomeration of five buildings," and that it had "corridors and light wells upstairs and...odd and irregular rooms [that] made the name quite appropriate." Most of the buildings were six stories in height, and one, on Howard, varied in height over the years from two to five stories. The corner building at Howard and Riverside had a rounded corner and tower. Most of the buildings were torn down in 1933, though a Sprague Avenue extension was left standing.

The old Rookery was replaced that year by the three story, Art Deco **new Rookery Building**, still on that corner. Designed by Gustav A. Pehrson, it has intricate carvings on its facade that are said to be reminiscent of ancient Egyp-

Detail of exterior of Spokane and Eastern Trust Company Building. *(Eastern Washington State Historical Society, Spokane, Washington, Detail of photo L87-1.81233-55)*

tian carvings.[29] Most of these were installed up-side-down, according to Hyslop, but since the effect was acceptable except for the top course, they were left in place. During construction, a few newly designed ones were made and placed at the top.[30]

On the southwest corner of Howard and Riverside was the **Spokane and Eastern Trust Company Building**. A handsome Art Deco building, it was described in *The Spokesman-Review* soon after it opened in 1931: "Architecturally, it is one of the most distinctive buildings in the northwest. Seven stories high, it is a moderne type, with straight and simple lines stretching from the sidewalk to the roof. The bulk of the exterior is of soft cream-colored terra cotta, laid in large smooth blocks. By way of contrast, the structure from the street level to the second floor

is chiefly Rainbow granite in brilliant mottlings of rose and metallic gray. Between the windows are spandrels of cast aluminum."[31] This aluminum decorative effect was an "art nouveau expression derived from imagining Egyptian papyrus scrolls being flung out vertically."[32]

This building had a touch of mystery for me as a child. It had doors that seemed to open magically as you approached the entrance to the bank. Nowadays every supermarket has similar doors, but then they seemed a marvel of technology. It was an absolute wonder to open a door by walking in front of a beam of light. We didn't dream that such doors would be commonplace in the future.

In the marble-lined foyer, brilliant iron and nickel silver elevator doors repeated some of the exterior patterns with the addition of floral designs.

Scrolls, geometric patterns, sunbeams, and chevrons lavishly decorated the front doors and windows of the Spokane and Eastern Trust Company. *(Eastern Washington State Historical Society, Spokane, Washington, L84-197.1)*

The interior had a number of chandeliers hanging from its beautifully detailed ceiling, which was decorated with flower and leaf patterns along with chevrons. A band at the top of the walls had yet another display of ornamentation. Ornate grillwork surrounded banking desks and tellers' cages.[33]

In 1951, the building was extended to Sprague Avenue, approximately doubling its size. The entire building was duplicated in style on the outside. At this time the lovely Art Deco ornamentation in the interior banking area disappeared. The exquisite old ornate ceiling on the main floor was covered, and the ceiling lowered. Chandeliers were eliminated in favor of recessed ceiling lights behind glass, charming wall decorations were removed, and sleek rounded counters replaced the areas with grillwork. Wide bands of decoration across the windows on Howard Street remained, probably because they

could not be destroyed without structural damage.[34]

Joel E. Ferris was manager of the Spokane and Eastern, and a vice president of Seattle-First National bank from the time this building opened until well into the '50s. Mr. Ferris was involved in civic and regional activities to such an extent that it is a wonder he had time for a life of his own. A partial list of his activities is: Trustee of the Hutton Settlement, of St. Luke's hospital, and of Eastern Washington College of Education; President of the Friends of the Library at Washington State College, Overseer of Whitman College, Chairman of the Pacific Northwest Conference of Banking, President of Eastern Washington State Historical Society, Member of the Boards of the Camp Fire Girls, Red Cross, and Salvation Army. He was on national boards of several of these. In addition, he privately and substantially helped finance archaeological digs of several pre-

The interior of the Spokane and Eastern Trust Company, 1931. *(Eastern Washington State Historical Society, Spokane, Washington, L84-197.2)*

historic Indian sites that were to be covered by Coulee Dam flooding, thus saving at least some knowledge about these people. He also wrote monographs on historic places and events.[35]

The well-known murals on the west wall of the bank's interior, now in the Cheney Cowles Museum, were not installed until 1953. The Spokane and Eastern Building was the last to go when the entire block was demolished for construction of the SeaFirst Bank Building. Banking continued here while other parts of the new building were constructed. The old building was torn down in 1981.[36] The area where the bank had stood (before the extension), became a sidewalk and garden area leading to the entrance to the SeaFirst Building.

The **Washington Trust Bank** was located in the middle of the block on the south side of Sprague between Post and Wall and between John W. Graham and the Bandbox theater. The building was built for the Spokane Savings & Loan in 1919; the Washington Trust Company moved into it in the early '30s and it became known as the Washington Trust Building by the late '30s.[37] A handsome six story concrete structure with a white terra cotta front, the building had interesting detailing in the cornice area, and in elaborate spandrels above and below most of the windows. Four rather small pilasters at the street level were repeated in six tall pilasters on either side of the windows in the upper four stories. The building was razed in 1972 for the construction of the Washington Trust Financial Center which covers the entire block.

The **Ziegler Block** was a five story structure on the northeast corner of Howard and Riverside built to replace an earlier wood frame Ziegler Building that was lost in the 1889 fire.[38] The Ziegler Block was an attractive building in many respects, especially because of its contrasting light and dark detail. It had an elaborate Beaux Arts cornice, and distinct horizontal divisions. The building was torn down in 1952 to make way for construction of the Fidelity Building.

One last memory about the buildings of that period. It was common to find spittoons, usu-

The Washington Trust Bank Building, between John W. Graham and the Bandbox theater. *(Eastern Washington State Historical Society, Spokane, Washington, L87-1.65849-51)*

The Ziegler Block was a mix of many styles with a different window treatment on each floor. *(Eastern Washington State Historical Society, Spokane, Washington, L87-1.16652-39)*

ally made of brass, next to the elevators. Buildings with a bank of elevators had one by each elevator on each floor. They were in the Old National Bank Building, the Paulsen Building, the Mohawk Building, The Davenport Hotel, and many others. They were probably left from an earlier time when tobacco chewing was more common. I don't believe I ever saw one being used.

RAILROAD STATIONS

In addition to the **Northern Pacific** sta-

tion (now Amtrak) that is still in existence near First Avenue and Bernard, we had the *Great Northern Depot*, the *Union Station*, and the *Milwaukee Freight Office*. All three of these were demolished in 1973 to make way for EXPO '74, and then for Riverfront Park.

Efforts to save the *Union Station* and the *Great Northern Depot* were made by The National Railway Historical Society's Inland Empire Chapter, the Save Our Stations Committee, and the Sierra Club. Architects Kenneth Brooks and Warren Heylman suggested possible uses for the buildings might be a visual arts center, a place for social services or enrichment programs, or a food fair, but most people were not yet interested in historic preservation and these ideas were rejected.[39] A compromise was made by keeping the Great Northern Tower. It is the sole symbol of railroading in this area that once was teeming with railway activity.

The **Great Northern Depot**, built in 1901,was located on what was then called Havermale Island.[40] The building, Romanesque in style, was an austere three story tan brick structure with a hip roof. It faced the south channel of the river between Washington and Stevens. The splendid tower that still graces a meadow area of Riverfront Park, with its four huge clocks, was at the center front of the building. The upper part of the tower looks the same today as it did when the entire building was there, though there was a very large G N on each side of the tower between the roof and the arched area below.

Entering the main doors of the building on the east and west sides of the tower, one turned immediately north, then entered a white glazed tile waiting room that had large wooden benches. A ticket office and baggage checking area were on the right side, an eating area and cigar/magazine counter on the left. The tracks were at ground level on the north side of the building. Between the building and the tracks were train sheds—covered areas next to the tracks that kept passengers and their companions protected from rain and snow.

The **Milwaukee Freight Office**, a brick building with attached freight loading docks on either side, was located on the north side of Trent (Spokane Falls Boulevard), two blocks west of Division. According to Hyslop, this building was probably built in case there were difficulties in the Milwaukee railroad (Chicago, Milwaukee, St. Paul and Pacific Railroad) getting continuous use of the Union Station. He writes, "This problem did not arise, and the Milwaukee building, along with its one-story wings and wagon [later truck] loading along Trent (there was no sidewalk) served as the freight office for the railroad...A name panel 'MILWAUKEE' in terra cotta was across the top center of the two-story building."[41] The building and loading docks were razed in 1973.

The **Union Station**, built in 1914, was located on the north side of Trent (Spokane Falls Boulevard) between Stevens and Washington. The station was sometimes erroneously called the

The Great Northern Depot on Havermale Island. (*Northwest Room, Spokane Public Library*)

Milwaukee Station as the "Milwaukee Road" used this depot.[42] This building was more ornate and elegant than the Great Northern Depot. It was four stories tall, red brick and white stone, with terra cotta trim on the front. A large marquee was suspended from the building with chains and above it were huge arched windows. Inside was a waiting room where the arched form was repeated in niches around the room. The area was

The Milwaukee Freight Office. In this 1929 picture by Charles Libby, it appears there were 14 loading docks on each side of the main building. *(Eastern Washington State Historical Society, Spokane, Washington, Detail of photo L87-1.40677-29)*

The Union Station. Many wood-framed glass entrance doors were across the front of the building under its marquee. *(Northwest Room, Spokane Public Library)*

grandiose, with immense chandeliers, high ceilings, and a wide staircase coming from the large entrance lobby below.[43] On the north side of the building were the tracks, which were elevated, making it necessary for passengers to take another set of less grand stairs to that level.

HOTELS

(Dining areas of some hotels will be found in the chapter on restaurants.)

The brick **Coeur d'Alene Hotel** is still on the southeast corner of Howard and Spokane Falls Boulevard. Built in 1890 as the four story Loewenberg Building, it was later acquired by "Dutch" Jake Goetz and Harry Baer, two men who made money in the Coeur d'Alene mines. After the purchase, the building had a colorful history which involved gambling, dance halls, and theaters, not unlike several such places in Spokane. Public protests after the turn of the century soon closed the places. In 1910, the two owners added two stories and remodeled it into the Coeur d'Alene Hotel with its famous Silver Dollar bar.[44]

Even though this was not a desirable part of town by the '40s, the Coeur d'Alene was by far the most attractive of the row of hotels along Trent Avenue. Guests were readily available as the hotel was close to railroad stations and the intercity bus depot. Hotel operations continued in the building until 1977. The Coeur d'Alene was remodeled into apartments in 1980.[45] It is now called the Coeur d'Alene Plaza Apartments.

THE DAVENPORT HOTEL

Louis Davenport started as a restaurateur right after the 1889 Spokane Fire. Around 1890, he moved his operation from the site of the Whitten Block, where he had a waffle restaurant in a tent, to the two story building on the southwest corner of Sprague and Post. He built the 12 story Davenport Hotel on that block in 1914. At this writing, The Davenport Hotel has been closed for twelve years. The new owners have restored the lobby, the Marie Antoinette, Elizabethan, and Isabella rooms and they are used for weddings, receptions, parties, and dances. The owners have plans for renovating the hotel, restoring it to its original grandeur; it is due to reopen in 1999.

The Davenport Hotel, the grand landmark hotel of Spokane, was still in its golden years at the beginning of the '30s. The magical aura that surrounded The Davenport in those years came from its elegance, its reputation for only the finest service, its celebrated epicurean dining, and from its luxurious pampering of guests. There were also unique features that became legendary. Among them were polished money, singing birds, a profusion of blossoming flowers, soft water from a well beneath the building, and fish in glass columns.

As mentioned earlier, I remember as a child looking out a window from the Radio Central Building at the white stucco, gables, red roofs, corner clock with little columns around it, and the tiny columns next to the windows. It was a little fantasy land. Beyond this Spanish portion of the building could be seen the taller and newer part of the hotel. I studied the lighted vertical letters that spelled the word "D A V E N P O R T" on the north edge of the west side of the building. Above these letters, a small American flag, shaped as though it were waving in the breeze, flashed in red, white, and blue light bulbs.

Kirtland Cutter, architect of The Davenport, is well-known to Spokanites for his many outstanding buildings and homes in our area. According to Henry Matthews, professor of Architectural History at Washington State University, Cutter knew "how wealthy people lived... [and] wanted to create new heights of pleasure for them in their homes and places of entertainment."[46] Louis Davenport apparently did not want to intimidate customers with the opulent architecture of the hotel, however, as a frequently heard phrase in the hotel's advertising in early days was "Come in just as you are."

The Davenport was the center of much of the social life in Spokane. Louis Davenport's policy was to encourage people of the community to use the hotel. It was not just for the use of the hotel's guests; its lobby was used by many as a meeting place. People would say, "I'll meet you by the fireplace," or "I'll be waiting near the fountain." Friends could meet on the mezzanine where there were chairs and small tables and they could watch the scene below or write a letter on The Davenport stationery that was provided at the tables.

The Davenport was a showplace to which we took out of town visitors. Most of us were unaware of the symbolic and mythological references to protection, determination, and decent competition of trade when we looked at the figures on the exterior—armored heads of knights, swords, Bighorn sheep alternating with scrolls, and above these a staff with twisting serpents.[47] We simply felt proud of this fine building in our city.

Inside the hotel we entered the elegant **Spanish Renaissance lobby**, reminiscent of a Spanish patio but with a skylight of green opalescent glass rather than actually being open to the sky. It gave us pleasure to show the lobby's central spouting marble fountain, its pool at times

Detail of one of four large floor lamps in The Davenport Hotel lobby. *(Family Collection)*

filled with goldfish, at other times with fragrant flowers. The lobby was known for the profusion of fresh flowers that graced the area especially at Easter time.

We made sure that our friends saw the fireplace with its glowing blaze that was never allowed to go out, and the cages that held a wide variety of birds. Guests who stayed at The Davenport told us that the birds tried to outdo each other with their bright and cheery songs when the sun streamed through the skylight each morning. We walked by the four magnificent floor lamps—twisted and spiraled gold columns embossed with entwined grape vines, each mounted on stone and crowned with alabaster shades—two of which were at each end of the lobby. Up on the mezzanine we pointed to wonderfully crafted beams, with their griffins, dolphins, coats of arms, and seemingly endless beautifully worked figures, again filled with symbolic references to strength, swiftness, sociability and protection.[48]

Not only was there regular hot and cold water in the taps in the hotel's more than 400 guest rooms, but there was also an additional tap that brought ice water. We bragged of the hotel's using only new crisp currency bills, and its unusual habit of washing and polishing coins so that they were shiny bright before they were used for change. This cleaning and polishing of coins was done in a specially designed machine that was located in The Davenport basement. It was carried out for over fifty years by John Ungari. Federal agents at one time came to the hotel and questioned the practice of washing the money, saying it might damage it. Ungari asked the agents if they would be satisfied that the coins were not being damaged if he could put a fresh egg through the machine without breaking the egg. The agents agreed. Ungari got two eggs from the kitchen and let the federal agents select one. He then broke the other to prove that the eggs had not been cooked. The remaining egg was put through the machine. It did not break, and the federal agents went away satisfied.[49]

What a delight it was to go to The Davenport for banquets, proms, luncheons, wedding receptions, Christmas parties, fashion shows and other special occasions. We might go to the Spanish style **Isabella Room**, with Corinthian columns and a frieze around the room decorated with rabbits, foxes, turtles and boys, and with walls ornamented with turkeys. Dressed in formal gowns, we would go to the exquisite ivory and gray French style **Marie Antoinette Ballroom**, with its French crystal chandeliers, a gallery decorated with plaster court jesters, and springs under the dance floor to cushion the feet of the dancers. Being in these elegant surroundings was like being transported to a radiant dream world and the soft lights, music, shining silver, polished brass, and sparkling crystal added still more to this brief fairy tale existence.

The **Italian Gardens**, on the southwest corner of Sprague and Post, was the site of the original Davenport's Restaurant. It was Davenport's Restaurant, then the Italian Gardens, and later the Crystal Room, the Matador, and finally Louis D's. The Italian Gardens is the place that most of us remember not only as the height of formal dining, but also as the place where we took the most special guests.

Large glass fish tanks were found in several places in the hotel, but the ones most remembered were those in the Italian Gar-

The Italian Gardens in 1938; the two glass columns of fish frame a large mirror. The Roman Corinthian column was one of many along the north wall. *(Eastern Washington State Historical Society, Spokane, Washington, L87-1.13842-38)*

dens.[50] These were two large crystal columns that contained tropical fish. (Some sources say goldfish.) They were located in the northeast corner of the room, directly across from the main public entrance to the restaurant which led from the foyer that also served the Coffee Shop. In early days these glass pillars were in front of an elaborate marble area of carved garlands, mirrors, and a cupid, and were centered on a wide wall in another part of the room.[51] When they were moved is uncertain. A Davenport booklet published about 1928 describes the area as a "garden spot of flowers" with a spouting fountain and changing waves of light playing over all.[52] The fish-filled columns were retained through the '30s/'40s era. John Luppert, musician there from 1937 to 1942, has said, "When I think of the Italian Gardens I remember the smell of fresh flowers and Havana cigars."

Delicately painted urns, deer or antelope, flowers, leaves, and dainty birds were painted in muted shades on the walls. Black and white checkerboard patterns were on the dance floor and entrance area.[53] Roman columns along one

wall, many plants and exquisite flora and fauna motif were fitting for an "Italian Garden."

If we were lucky enough to go to the **Hall of the Doges** for a special banquet or dance, we would find ourselves on the second floor of the original east end in an elaborate Italian style room covered with ornamentation. Three large crystal chandeliers hang from the ceiling. Cherubs, an angel, and a woman with two swans float in blue in a circular ceiling mural. This and the vaulted ceiling with other painted figures are suggestive of the interior of the Palace of the Doges in Venice. Arches in all walls of the high-ceilinged central room led to surrounding areas; at some point over the past 40 years the arches were enclosed, but the new owners plan to restore the room to its original open-arch plan. Above the arches, behind miniature faux balconies, are windows and smaller arches that resemble those on the exterior of the Venetian palace.

We also liked handsome areas such as the oak paneled **Elizabethan Room**, decorated in Tudor style, with its silver chandeliers. There were 15 private banquet rooms available during most

The Hall of the Doges. (*Courtesy of The Davenport Hotel*)

of the time the hotel was open.

We could hear piano music played on the mezzanine of the lobby by Arthur Zepp, well known Spokane pianist, who played there beginning about 1936.[54] The job was agreed upon by bartering; in exchange for playing several times a day, Zepp and his wife got their meals and lived in one of The Davenport's rooms. As far as the Zepps were concerned, it was a splendid plan, as earning a living was not easy in those Depression days. Mr. Zepp played several types of music, familiar classics by Chopin, Brahms, Debussy and Schumann, and melodic popular songs. Zepp remembers: "I had instructions to play something by Stephen Foster if I noticed that Louis Davenport was in the lobby."

Mrs. Zepp often sat near him and knitted or did mending. On one occasion, a stranger came and sat next to him on the piano bench while he was playing. Zepp felt somewhat irritated as it is difficult to play if a person sits so close, so he stopped playing. The man asked him

if he smoked. Zepp answered: "No, I can't afford it." During their conversation Zepp mentioned it was his wife sitting nearby. When the man left, he slipped a ten dollar bill into Mrs. Zepp's sewing bag. Ten dollars represented a lot of money then.

Zepp liked trading music for room and board and would have continued it; however, in 1937 there was an Amalgamated Laundry Workers strike.[55] Zepp recalls the strike as an ugly affair in which stink bombs were thrown in the lobby, killing some of the birds in their cages. As a consequence of the strike, The Davenport went nonunion. Although he hated to go, Zepp and others were forced to leave the hotel.

By the '30s, a large pipe organ in the east end of the lobby had been replaced by a Hammond organ, played by Frances Tipton. John Luppert recalled one day when Tipton, a well-known organist in the community who prided herself in her abilities, became infuriated with Mr. Davenport who remarked, "You know, you're getting quite good on that thing!"[56]

Sometimes the Davenport lobby would be given over to special events, perhaps a convention, a large banquet, a style show, or to music performances. Some of these performances were carried live over the radio.

On the north side of the lobby was a small candy shop tucked almost under the stairs leading to the mezzanine, in front of what had, in the '30s, been the entrance to the "Fountain Room." (See restaurant chapter.) One of the specialties sold there was a thick candy bar called the Davenport Bar, made of two layers of baked fudge with a jam filling. The bar was then dipped in chocolate and was wrapped in one of three colors of foil, the color designating the flavor of the filling, raspberry, pineapple, or lemon. Many of the candies were made in the basement candy factory.[57]

Bellhops wore flat-topped pill-box caps and blue uniforms with brass buttons; they carried a silver tray to hold messages like the famous page boy in the Phillip Morris advertisement.[58] They could be heard calling out as they walked through the lobby, "Paging Mr._____! Paging Mr. _____!"

Much of the basement of The Davenport was white marble. In the '30s, a large billiard room with twelve tables could be seen from a hallway through leaded glass windows.[59] A bowling alley was also located in this lower level.[60] There were also the small candy factory, the **Pompeian Barber Shop**, a nail salon, a shoe shine shop, employees' rooms, a storage room for trunks, and the **Equerry Dining Room** to serve traveling servants of guests. The basement men's room contained one of the many aquariums in the building.

Through the years, guests at The Davenport included many well known people. With the exception of Eisenhower and Carter, all U.S. presidents from Taft through Gerald Ford visited or stayed at the hotel, though both Reagan's and Bush's visits were before they became president. Heads of state, movie stars, other entertainers, and sports figures stopped at The Davenport. The following hotel guests are said to have been there during the '30s and '40s: General George Marshall, Maurice Evans, Zane Grey, Jack Benny and his wife Mary Livingston, Bing Crosby, Fritz Kreisler, Clark Gable, Woody Guthrie, Dennis Day, Jeanette MacDonald, Nelson Eddy, Betty Hutton, Alfred Lunt and Lynn Fontanne, Benny Goodman, Gene Autrey, Charles Boyer, Robert Taylor, and Capt. Eddie Rickenbacker.[61]

The well in the sub basement was dug beneath the hotel at the time it was built. James A. McCluskey, who worked at the hotel from the time it opened until he retired as vice president and managing director in 1952, said the well was 1,606 feet deep and was located in the third level basement. According to McCluskey, the water was too cold for drinking, but was heated from the Central Heating Plant and used for bathing, laundry, washing dishes, running the elevators (which were operated by a hydraulic system), and all other non-consumptive uses. Many of the hotel guests loved bathing in this soft water, and some claimed to extend their stay because of it. In the 1950s, use of the water from the well was discontinued.[62]

In 1933, when Prohibition was repealed, Harry Jones recalled that the Old National Bank lent money to the Bohemian Brewery to get that operation started. The Davenport Hotel management wanted to have beer on hand when the first day of legalized drinking arrived. On the day before Prohibition was to end, still an illegal time to drink, beer was delivered to The Davenport with a police escort.

Many couples from Spokane and the Inland Northwest spent their wedding nights at The Davenport. A charming memory of their 1939 wedding night comes from Don and Lillian Sperry. They had a reservation, but when they reached the room they were surprised to find that it was the Bridal Suite. They describe it as a lovely large room with a chaise longue, and decorated with a beautiful bouquet of fresh flowers. As they had not asked for the Bridal Suite, they became concerned that they wouldn't have enough money to pay for it. In the morning, Don went downstairs to check out and was told that the room was "free"! Don's father was a personal friend of Louis Davenport, but the Sperrys didn't ever find out if this was a gift from Mr. Davenport or from one of their parents.

ALTERATIONS TO THE DAVENPORT DURING THIS PERIOD

Shortly before 1930, plate glass windows and large ornamental doors were installed in the Orange Bower restaurant, located in the center of the Post Street side of the building, and in the Delicacy Shop that was just south of the Orange Bower.[63] Until this time there had been no entrance at First and Post in the corner of the Delicacy Shop. The new entrance was described as being a "dome-shaped structure of oriental de-

Large glass display cases on black marble bases in the Arcade. The richly ornamented filigree decoration was repeated in the chandeliers and in a gate-like door to another area.[64] *(Eastern Washington State Historical Society, Spokane, Washington, L86-859)*

sign." In addition, "a new American soda fountain completely equipped with the latest refrigeration system" was installed, probably in the Orange Bower area as there was a soda fountain there in the '30s. What a history of names this room had; it was the Orange Bower Men's Bar, then simply the Orange Bower (probably because of prohibition), and later the Apple Bower, the Copper Strike, the Tap Room, and the Audubon Room.

In the spring of 1930, Great Northern Railroad opened a ticket office in the hotel, and an existing flower shop, located near the coffee shop on the north side of the building, was reduced to a "flower corridor." This provided space for a small foyer at the east end of the hotel corridor. Fresh flowers were sold at a black marble counter in this area, which was sometimes called the Arcade. Around 1937, a roof garden restaurant adjacent to the skylight was closed.[65]

In 1939, Davenport announced a $100,000 remodeling of the basement for the addition of an 80 car garage. Cars would be lowered to this level by two elevators.[66] An air conditioned kennel for dogs was to be added as well. The "**Early Birds Breakfast Club**," a private club that had previously met in the Desert Hotel, moved into the lower level. These facilities were

in space that had been occupied partly by the baggage area, a carpenter shop, a laundry, the billiard room and part of the candy factory. The laundry moved to an area on the Post Street side of the basement that was formerly occupied by the bowling alleys.[67] The twelve tables of the billiard room were taken out, and the other facilities were moved to an area under the Italian Gardens.

There was still not enough parking at the hotel, and it was announced in 1940, before the above basement parking area was finished, that The Davenport would build a parking garage opposite the hotel entrance on First Avenue.[68] The facade of the garage was described in the newspaper—"fluted concrete columns of an unusual design, illuminated with concealed lights...an opening, 40X30 feet in height...done in aluminum and plate glass."[69]

In 1947, the parking area under the hotel was demolished and the Early Birds Club was expanded to nearly three times its original size. About the same time, sixteen new hotel suites were added on the fourteenth floor, changing the rooftop skyline and eliminating a public area that had once been tennis courts.[70]

During World War II, misplaced patriotism led to vandalism in the hotel. Several Chinese jardinieres that were displayed on stairway landings were smashed as they were thought to be Japanese.[71]

The most significant changes began when Davenport decided to sell the hotel in 1945. He was nearly seventy-seven years old, perhaps ready to retire, and he may have anticipated changes in the hotel business as motels began attracting more people. For whatever reason, he sold the hotel. This was the beginning of a precarious period. The hotel would sell again in 1947, in 1948, and still again in 1949. The Davenport would have nine different owners from 1945 to 1990. During this time, changes were made that destroyed forever some areas of the beautiful old building. New owners would usually announce plans to return the hotel to the grand and elegant place it had been, but remodeling efforts were at times ill considered. Many original furnishings were lost and the hotel began to decline.

Late in 1948, Washington State liquor laws were changed, so that for the first time, mixed drinks could be served at places other than at private clubs; The Davenport put in a cocktail lounge in 1949. Major alterations were made to the Italian Gardens and nearby areas. Perhaps it was at this time that remaining aquariums were removed. The Italian Gardens would now be called the **Crystal Room**. It was decorated with chandeliers of cut crystal and with wallpaper panels that were copies of the famous unicorn tapestries at the Metropolitan Museum of Art. A place for an orchestra was still there, and the carpet was laid so that it could be removed for dancing.[72]

A new entrance on Sprague at Post Street led to the **Fountain Room**, the new cocktail lounge. According to *The Spokesman-Review*, February 13, 1949, the room had been named for a small spouting fountain that featured a little boy statuette that had been in the Italian Gardens for many years, and was now to be in the new lounge, but the name must also have been reminiscent of the old Fountain Room soda fountain. (See restaurant chapter.) Cocktails were also available in the Tap Room, the former Apple Bower. The coffee shop was also transformed. The east wall was removed and "except for wide-spaced pillars, there...[was]...no demarcation between the Crystal room and the coffee shop." New paneled walls in the coffee shop showed stylized apple trees and apple pickers. All of these rooms were to be fully air-conditioned.[73]

Fortunately the beautiful detail in the lobby, mezzanine, grand ballrooms, and smaller banquet rooms remains, much as it was in the '30s and '40s. The new owners, Sun International

In the Italian Gardens for many years a small statue of a boy poured water from a jug on his shoulder. *(Eastern Washington State Historical Society, Spokane, Washington, Detail of photo L85-295)*

Hotels Ltd. of Hong Kong have begun restoration of the hotel.

The **Desert Hotel**, built as the Pacific Hotel in 1890, was a three story building that was located on the southeast corner of First and Post. It was named for its owner, Victor Dessert, pronounced Desert, and though the hotel used two s's in the name in early years, by 1939, one "s" was dropped.[74] A desert theme was used in its main dining room, the *Oasis*. (See restaurant chapter.)

A **Rathskeller** room "with rough stone walls and heavy adzed wood doors and sills" that included a bar and "a polished floor for Saturday night dancing" was put into the basement in 1933 after the repeal of prohibition. This room was "patterned after an old German taproom" and featured steins, goblets, kegs, and beer bottles in decoration, and German dishes in fare. At the same time, three dining rooms, each with a special theme, and a kitchen were added to this lower level.[75]

The Roundup Room in the Desert Hotel was paneled with mirrors, had indirect lighting, neon lights on the bar, and pastel colors on the ceiling. *(Eastern Washington State Historical Society, Spokane, Washington, L87-1.5495-35)*

Said to be "the last word in modern, artistic decoration" when it opened in 1934, the **Roundup Room** was "an elaborate cafe and night club" that seated 250 people. A concert pipe organ, "the only hotel pipe organ north of San Francisco and west of St. Paul" was on a stage that also had space for an orchestra.[76] This room, I am told, was the same location as the Rathskeller, above.[77] This means that the Rathskeller was very shortlived, having been put into the hotel only a little over a year earlier. It is probable that a more stylish and sleek environment evocative of the Art Deco 1930s was desired.

In 1936, the Dessert did extensive remodeling to its guest rooms. Chief among the improvements was that it became "the only hotel in Spokane air-conditioned above the second floor." Fifty bathrooms were added so that there was one for each room. This major renovation also included lowering of ceilings, replastering, new wood trim in all rooms, and redecorating. New furniture was purchased in "modern" and in "California Monterey" styles.[78]

A **Desert Hotel Cigar Shop** was located on the northwest corner of the building and the hotel lobby was next to it on the Post Street side of the building. The lobby was almost square in shape and rather small, especially compared to the spacious lobby of the nearby Davenport. One could reach the Oasis dining room from the lobby by going through a wide doorway. In 1949, after state liquor laws were changed so that mixed drinks could be served in places other than private clubs, the Desert put in a cocktail lounge called the **Mirage Room**.

The Desert Hotel was demolished in 1961 and replaced by a Desert Saharan Motor Lodge in 1962. The Desert Saharan Motor Lodge closed in 1978 and was razed.[79]

The **Spokane Hotel** was on the south-

The Spokane Hotel. The sign across the street on the far left was for the Okanogan Valley Bus Lines. *(Eastern Washington State Historical Society, Spokane, Washington, L85-143.74)*

west corner of First and Stevens. It was six stories tall and was built in 1889.[80] What Spokanites probably remember most about this hotel was its well-known *Silver Grill* restaurant. (See restaurant chapter.) A marquee, decorated with metal filigree, hung on four large chains above the outside entrance to the Silver Grill. In the '30s, the hotel's lobby had a number of heavy columns that were decorated with rosettes around the capitals. The tops of the walls and the beams were ornamented with festoons. At an earlier time, a stuffed elk was in the lobby, and may have been there in the '30s.[81]

In 1942, the lobby, coffee shop, and parts of the main dining room were remodeled. Described as modernistic, the lobby's fixtures were all new, its columns were "finished in marble," and the ceiling was of redwood. A large old foyer to the Silver Grill was converted to a modern coffee shop, and areas near the Silver Grill itself

were remodeled to provide several carpeted dining spaces that could be closed off from each other with folding doors.[82] Just as The Davenport and the Desert Hotels had put in cocktail lounges in 1949 after liquor laws changed, so did the Spokane Hotel, adding the **Silver Room**.

The Spokane Hotel was purchased in the early '60s by the owners of the Ridpath. It was then torn down and replaced with the Ridpath Motor Inn Annex, now called the Ridpath Executive Court.

The **old Ridpath Hotel** was a five story building that was located in the middle of the block between Howard and Stevens, and extended from Sprague Avenue through the block to First Avenue. (This is now the location of the **new Ridpath Hotel**.) The old Ridpath was not distinctive architecturally. Hyslop describes it as being "remarkably clean and simple for its date of construction," which was 1899.[83] In 1938, the

The lobby of the Spokane Hotel in 1938. *(Eastern Washington State Historical Society, Spokane, Washington, L87-1.13635-38)*

Ridpath acquired the **St. Nicholas Hotel** on the northwest corner of First and Stevens, added it to the Ridpath, and put floors and fire doors in place between the two buildings. The **YWCA** had been located in the St. Nicholas. It moved at that time to its next location on Main and Monroe in the former Spokane Amateur Athletic Club building.

The Ridpath was a residential hotel in the '30s and '40s, having been converted to 31 apartments in 1926.[84] On February 28, 1950, a spectacular fire swept from the basement up through the elevator shaft. Smoke and fire poured out of the top of the building, leaping as high as 60 feet according to articles that appeared in *The Spokesman-Review* of March 1, 1950. The fire destroyed most of the wooden interior of the building, leaving brick exterior walls standing. The annexed portion of the building was saved because of the fire doors at each level. The present Ridpath

Hotel was built on the site in 1951.

The **Victoria Hotel** was a quaint building of seven stories that stood on the northeast corner of First and Wall. Designed by Hermann Preusse and Julius Zittel and built in 1903, it had elements of Victorian and Renaissance Revival Styles. The building had a long marquee covering the sidewalk that extended in both directions from the corner. Hyslop describes it as having a deck "at the second floor level, surrounded by ornamental wrought iron railings, and supported on delicate cast-iron columns at curbside, all suggesting a New Orleans flavor."[85] The cast-iron columns were painted dark green, as I recall, and at some time the street level of the building was painted a pale green. A mansard style roof was handsomely decorated with elaborate dormer windows and turrets. Fire destroyed the top floor in about 1960, and the elegant turrets were replaced by a rather plain roof line.

The Victoria Hotel, showing part of the ornate marquee. (*Northwest Room, Spokane Public Library*)

This charming building had a lower level, about halfway below grade level, that could be reached by going down a few steps next to the building on the Wall Street side. Large windows in this lower level revealed a barbershop and a barber pole with its endlessly rising and turning red and white stripes. The Victoria Hotel was torn down in 1979, along with the entire block, for construction of a parking facility for the SeaFirst Bank.

OTHER BUILDINGS

Two immense and graceful smokestacks have been part of the downtown skyline for many years. These tapered twin towers, with their brick patterned bands near the top, are 235 feet high and 12 feet in diameter at the top. They belong to what was the **Central Heating Plant**, or **Steam Heat Plant**. The building which housed the plant is located just south of the Amtrak elevated tracks between Post and Lincoln. Most of the building was hidden in the middle of the block during the '30s and '40s, though it is now more exposed. Built in 1915 and probably designed by Cutter and Malmgren, this facility was the heat source for the majority of downtown buildings for decades. In 1948, for example, it was used to heat 355 office buildings, hotels, stores, and railroad depots.[86]

During its operation, fuel was provided at various times by coal, oil, compressed wood waste known as hog fuel, electricity from dams when the river was high, and natural gas. Steam was generated in eleven immense boilers, then transported through a maze of mains and tunnels in ten miles of pipes buried 12 to 18 feet under downtown streets.

The Central Heating Plant provided heat, hot water, air conditioning, steam baths in downtown clubs, and heat for railway cars when they were not attached to engines. Copper pipes beneath sidewalks and driveways carried steam that melted snow. Miles of pipes beneath the streets also provided some undesirables...rats. Two people have told me of seeing rats in the basements of downtown buildings in those days, and while that may be common in old buildings, the rodents probably traveled from one building to another via the plant's underground tunnels.[87]

Leaking steam pipes eventually made the system too difficult to maintain and repair. The thick wood insulation enclosing the pipes began to rot and the pipes corroded after many years of use. In addition, the pipes were buried quite deep, often under communication, gas, water, and electric lines, making repairs expensive. Heat was supplied to EXPO 74, but operations were stopped in 1975. The tunnels and pipes still lie beneath our streets.[88]

On the southwest corner of Wall Street and Trent (Spokane Falls Boulevard) is the location of the old **City Hall**. The building, completed in 1913, has been described as having a spartan appearance by a local architect. Though no longer our City Hall, the building has been renovated and today houses offices, shops, and restaurants. In the '30s and '40s, the City Hall housed municipal offices; on the sixth floor the City Council Chambers were located, and a court room for criminal and traffic offenses. Most of the police department was located on the first floor. An emergency hospital for jail inmates was on the fourth floor. Two sets of elevators were in different locations of the building; one used by the public, the other was used to take inmates to and from areas of incarceration. The jail areas, on the south side of the building, were on the second floor for men and on the third floor for women. Jim Read, policeman in those days, recalled: "We used a paddy wagon, it was sort of a police ambulance, to pick up 'drunks,' or sometimes people that had been hurt in fights."[89]

During the '40s, the city jail had a food contract with a restaurant called the **OK Coffee House**, located on Trent (Spokane Falls Boulevard) between Stevens and Washington in the middle of the block. Frequently the food for the jail was hamburgers which contained a sort of hash with crumbs, meat, and vegetables. The inmates complained about the food, calling the hamburgers "breadburgers," but their protests were pretty much ignored. The food may not have been very good to start with, but part of the problem may have been that the meals were brought 3 blocks from the restaurant in a metal cart in every kind of weather.

The city's central fire station was located on the first floor in the northwest corner of the City Hall building. On warm summer days it was common to see firemen sitting outside on this side of the building near the large firetruck doors. In the '90s, renovations of large windows on the north side of the building have replicated doors that were used by early day fire trucks.[90]

Historic **Fire Station No. 1**, on First between Stevens and Washington, is a small two story brick building that was built immediately after the Spokane Fire. It was used as a fire station from 1890 until 1938, as a boys' gymnasium in 1939, and was the home of a candy company from 1945 to 1965.[91]

The **Masonic Temple**, in the 1000 block on West Riverside, was a major location for recitals, plays, ballet and other dance performances, and many kinds of music programs. It was also used for dances and "mixers," dances where people went without a date but mixed and danced with different people.

The interior of the Masonic Temple has been called cavernous. It can be confusing unless you know the building well, as two of the public rooms, "The Auditorium" and "The Commandery" are nearly alike except for size. Each room has a large open area in the center with a stage opposite the entrance. Permanent seats are located on the sides of each room and on balconies. The large center area of each room can be filled with more seats or left open. Seating varies from 1,000 to 1,600 in "The Auditorium," and from 300 to 600 in "The Commandery."[92] Because of the flexibility of the performing areas, it was used in countless ways in earlier years.

In celebration of the Golden Jubilee of Washington State, the Masonic Temple was used every night for more than a week in May, 1939, with concerts by every imaginable music group in Spokane. Memorable civic choruses—the Mendelsohn Club, the Spokane A Cappella Choir, the Bel Canto Club, and the Lorelei Club, per-

The Sartori Building on Wall Street. The narrow building was between the Hyde Building on Riverside, and the Title Building on Sprague. *(Eastern Washington State Historical Society, Spokane, Washington, L87-1.61706-49)*

formed. School instrumental and vocal groups, from elementary to college level, participated. Spokane's orchestra of the time, the Spokane Civic Symphony Orchestra played. Massed church choirs sang. Student contest winners performed—pianists, violinists, and vocalists. Private piano teachers had their night with "unique piano ensembles" when thirty pianos were placed in the open area of "The Auditorium." Several student groups performed, with two people at

each piano. My sister, Marianna, was in one of these groups. Finally, a group of teachers played Chopin, Debussy, and von Weber. The printed program billed the event as "30 pianos—240 pianists."[93] Only the Masonic Temple would have been suitable for such a performance.

In "The Auditorium," the Spokane Philharmonic Orchestra, forerunner of the present Spokane Symphony Orchestra, presented its first concert on December 18, 1945, under the direc-

The Washington Water Power Building shown at Christmas in 1939. The entrance, on the east end of the Trent side of the building, was reached by going up six steps. *(Eastern Washington State Historical Society, Spokane, Washington, L87-1.17241-39)*

tion of Harold Paul Whelan. Though it is generally thought that this was Spokane's first symphony orchestra, several civic orchestras were organized and performed earlier. In the '20s, a chamber orchestra under the direction of Ralph Bovee performed regularly at The Davenport Hotel. It was considered *the* orchestra in Spokane at the time. In the '30s, there were orchestras directed by Gottfried Herbst and later George Poinar. In the early '40s, there were symphony orchestras under the direction of Arthur Uhe and Francis Baxter.[94]

The **Sartori Building**, housing a jewelry store, was a charming Italian and French Renaissance style building located in the middle of the block on the east side of Wall between Riverside and Sprague. This unusual building stood in what was to have been an alley. Though it was only 16 feet wide, it had seven stories sandwiched be-

tween the Hyde Building and the Title Building. The entire front was decorated with smooth cream terra cotta ornamentation. The building was torn down in 1979 for the construction of the SeaFirst Bank.[95]

The **Washington Water Power Building** was on the southeast corner of Trent (Spokane Falls Boulevard) and Lincoln. A four story building of brick and stone, it was designed by Cutter and Malmgren and built in 1907. Spiraled brackets decorated the building and flanked the arch above the doorway. In 1939, a fifth floor was added. It was set back from the other floors so that it would not conflict with the architecture of the rest of the building.[96]

On the main floor were several "cages" where people could pay their electric bills. Various electric appliances were also displayed in this area: coffee makers, waffle irons, toasters, stoves,

This building housed Spokane's YMCA for 57 years, from 1907 to 1964. *(Eastern Washington State Historical Society, Spokane, Washington, L87-1.18657-20)*

washing machines, and one of the new dishwashers made with a glass top so that a person could look down inside and watch it as it ran.

In the late '50s, the Washington Water Power Company moved out of the downtown area and gave this building to School District #81 to be used for its administration building. The building was destroyed by fire on a weekend in 1979. The location is currently a street level parking lot.

The **YMCA** Building, in those days located on the southeast corner of First and Lincoln, was a five story gray brick building trimmed with darker gray sandstone. The main entrance was at the center of the building on First Avenue

where there was a flight of steps extending on the sidewalk. Another entrance, on Lincoln, was the Boys' Department entrance, which led to a two story gymnasium. Below this was the swimming pool.[97] The building was torn down in 1964.

In 1904, the **Spokane Amateur Athletic Club** constructed a building at Main and Monroe.[98] In 1938, it became the home of the **YWCA**. This tan brick building, with its graceful birch trees across the front, holds memories for many women of Spokane who went there as children.

In the '40s, I went to summer "day camps" lasting a week or two in the "Y" building. Drama, music, mime, exercise, swimming, volley ball, dance, and art classes were among the choices offered. We brought sack lunches, ate them at wooden tables in stark rooms, and went home in the afternoon exhausted but happy.

The smell of the building was heavy with chlorine and steam from the rather small swimming pool that was located on a lower level. Some girls wore the "Y's" dark blue scratchy wool swim suits. Because of pool rules, we all wore tight white bathing caps.

The first floor of the YWCA had a reception desk, a gym, and some plain rooms that were nameless as far as I know. Wide carpeted stairs and dark, heavy wooden bannisters led to the second level with a large carpeted area and old-fashioned easy chairs, a sort of sitting room for the young women who lived on the three floors above. Temporary wood walls could be pulled between large square columns in several places to divide this big room into smaller areas, making meeting rooms or smaller lounges possible. Because this room had a grand piano, it was also used for student recitals. The YWCA building was demolished in 1966 to make way for the Federal Building.

ON THE FRINGES OF DOWNTOWN

The Armory, at W. 202 Second Avenue, has not been used as an armory since 1977, but the name "State Armory" is still displayed in cast lettering at the center of the building just below the roofline. A sculpture of an eagle with raised wings, and a flagpole were once on the roof above the name, but these are gone today. Built in 1908, and designed by Preusse and Zittel, the official use of the Armory was to provide a place for drilling the Washington National Guard. During World Wars I and II, the building was also the regional location for draft registration.[99]

In the years 1935 to 1941, the Armory was used as "station X," a special Christmas post office for handling extra incoming Christmas packages and other mail. Mail was taken directly from trains to the Armory and carriers distributed it from there.[100] This may have continued beyond 1941, but it is unlikely, as the Armory had military uses after that.

The Armory's barnlike interior was used for many large civic events and performances before the Coliseum was built in 1954. (The Coliseum was replaced by Spokane's Arena in 1995.) Bleacher seats could be added so that many spectators and participants could be accommodated. In the '40s, I was in several large group music

events that rehearsed and performed in the Armory.

The Armory was the setting for a special concert by Spokane's Patrice Munsel in 1943. This performance was for servicemen, their guests and, according to an article in the *Spokane Daily Chronicle*, June 18, 1943, "any lucky civilians who were able to crowd in." This concert and a prior one at the Fox theater were a benefit for the Red Cross. Earlier that year, Munsel, at age 17, had become the youngest singer ever to sign a contract with the Metropolitan Opera Company of New York.

Other events held at the Armory were the Camp Fire Girls' yearly Grand Council, some of the high school basketball games, and some public dances. The State Republican Convention was held in the Armory with an attendance of 1,121 in the spring of 1936.[101]

The **Carnegie Library**, located on the west side of Cedar between Riverside and First Avenues, was Spokane's central library. This handsome building was designed by Preusse and Zittel, and constructed in 1905 with help from philanthropist Andrew Carnegie.[102] Seven fireplaces are in the building, each distinctly different from the other. Four Doric columns in a central area support a second floor balcony, which in turn supports smaller columns that rise to a high ceiling and a large square skylight. Around the balcony are wood railings with black wrought iron filigree. Rosettes on columns and arched doorways are repeated in patterns in subtle colors on the tile floor.

The main desk for the library was in the central area below the skylight. By the '40s, the beauty of the architecture was lost for many of us as the building had become dark, dingy, and gloomy. It was also overcrowded, even though a substantial addition had been made to the building in 1929. The fireplaces were nearly hidden, some because they were in remote areas, but most because they were behind bookshelves.

The library moved from the building in 1963. The building was then used by several education groups, most notably the Spokane Center of Washington State University, and the Intercollegiate Center For Nursing Education.[103] During that time, partitions were added, ceilings were lowered and lighting was changed. The building was left empty in 1979, after which it was ravaged by time, vandals, neglect, pigeons, and a fire. It was finally purchased by Integrus Architects and beautifully renovated in 1992-93 to its original elegant grandeur.

After the repeal of Prohibition in 1933, several large breweries opened in Spokane. One was the **Golden Age Brewery**, which used the old Schade Brewery Building. This interesting building with its huge arch on the left and high stepped gabled roof line on the right, is at E. 528 Trent. When I was growing up, a huge clock, which could be seen and read from Division, was in the large window between the gables. The building is an exact replica of a brewery in Europe and was constructed in 1903 by Bernhardt Schade.

The railroad tracks were well below ground level in this part of town because, when the tracks were laid around 1910, the brewery stood directly in their path. Schade's asking price for the building was $1 million; he refused to budge from this price. The railroad management decided to go underground just to the south side of the brewery with their tracks. A huge, wide trench for the tracks was dug just across from the brewery and the tracks continued west in this immense ditch for several blocks next to Trent, then went under Division. Near Bernard, the tracks rose to the elevated level.

A memorable billboard advertising Golden Age Beer sat diagonally on the northeast corner of Division and Trent. This fascinating advertisement had a tilted brown beer bottle that seemed to endlessly pour beer into a glass. The sign was lighted in such a way that golden beer appeared to flow out of the bottle, the glass lighting up slowly from bottom to top, the beer appearing to rise in the glass. White lights topped it off with a head of foam. All of the lights would then go off, the sign would be dark for a moment, and the glass would fill again. During part of the Prohibition period, soda pop was made in the building. Golden Age at one time called its brew "the beer that makes Milwaukee jealous."[104] It operated as a brewery from 1934 to 1959 under various labels.[105]

Gonzaga University Stadium played such a big part in our lives in the '30s and '40s that it seems to belong here. Unofficially, it served as our civic stadium before Spokane built Albi Stadium in 1952. The Gonzaga Stadium, with a seating capacity of around 5,000, was built in 1913. In 1925, the capacity was enlarged to 10,400. The stadium was located on the east end of the campus between Standard and Dakota Streets on the east and west, and between DeSmet Avenue on the north and an area near the river then occupied by the McGoldrick Lumber Company on the south. A financial drain on the college from the time of its enlargement, the stadium was torn down in 1949.[106] The Foley Center Library now occupies the approximate center of the stadium area.

The Gonzaga Stadium was used for many citywide events and for some traveling performances. I remember seeing a high wire, acrobatic, and juggling performance there. Wild West shows, Shrine football games and many high school football games were held in the stadium.[107] Bob Hope appeared in the stadium in the '40s.

Probably most memorable of the high school games played at Gonzaga is the **Merry-Go-Round Game**. This annual event opened the high school football season every year beginning in 1938. Sports booster Vic Dessert, of the Desert Hotel, was the father of the idea.[108] The four high schools then in the football league, Gonzaga, Lewis and Clark, North Central, and Rogers, all participated. The two teams that played in the first quarter were selected by a draw. The remaining two teams played the second quarter. The third quarter was played by the losers of the first two quarters, followed by the winners playing the final quarter.

The Merry-Go-Round Game was eagerly awaited and well attended by students from all the schools. Each school's marching unit and band performed at half time. The winner of the Merry-Go-Round Game seldom ended as the top team of the season, as I recall, but school spirit was high at the Merry-Go-Round Games, and many people who grew up in Spokane will remember the game as a highlight of the beginning of each school year. The Merry-Go-Round Game was discontinued in the early '60s when there were more than four high schools in the football league.

CHAPTER
4

RESTAURANTS

Adventures in Good Eating was its name, and its author was Duncan Hines. It was a book about restaurants in the United States, or as its subtitle stated: "Good Eating Places Along the Highways and in Cities of America."[1] Spokane is listed in several editions as being on highways 10 and 195, 302 miles east of Seattle. Highway 10 became Interstate 90 and with modifications cut 22 miles from the distance. New editions were published each year at least from 1936 through 1950. The 1938 edition, the earliest available to me, lists only *The Davenport Hotel* for Spokane: "This world famous hotel seems to have corralled just about all those looking for good meals in Spokane. With its several dining rooms, catering to all tastes and purses, it covers the eating question here."[2] The 1945, '46 and '47 editions list *Bob's Chili Parlor*, *The Davenport*, and the *Silver Grill* in the Spokane Hotel. By 1950, The Davenport had been dropped—quite a comedown from having covered "the eating question" in 1938. *Bob's Chili Parlor* and the *Silver Grill* retained their places in the book.

Restaurants in the '30s and '40s were different in many ways from those of today. Except for the *Italian Gardens* at The Davenport Hotel and the *Silver Grill* in the Spokane Hotel, most eating places in Spokane had no waiters, but had only waitresses. All waiters at the *Silver Grill* were African American. Waitresses in all eating places usually wore a uniform, often a plain black or white cotton skirt, blouse, and bib-less apron and a small, stiffly starched semicircle headpiece that was attached to the hair with bobby pins. Sometimes there was a bit of color on the apron or headpiece.

There was no such thing as "fast food" with its rather limited menus. We knew nothing of pizza, tacos, or baklava, as there were few ethnic or foreign restaurants in Spokane except for Italian and Chinese places. Typically first class res-taurants had very long menus with many choices, and since frozen food and mixes weren't invented until later, everything was made "from scratch." Vegetables were usually from a can and were limp and tasteless, often having sat for long periods on steam tables. One wonders how restaurants could provide such a wide variety of foods before the advent of frozen food.

Downtown Spokane could boast of some wonderful places in which to eat, and we could find delectable items that are seldom seen today. Savory chicken croquettes, scrumptious olive-and-nut sandwiches, crackly "hard rolls," rich fruit pies, melt-in-your-mouth mocha log, luscious cream pies, tender layer cakes, and a delightful variety of ice cream specialties come to mind.

The soda fountain was found in both casual eating places and in many of the more sophisticated restaurants. A conservative estimate is that there were some 100 soda fountains in Spokane in those years with about 30 to 35 of them located downtown.[3] Made of stainless steel, chrome, and at times with porcelain trim, the soda fountain had many spigots, deep wells for varieties of ice cream, special areas for flavored toppings, chopped nuts, and cherry garnishes. Whipped cream was at the ready, and soda dispensers gave that "extra fizz." Out of the soda fountain came sundaes, ice cream sodas, cherry, lemon, and other flavored cokes, banana splits, and "black and whites" (vanilla and chocolate ice cream with chocolate syrup and marshmallow cream), most served to us in thick, stemmed glassware. Nearby were the milkshake machines, cones for ice cream, and a tall glass container with a shiny metal top that could be pulled up by a button on the top for easy access to a bunch of drinking straws. We took it for granted that the soda fountain would remain a part of our culture.

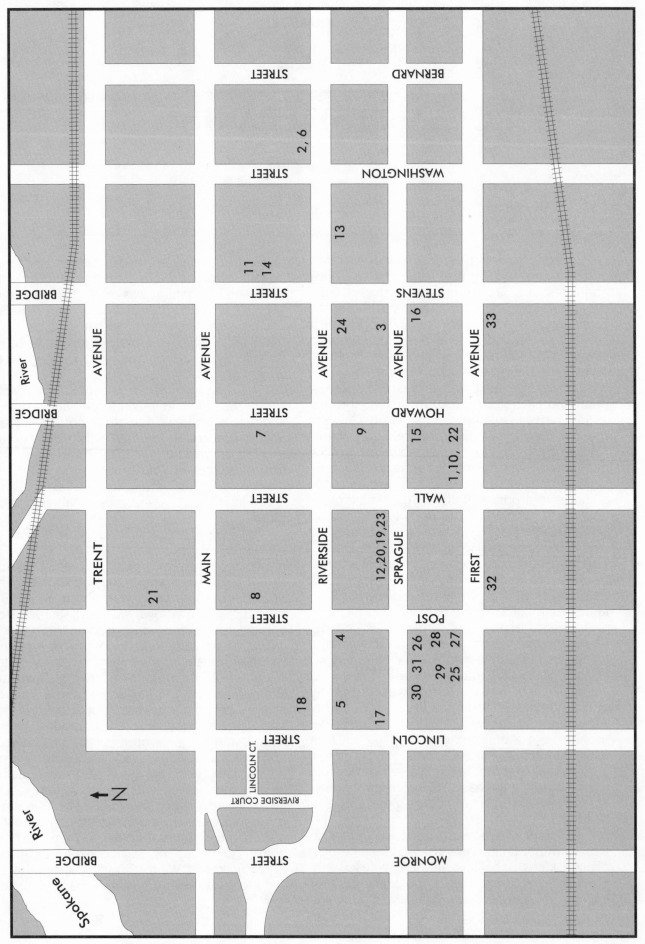

RESTAURANTS & DINING ROOMS

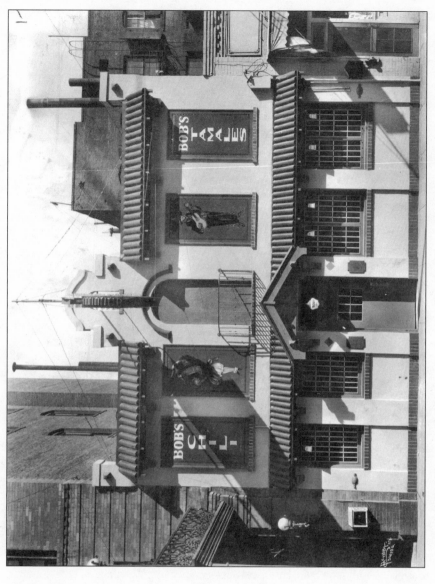

Bob's Chili Parlor as it looked in the '30s and '40s. A bell hung in the small tower over the center of the roof. The building had this facade until the late '40s.[4] *(Courtesy of Margery Nobles McIntosh and Barbara Nobles)*

1. Bob's Chili Parlor
2. Coney Island Sandwich Shop; New York-Coney Island Sandwich Shop
3. George's Coney Island
4. Cooke's Nut Shop
5. Cooke's Nut Shop, later location
6. The Fern
7. Hil-Mar Dinette
8. Mannings; Lutz Home Made Food Shop; Tony's Big Seven Delicatessen
9. Tony's Big Seven Buffet
10. Malcom Stalker's Fish and Chips
11. Mey's Lunch
12. Model Cafe
13. Modern Maid Ice Cream (Sweet Maid Ice Cream)
14. Nim's Cafe
15. The Percolator
16. The Rockaway
17. The Outside-Inn
18. The Aster Tea Room
19. Al's Sandwich Shop
20. ChungKing Inn
21. Elliot's
22. Lloyd's Cliff House
23. Mandarin Cafe (upstairs)
24. Schaefer's Fountain Lunch

HOTEL DINING ROOMS

THE DAVENPORT HOTEL
25. Isabella Dining Room
26. Italian Gardens (later, Crystal Room, Matador Room, Louis D's)
27. Delicacy Shop
28. Orange Bower (later, Apple Bower, Copper Strike, Audubon Room)
29. Peacock Room
30. Fountain Room
31. Coffee Shop

THE DESERT HOTEL
32. Oasis

THE SPOKANE HOTEL
33. Silver Grill

"Bob's Tamale Department" in 1929. (Eastern Washington State Historical Society, Spokane, Washington, L87-1.38247-29)

INDIVIDUAL RESTAURANTS

The Polk City Directory lists around 155 restaurants in the downtown area in 1939. Of these, approximately 70 were in what most of us considered the skid row area, roughly bounded by Washington, Trent, Division and Main. This left 85 large and small cafes, lunchrooms, and dining rooms in the nicer part of town. The following restaurants are limited to those that I remember and to a few that others have told me about.

Anyone who ever tasted the lip-smacking tamales or zesty chili from **Bob's Chili Parlor** probably still salivates at the thought! This little hole-in-the-wall place was located on the north side of First Avenue between Howard and Wall next to the Victoria Hotel, and had been in business since the early part of the century. Owner "Bob" was long gone in the '30s/'40s era, and menus and a sign on the wall announced: Harry Nobles, Proprietor. Early pictures of the exterior of Bob's Chili Parlor show that it had several faces.

As I recall from the early '40s, when one walked inside Bob's Chili Parlor, the floor was so uneven you felt as though you might end up in the basement! The building was replaced around 1950, and both inside and out the little structure could have been characterized as nondescript. Not, however, the food! Featured items were chili—which came in three varieties—Hot, (and it *was* HOT!), Medium, and Mild—and the delicious tamales! *Adventures In Good Eating* wrote: "Open all year. 10 A.M. to 1 A.M. For their tamales, they use over two carloads of cornhusks a year and ship as far east as Montreal and all over the country. I assure you they are quite unusual.

Decorated with baskets of flowers, Cooke's Nut Shop is shown during its Grand Opening at the W. 803 Riverside location. Its black glass candy counter can be seen on the left, the fountain/lunch counter on the right. (Eastern Washington State Historical Society, Spokane, Washington, L87-1.2362-33)

Soup, chili, and few sandwiches round out their menu. Prices moderate."[5] The thought of Bob's Chili Parlor evokes far off looks and mouthwatering memories for many of us. There were no Mexican restaurants in Spokane then, and this food was not only savory, but unique.

A Coney Island, a hot dog on a bun served with a sauce made with ground meat, onions, and seasonings, was very popular. The **Coney Island Sandwich Shop**, in some years called the **New York-Coney Island Sandwich Shop**, at W. 336 Riverside, and **George's Coney Island** at W. 514 Sprague, sold this succulent item. The shops were owned by brothers, George and Ernie Pappas.[6] Sizzling wieners cooking on rotating rollers in the windows tempted customers to come in. It is somewhat surprising to realize that Bob's Chili Parlor was open until 1 a.m. and George's was open until 2 a.m.[7]

Cooke's Nut Shop was a combination restaurant and candy shop. Cooke's had a dizzying number of locations during the late '30s, with addresses listed on Sprague, Howard, and two on Riverside. Most of these were probably simply candy outlets. It is the restaurant near the southwest corner of Riverside and Post, at W. 803 Riverside, that most of us fondly remember. Inside, the irresistible aroma of chocolate filled the air. I believe they featured nuts, and chocolate covered nuts, but also made other candies. Chocolates and candies purchased at Cooke's came in elegant boxes with gold lettering that said, "Cooke's Home Made Candies." The hand-dipped chocolates and other candies were made on the second floor. Their irregular slabs of milk chocolate covered almonds were especially tantalizing.

Cooke's art deco atmosphere seemed very glamorous, with black leather stools and booths, and extensive use of black and white tiles, mirrors, and chrome. To the right was a fountain/lunch counter, and in the back were black leather booths. More booths were on the second floor.[8] Sandwiches, sodas, and ice cream were served. "But what people really talked about was the Red Devil's Food Cake," recalls Carole Cooke Jones, daughter of the owners. Imagine trying to resist that temptation in this environment of fragrant chocolate!

In 1936, an advertisement appeared in *The Spokesman-Review* for Cooke's Nut Shop saying: "Appetising Breakfasts, Tasty Lunches, Dinners That Please, Home Made Nut Candy, Salted Nuts, Home Made Ice Cream, Halloween Favors, Bridge Party Candies, Gift Boxes—Nuts and Candies...We Deliver We Wrap for Mailing Open 'til Midnight."

Another ad from November, 1938 says: "That Great Big 50¢ Turkey Dinner 50¢ [twice for emphasis] Roast Young Turkey, Dressing, Cranberry Sauce, Candied Sweet Potatoes, Vegetable, Roll and Butter, Drink and Peanut Brittle Whip Pudding or your own favorite Ice Cream. Saturday Lunch, 11 o'clock to 2, also on evening Dinner 5 o'clock to 7...50¢." In the same ad: "Cooke's New Breakfast Special Try our Golden Brown Hot Cakes or Waffles with that Delicious New Butterscotch sauce and a Cup of real Silex Coffee...20¢." UMMM! Doesn't it all sound good?

Soon after the war, Cooke's moved down the block to a new location near the Granada theater where, in a joint venture with Peters and Sons Florists, they constructed a new building. There had been no construction during World War II, and the building was started as soon as possible after the war.[9] Here, Cooke's had a lighter, brighter and more up to date environment, but I missed the splendor and glamour of the earlier location less than a block away. In this last location the candy business was featured more than the restaurant.

Far too many confectioners and ice cream places were in the downtown area in those days to name, but these were very popular and many of them also served uncomplicated sandwiches and light salads along with the various ice cream delights. The **Fern**, at W. 332 Riverside, served only ice cream dishes and sold candy. It was located on the north side of Riverside, a few doors from Washington Street, near the Rex theater. Here the decor featured old-fashioned "ice cream store" wire chairs with heart-shaped backs, and tables with twisted wire legs. A "soda jerk" dispensed ice cream sodas, sundaes, and fancy concoctions. One former customer remembers that they had a candy factory in the basement, and also recalls being served a soda that was called a David Harem, which she describes as ice cream with a "squirt of this and a squirt of that," which cost 15¢.[10]

The **Hil-Mar Dinette**, I was told, was named for its partners Hilda and Martha. It was located on Howard Street across from the Orpheum theater in the charming little building that is still next to the alley. This building had a false wooden front at the time, and was painted gray with white trim. The door was centered on the front, and there was a tiny porch with steps leading up from either side. This place had a tearoom atmosphere and was open only for lunch.

On the east side of Post and in the middle of the block between Riverside and Main was an establishment that rented a large square area to several small businesses. Though the businesses changed from time to time, some of them were: **Mannings, Inc.** (coffee), the **Model Bakery**, **A. E. Post Butter and Eggs**, **Lutz Home Made Food Shop**, and **Tony's Big Seven Delicatessen**. **Tony's Big Seven** was also at S. 12 Lincoln, and there was a **Big Seven Buffet** at N. 7 Howard, apparently the origin of the name. The latter sported a huge neon numeral 7 out front.

Food was served cafeteria style at the delicatessen, and there were high tables at which one could stand or sit on tall stools. By the early '40s, in a window to the right of the doorway, was an automated stainless steel doughnut machine. The exact amount of doughnut batter would ooze out and drop, perfectly shaped, into hot fat. This doughnut would take its place behind a parade of doughnuts that were making their way, single file, slowly around the machine. About halfway through the trip, each doughnut would magically turn itself over and begin its way toward the front, where, perfectly browned, it would drop into a waiting basket. It was quite entertaining; when the machine was turned on, there was always a group of three or four people standing and watching in front of the window.

Malcom Stalker's Fish and Chips was a Mom and Pop restaurant located just east of Bob's Chili Parlor in the late '30s. Inside was an old fashioned counter along the right wall, with high shiny wooden booths to the left that were painted gray blue. Here they served perfectly cooked, thick and flaky pieces of fish, the best fish and chips imaginable. A large order was 65¢,

Stevens Street looking north from Riverside showing Nim's Cafe on the right and Mey's Lunch just beyond it, ca. 1929. Note elevated railroad tracks at the end of the street, and also that there is no door on the Stevens Street side of the Old National Bank Building to the right. *(Northwest Room, Spokane Public Library)*

a smaller one, 35¢. We would often go there after a Saturday afternoon movie. My sister and I would be *so* hungry and thought we could eat the larger order, but the 35¢ plate filled us completely. How I would like to taste those fish and chips again! Stalker's moved and built a new place on North Monroe in the early '40s.

Mey's Lunch was located at N. 128 Stevens, just north of the better known Nim's Cafe. A green neon sign hanging above the sidewalk spelled out the name "Mey's Lunch" and could be read from either direction. It was a small Mom and Pop restaurant, owned by a German couple with heavy accents. He, who seemed to be always smiling, cooked in a large floppy chef's hat behind a pass-through at the back. She, who often wore a worried expression, waited on the counter and tables. Despite the restaurant's name, they were open for lunch and dinner. I do not remember that there was any featured German food, but rather it was a fairly large American menu. My parents knew the Meys, and occasionally when we ate there, he would come out afterward and tell us with twinkling eyes that it was "on the house."

The **Model Cafe** was on the north side of Sprague between Wall and Post. In the late '30s it had small-paned windows across the front. The interior was rather dark, and there was dark woodwork with wooden tables and booths. Later remodeled, a picture from 1945 shows a light interior with three U-shaped counters and booths

along one wall, but no tables.[11] Open for both lunch and dinner, the cafe had a long menu. Steak was a dinner specialty. In 1933, they advertised "A Well-Balanced, Satisfying Lunch for 20¢" of Corned Brisket of Beef Sandwich, Cole Slaw, French Dressing and beverage.

Known as **Modern Maid Ice Cream** when established in the late '30s, and becoming **Sweet Maid Ice Cream** in the '40s, this "fountain-lunch" was located in the Paulsen Building, mid-block between Washington and Stevens, with a street entrance on Riverside. Its black, medium blue, and chrome art deco booths and slightly curved counter were smartly styled, bright, and inviting against its pale beige walls and high ceiling. Lunches featured sandwiches and ice cream dishes. It was not open for dinner. This was the first place I ever saw or tasted soft ice cream. The flavor was chocolate and it was served in a tall, shiny, metal parfait shaped dish and came with a long spoon.

Nim's Cafe was located at N. 118 Stevens, directly behind the Old National Bank. "Nims Cafe" was spelled out with a refrigerated coil in thick, frosty script in one of the windows.[12] The combination of heat from the cooking and the presence of this frozen coil created perpetually steamy windows. A sign above the sidewalk had a series of lightbulbs forming the letters "Nim's Cafe" on it. Nim's catered to business and professional people for lunch and dinner.

Who could forget the **Percolator**, located on the south side of Sprague, between Howard and Wall, at W. 603 1/2 Sprague? The address gives a hint of the narrowness of the establishment. A picture taken by Libby studio in 1949, shows the Percolator with a plain, dark, possibly tile exterior. It is squeezed between Rowles Market and "The Rendezvous." A neon sign in script saying simply "Percolator" is above the door. In the early '40s, it had small ivory framed window panes and similar panes in the door with an interior painted white or ivory. A single long and low counter extended from front to back, with *just* enough room for waitresses on one side, and seated customers on the other. Waiting customers stood in a restricted space along the wall behind those who were eating. It was a very popular eatery, and at lunch time was packed with people. The Percolator served sandwiches, salads, and such delicacies as chicken a la king, but most memorable were the several glass-domed covered plates holding cakes that sat along the counter. Five to seven layers tall, these huge mounds were feathery light, had luscious fillings, snow white frosting, and were baked fresh each day.

The Rockaway was on the southwest corner of Sprague and Stevens. The exterior walls had two long rows of nearly square windows, one row at eye level and the other very high. Each window had many small square panes.[13] All of these windows made the inside seem quite bright. Much of the interior was an apple green; the tables and counter were both varnished wood. A hallway along one side led to four or five small private dining areas. Each room had walls of ivory and green "jazz plaster," and a small rounded arched doorway with dark green (perhaps velvet) swag curtains tied back on either side. How exotic! I did not eat at the Rockaway often enough to remember the food. In earlier days they featured "oysters a la Rockefeller," giant oysters served on the half-shell.[14] This may have been a specialty in the '30s-'40s era too. Jay J. Kalez wrote in the *Spokane Daily Chronicle*, December 30, 1972, not long after the Rockaway closed, that many of the customers had looked forward to the Hungarian goulash served at lunch.

Members of the Travo family owned and operated restaurants in downtown Spokane for many years, beginning in 1936 when they opened the **Outside-Inn** on the northeast corner of Sprague and Lincoln.[15] It was rather small, according to Della Travo, one of the owners. They served only sandwiches, beer, and soda fountain items. They also made and sold candy there until

they opened their next restaurant in about 1940, the **Aster Tea Room**. This restaurant was located on the north side of Riverside, just west of Lincoln. The name was later changed to the **Aster Cafe and Candy Kitchen**, but most of us called it simply the **Aster**. Here, Mrs. Travo says, they made all kinds of candy in their basement. This included hard candy, chocolates and large candy canes for Christmas. At the Aster, Mrs. Travo recalls, there was a baker who made all of the pies, breads and cakes. They also made their own ice cream, both hard and soft. I especially remember their tasty sandwiches and delicious crab salad.

In 1946, the Aster was remodeled and there was a grand re-opening. An ad told about the "newly decorated interior with the latest Zeon overhead lighting, air conditioning with water cooling system, new counters and tables with beautifully upholstered red and blue leather seats." Later, the ad continues in this way: "We will continue to feature homecooked food with home-made biscuits, rolls, pies, and cakes and to the best of our ability we will endeavor to supply the demand for our high quality candies." In another ad: "As a token of appreciation" was the following "Opening Special...Virginia Baked Ham with Fruit Sauce, au gratin potatoes, sweet corn, Rolls and Butter, Drink and Pudding or Sherbet.....49¢ ."

In 1949, the Travo family was still operating the **Aster**, but they closed the Outside-Inn and reopened it as **Travo's** on July 6th, 1949, and continued in operation until the early 1990s when the restaurant was sold. On Jan. 15, 1996 the family opened Travo's Outside Inn at the same location.

Other restaurants that may be remembered are tiny **Al's Sandwich Shop**, at W. 704 Sprague, that served 5¢ hamburgers at a counter and in narrow booths that had room for only one person on a side; the **Chungking Inn** at W. 710 Sprague, where we sat in one of the booths that were in rows eating American Fried Noodles, Chow Mein and other Chinese American food; **Elliots**, (listed as **Elliot's Fastway**) at N. 218 Post, where hamburgers were deep-fried (imagine!) and crispy crunchy; **Lloyd's Cliff House**, at S. 14 Howard, where there was a diagonal door on the corner and one could get a fast lunch; the **Mandarin Cafe**, on the second floor of the northwest corner of Sprague and Wall with an entrance on Sprague up a narrow stairway—my order was always Pork Fried Rice; **Marnell's**, a small breakfast, lunch, and dinner restaurant on the east side

The Aster in 1946 after remodeling. The long candy counter was on the right, the soda fountain on the left. Booths were in the back. Before remodeling, huge apothecary jars filled with many colors of hard candy were above the candy counter. The new "Zeon" lights can be seen on the ceiling. *(Eastern Washington State Historical Society, Spokane, Washington, L87-1.47521-46)*

of the street, just south of Howard and Riverside; and in the early '30s, **Schaefer's Fountain Lunch**, at W. 507 Riverside, where magazines and newspapers were for sale and displayed outside.

HOTEL DINING ROOMS

The Davenport Hotel had several places in which to eat, from very formal to casual. By 1945, the wording in *Adventures In Good Eating* had changed somewhat from what was mentioned at the beginning of the chapter: "Open all year. The dining facilities here are too well known to need extended comment: A coffee shop, open 24 hours daily; a delicacy shop, serving L. and D. [lunch and dinner], up to 75¢: fountain room—light lunches, sodas, etc. 'Apple Bower', serving mostly plate meals; Italian gardens (dancing), a la carte; and the main dining room, 'Isabella', mostly a la carte, but D. [dinner], $1.25 to $1.75." One wonders how accurate Hines was, as the Isabella Room had not

been open as a dining room for around 15 years; also prices did not change in successive editions.[16]

A single kitchen was used for all dining areas in The Davenport. The kitchen was presided over for most of the era by French Chef Edward F. Mathieu. He became chef at The Davenport soon after the hotel opened in 1914, and retired at the end of 1945.[17] Chef Mathieu, in his extra tall white chef's hat, reigned in a supreme manner over everything that went on in the kitchen. He also ruled indirectly over the waiters and waitresses. If Mathieu did not like one of them he would not let them come into the kitchen, forcing them to quit.[18] After 1945, the kitchen was in the charge of Chef Frank O'Malley. Around 1948, Chef O'Malley was enticed away from The Davenport by owners of a new but short-lived restaurant on the east side of town, who named their establishment after him, calling it "The Chef O'Malley."

The grand **Isabella Room**, on the south side first floor of The Davenport, is still a glorious room that has changed little. Gerald S. Hartley recalls that his father, Fred Hartley, directed an orchestra that played nightly in the Isabella Room for dinner. He remembers that the room closed as a dining room about 1930 as a result of the Depression. The orchestra then moved to the Italian Gardens.

An undated menu from the Isabella Room (probably late '20s or early '30s) is large and everything is a la Carte.[19] If you were spending liberally you could have feasted on imported foie gras for $1, followed by Special onion soup, au Gratin, 45¢, then Hearts of Palm salad, 75¢, with Russian Dressing, 50¢ , then porterhouse steak, $1.40, with Au Gratin potatoes, 20¢, and String Beans, 20¢ , finished with Assorted French Petit Fours, 25¢, adding up to the truly astronomical price for those days of $4.75. Or you could have been more careful with your money and ordered a meal such as Consomme Bellevue in Cup, 20¢, Omelette with Virginia Ham, 75¢, Sliced Tomato, 30¢ and Green Apple Pie, 10¢, for a total of $1.35. After it closed as a dining room, the Isabella Room was used for special banquets, receptions, club lunches, and dances.

Looking back at the celebrated **Italian Gardens** dining room at about the mid-'40s, I recall green potted palms and other plants, a number of slender columns in the room, white linen table cloths, live music for listening and dancing, and elegant service. Many of us remember as children that it was here that we first encountered finger bowls, and had to be told how to use them.

Waitresses in the Italian Gardens wore a bodice of pastel shaded velvet, knee-length skirts, white stockings, and a cap with a wide band across the top of the head with a ruffle on the back of the band.[20]

Exquisite and delectable food was served there. A menu from August 7, 1934 is very extensive and includes no less than 30 choices for the main course.[21] During Depression days, many of the dinners were not a la Carte and were less expensive than in earlier days. The price of entree included appetizer, soup, desserts, and beverage, and we find such choices as watermelon, honey dew or fruit juice, Essence of Celery (what would that be?) or Fresh Crab Cocktail; Potage St. Georges or Hot Bouillon; entrees such as Roast Spring Lamb with Potatoes Persillee and New String Beans for a total of 80¢ , or Prime Ribs of Beef with Steamed Potatoes and Corn Saute also for 80¢ . The top price in this group was $1.05

Menu cover from the Italian Gardens, dated August 7, 1934; it is richly colored in brown, two shades of blue, and touches of orange. (About 2/3 of its original size) (*Northwest Room, Spokane Public Library*)

The Apple Bower in The Davenport Hotel as it was in the '30s. In this intimate atmosphere light lunches and tempting fountain items were served. *(Eastern Washington State Historical Society, Spokane, Washington, L94-36.78)*

for yearling T-Bone steak broiled on charcoal with baked, French-fried, or au Gratin potatoes and heart of lettuce salad with 1000 Island dressing. Desserts with these dinners included Plum Cobbler, Chocolate Custard Pudding, Marshmalow [sic] Sundae, Choice of Ice Cream, Sherbet or Cut Pies, Cheese, or Layer Cake.

On still another page of this menu are a la Carte choices ranging from Baked Halibut in Casserole, 50¢ , to Broiled Imperial Squab, $1.25, fifteen vegetables, ten kinds of potatoes, sixteen salads with a choice of fourteen dressings, and 39 desserts plus choices of ice cream or sherbet, and eleven choices of dessert cheese. Such an array of gastronomical delights should have pleased most anyone and, if you tired of eating, you could always dance.

The **Delicacy Shop** in the southeast corner of the building, had a pleasant, airy and open look.[22] In this informal spot, one could eat not only flavorsome breakfasts, light lunches, and dinners, but also could buy bakery goods and box lunches. Tables were available at the street level and on the mezzanine. In the summer of 1939 they advertised: "Appetizingly cool menus for all palates and purses. Open 7 a.m. 'til 8 p.m." A "Cool, Delicious Delicacy Dinner special" for 50¢ was offered: "Cold Home-made Prime Beef Loaf, Spiced Crab Apples, German Potato Salad, Sliced Tillamook Cheese, Green Onions, Hot Biscuits and Rolls, With appetizers, soups, dessert and invigorating, sparkling ICED TEA and COFFEE!"

The **Orange Bower** became the **Apple Bower** some time in the early '30s.[23] As I remember, the restaurant was a small, nearly square area with a few tables and a counter along the north wall. A popular feature was ice cream that was packed for the customer in take-out containers.[24]

The Fountain Room in The Davenport Hotel, looking toward Sprague Avenue. (*Eastern Washington State Historical Society, Spokane, Washington, L87-1.17530-20*)

A menu from the '30s indicates that the specialty was green apple pie, a piece costing 10¢, but diners could take home a whole pie for merely 35¢. For 40¢ one could get a hot corned-beef sandwich, mashed potatoes with sweet relish and a beverage. English pea soup was 10¢ , lamb and veal pie was 30¢, and strawberry shortcake, 20¢.[25] Around 1946, the name of this room was changed again to the **Copper Strike** room. In the 1949 City Directory it is listed as a beer parlor.

The intimate restaurant called the **Peacock Room** was shaped and furnished somewhat like a dining car on a train, though it was a shorter area without windows, and each table seated just two people.[26] One end could be reached by going up a short stairway on the west side of the Coffee Shop; the other entrance was from the mezzanine of the Delicacy Shop.[27] A picture of the room dated 1908 shows a stylized peacock over one of the doorways with the peacock's long tail feathers fanned out and filling the arched area above it in a colorful display.[28] The vaulted ceiling is painted with a formal pattern of feathers. One would assume that the room was similarly

decorated for many years, as it continued to be called the Peacock Room.

The Peacock Room first began operating around 1904. There are no references to it in several books on the hotel written in the early '30s.[29] However, John Luppert, who worked as a musician in the Italian Gardens from 1937 to 1942, refers to it in an article he wrote about the hotel during that period.[30] Perhaps it was closed for several years and reopened. I have heard the area referred to as Peacock Alley. In the above article, Luppert called it simply "The Alley" and described it as "a very narrow room with curtained booths, which served as a posh, but very discreet dining area for quiet tete-a-tetes." It was destroyed in the 1950s.[31]

A soda fountain called the **Fountain Room** could be entered from the lobby under the stairs on the north side, or from a street entrance on Sprague Avenue.[32] The room was long and narrow with a single counter spanning its length. A number of pieces of beautiful Venetian blown glass in a variety of colors were displayed in glass cases in this room.[33] These were undoubt-

The Davenport Coffee Shop. A large aquarium that served as a divider between the foyer and the Coffee Shop can be seen between the entrances to the room. Live examples of local game fish, such as bass, perch, sun fish and trout could be viewed. *(Eastern Washington State Historical Society, Spokane, Washington, L94-36.384)*

edly brought from Italy by the Davenports. Exactly when this room was in use is difficult to determine, but it is listed in the City Directory in 1939.

The **Coffee Shop** was on the north side of the building. Just inside the double entrances beneath a small domed marquee was a rather large foyer serving both the Italian Gardens and the Coffee Shop. Straight south of this foyer was the Coffee Shop. Its counter was U-shaped with a service counter going down the middle on which sat large coffee brewing urns, refrigerated cases for pies and fresh fruits, and three elaborate, five foot tall silver candelabrums.[34] Since the Coffee Shop was open long hours, it was a wonderful place to go after a concert or movie for ice cream or hot chocolate.

The **Desert Oasis** was the dining room in the **Desert Hotel**. The restaurant, a large, nearly square room with high ceilings, was entered on the First Avenue side of the building. The room was rather colorless, having tan "antique sandstone" walls which were also described as having a "California stucco" finish when the room was remodeled in 1926.[35] Tiled floors are described as being black and white squares with a blue border. The most memorable part of the decor were the six large central columns, each of which had four gigantic Egyptian heads for capitals. These heads, one facing each direction, were said to be of the Egyptian goddess of light. They sat stony-eyed, soberly surveying the scene below. The main contrast to the wall color was the dark oak used in the counter and in the high booths. Though in a different arrangement earlier, by the late '40s, the booths were situated along the west and south sides of the area, and in rows in the middle of the room. They were extremely high, giving privacy to the occupants. A low rectangular wood counter had oak swinging chairs with arms. An additional dining room for extra busy times was at the back or south end of the room and was entered through two wooden swinging doors. Private dining rooms were reached by walking up stairs to the mezzanine.

The 1926 remodeling with the Egyptian decor was designed by G.A. Pehrson. The double-doored entrance from the street had a set of two doors, a small foyer area and then another set of doors. Inside this tiny foyer, hot radiators blasted away in wintertime, serving as an excellent insulator from the cold. Over the outside entrance was a hand-carved lintel embodying a winged disk, the sacred emblem of Egypt. Windows flanked the door with grill work over them. Tile also ornamented the area. Next to the entrance, a handy place to weigh oneself before or after a meal, a tall scale painted gold, with a huge round numbered "face," stood on the sidewalk.[36]

In 1934 the Oasis advertised a Thanksgiving dinner at the "Same Low Price, $1.00. Children, 50¢ ." This included crab, oyster or grapefruit cocktail, choice of soups, seven entree choices such as Roast Duckling, Wild Rice Dressing, Apple Sauce, and a choice of nine desserts, plus beverage. "Second helpings without charge." Also, "Turkey Plate Specials as Low as 40¢ ."

An advertisement in 1936 for the "Dessert Oasis" (note spelling) advertised "Thrift Dinner Still only 59¢ ...Featured Entree Sunday Roast Leg of Lamb with mint jelly." In 1940, the Desert Oasis (now using the other spelling) advertised Ham & Eggs with French Fried Potatoes, Buttered Toast, Marmalade or Jelly, 25¢ .

In the late '40s my high school girl friends and I used to go to the Oasis often. It was our "place." A logo of a sphinx was on all menus and on advertising at the time. Menus were printed daily. The menu was large, dinners ranging from 50¢ up to about $2.40. When we were not get-

Interior of the Desert Oasis before being furnished. On the beams and below large Egypian heads on the columns were lotus flowers, scarabs, pyramids, peacocks and human figures. A small fountain done in tile is shown at the base of one of the columns. *(Eastern Washington State Historical Society, Spokane, Washington, L94-19.75)*

Clarence Taylor carving turkey on the French silver traveling carver at the Silver Grill. *(Courtesy of the Spokane Northwest Black Pioneers)*

The elegant Silver Grill in the Spokane Hotel. Red tile walls with ornamental inlays were set off by white linen table cloths. (Eastern Washington State Historical Society, Spokane, Washington, L94-10.31)

ting items from the soda fountain, we often got a 49¢ turkey dinner plate. This included large slabs of white and dark turkey lying over bread stuffing, a round scoop of mashed potatoes with gravy, a small white paper container with cranberry sauce, a roll and butter. Chicken croquettes were another favorite, as was the wonderful mocha log for dessert. We watched our waitress when she gave us the bill, for on the back of the check was a statement which said that if the waitress failed to smile you need not pay! They must have all smiled; in any case we would not have dared to refuse to pay, but we always watched.

The Desert Oasis closed in 1961 and downtown Spokane lost a treasured restaurant. The area in which the Oasis had been remained intact for awhile after the hotel was demolished, but it was used as "a utility," probably meaning for storage, by the new Desert Saharan Motor Lodge.[37]

The **Spokane Hotel**, on the southwest corner of First and Stevens, featured a restaurant called the **Silver Grill.** Lillian Sperry's father was assistant manager and accountant at the Spokane Hotel, and she recalls that the name Silver Grill came from the fact that their prime rib dinner was brought to the table and carved with much flair and style on a large and beautiful French silver traveling carver.[38] Dining room steward Clarence Taylor presided over the carving. Taylor started working at the Silver Grill in 1902 at 12 years of age, turning and basting the meat on a spit over the fireplace. He was promoted to serving wine, then became a waiter, and was still there in 1958, working at the Silver Grill for at least 56 years.

The restaurant, designed by Cutter, had two large, high-ceilinged rooms with wood beams in the hipped ceilings.[39] Private dining rooms were on a balcony level. English in style, the rooms had wrought iron light fixtures and dark woodwork and beams.[40] The Silver Grill advertised "known from coast to coast for good food." Surely this boast was based partly on its inclusion in Duncan Hines *Adventures In Good Eating*. The 1945, '46, '47, and '50 editions are identical in what is said about the Silver Grill except for prices. "Open all year, 6 A.M. to 9 P.M. Mighty good and one of the favorites with Spokane people. If you happen to be a baked apple fiend, try them here. Such things as roast beef, chops, and a long list of other well-known dishes. D., [Dinner], 60¢ to $1.25."[41] In December, 1937, an advertisement urged people to come for Christmas Dinner for $1.25, and 75¢ for "Kiddies."

A poem was written in dark Old English letters on a side wall near the back of the main dining room above a large fireplace. Robert Hyslop recalls this as "a fine piece of decoration" and says it is from "Lucille" by Edward Robert Lytton.[42] People who remember the old Silver Grill will undoubtedly recognize these lines:

He may live without books
    - what is knowledge but grieving?
He may live without hope,
    - what is hope but deceiving?
He may live without love,
    - what is passion but pining?
But where is the man that can live without dining?

The Spokane Hotel's last day of business was Christmas Day, 1961.[43] The building was torn down in 1962 for the Ridpath Motor Inn.[44] Around 1985, the Ridpath Hotel named its former King Cole Room, located on Sprague Avenue, the Silver Grill.[45]

How nostalgic to think of the downtown restaurants of those days! Wishful thinking might make us want to go back to the prices in the restaurants then, but wages were much lower, too. We might long for the freedom to eat such delicacies as mocha log, fish and chips, and chocolate almond slabs without pangs of conscience because we knew nothing about the dangers of fat and cholesterol. It was a more innocent time.

An interior view of the Auditorium theater. *(Eastern Washington State Historical Society, Spokane, Washington, L87-1.35276-27)*

CHAPTER
5
THEATERS

THE AUDITORIUM

Imagine a magnificent theater of nineteenth century opulence, with plush and ornate furnishings, fine carved woods, shining brass, silver and jeweled chandeliers, stained glass windows, gilded pillars, one of the largest stages anywhere—a theater that attracted the world's foremost actors, musicians and entertainers to its stage. This was the **Auditorium** in downtown Spokane. How proud the people of the city must have been of this fine theater.

The building, constructed in 1890, was both an office building and a theater. Located on the northwest corner of Main and Post, the theater entrance was on Post Street at the north end of the building. A large lighted sign strung on wires high above the street, stretching from the entrance of the theater to the other side of Post, proclaimed in Old English style lettering, "Auditorium Theater."[1]

Above a door leading to the box office was a large transom window of stained glass with the words "Spokane Falls" emblazoned across it.[2] An outer vestibule and an inner vestibule each had two massive doors with stationary transom windows above them. The first window, framed in an elaborate pattern of stained glass, was a portrait of Shakespeare. The second contained a cut glass rosette. Inside was a long corridor which led to entrances to the auditorium. Other richly hued windows were in the building, notably one of Beethoven, and one of Spokane pioneers J.J. Browne and A.M. Cannon who had constructed the building. The Browne and Cannon window is displayed in the Cheney Cowles Museum.

The interior of the theater was rococo in style. Highly polished brass railings bordered two magnificent balconies. Sumptuous and ornate paired boxes were heavily ornamented "with scrolls, foliage, cherubim's heads, shells, fluting and curved mouldings, all covered with gold leaf."[3] Upper boxes were canopied with "an enormous shell in an upright position...[and] supported by massive carved cornices." Heavy tapestries in sage green draped the doorways of the boxes. Frescoed walls had wide borders in a floral scroll design.

Other furnishings included chairs of crushed strawberry plush; jeweled brass chandeliers, some with silver chains, some with drop globes; friezes of the masks of comedy and tragedy; and massive carved arched doorways supported by gilded pillars. Two grand stairways that led to the balconies and upper boxes were made of "solid live oak with heavy mound-shaped balustrades and richly carved newel posts...surmounted by combination [both gas and electric] upright lamps of a beautiful jewel pattern about five feet in height."

The original seating capacity of 1,588 was reduced to 1,256 after a fire in 1913. The stage was one of the largest in the world. On this subject, George L. Lufkin in *Spokane Spectacle*, a book on Spokane theaters, says: "For its first ten years, the AUDITORIUM was said to have the largest stage west of Minneapolis except for a theater in San Francisco."[4] Hyslop in *Spokane's Building Blocks* says: "The stage itself was larger than the seating area, the deepest in fact in the world when it was built, deliberately one foot more than the previous record holder in Chicago."[5]

Lillian Sperry recalls something that was rather odd in such a handsome atmosphere. This lovely theater had a large screen, probably of asbestos, that was often lowered at the front of the stage. Mrs. Sperry says: "The screen was filled with a sort of permanent collage of rather junky looking advertising."

In its heyday, huge traveling stage productions, such as "Ziegfeld Follies," "Ben Hur," "Bird

THEATERS

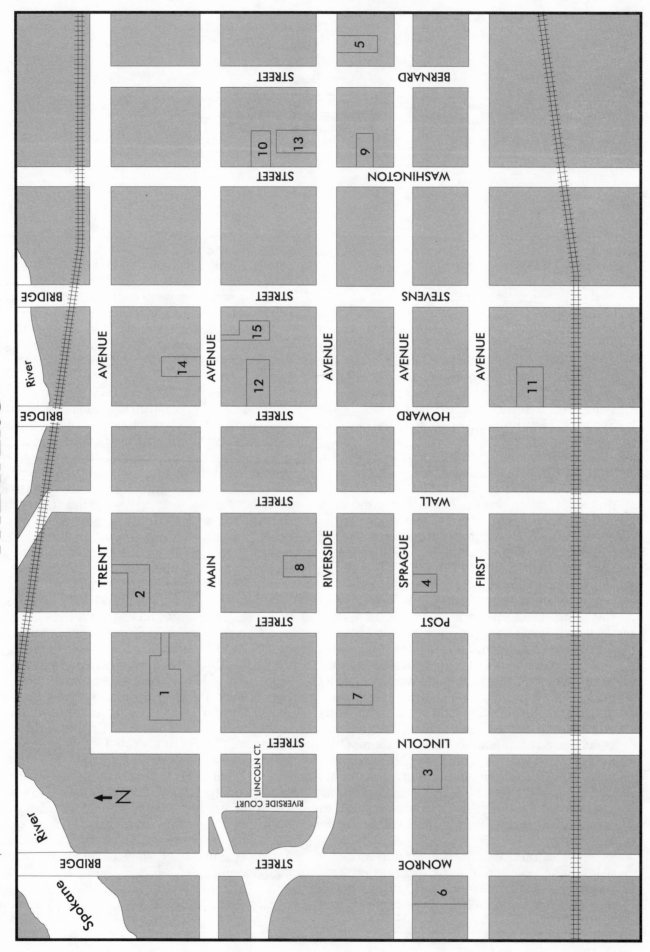

Each theater's first listing is its name in 1930. This is followed by other names used during the two decade period, and in the order that they were used. The bold type gives the name that was most frequently used during the period.

NON-MOVIE THEATERS:

1. Auditorium, (Demolished 1934)
2. Maylon. (The Post Street was used for four months in 1932 or 1933 by the Maylon Players, a popular local theater group.)

MOVIE THEATERS:

2. American/ Post Street/ (Maylon, see above)/ New American/ **Post Street**/ Post (Closed 1972, then demolished)
3. Audian/**State** (The Met, 1988)
4. Egyptian/**Bandbox** (Closed 1953)
5. **Empress**/ Studio (Demolished 1954)
6. **Fox**, Built 1931
7. **Granada** (In mid-'50s, the Riverside; Spokane Civic Theater, 1957-1966)
8. **Liberty** (Closed 1955)
9. **Lyric** (Burned 1931, then demolished)
10. Majestic/Diluf/**Rainbo** (Closed 1953, then demolished)
11. Music Box/**Avalon** (Closed 1933, then demolished
12. Radio-Keith Orpheum (RKO-Orpheum)/ **Orpheum** (Closed 1958)
13. Rex/**New-Rex**/Nu-Rex (in '60s, El Rey; late '70s, Studio. Demolished 1990)
14. **Ritz** (In '60s, Cinema)
15. **Unique** (In '50s and '60s, El Rancho. Demolished 1964)

Decorative work next to the stage and crowning a column in the Post Street theater. *(Eastern Washington State Historical Society, Spokane, Washington, Detail of photo, Favorite Theaters, Inc.)*

of Paradise," and "Hamlet" came to play at the Auditorium. Internationally known artists, lecturers, and musicians gave performances there during the time it was open. These included a lecture by Mark Twain, concerts by singers Ernestine Schumann-Heink, Nellie Melba, Mary Garden, Harry Lauder, Alma Gluck, by violinists Jascha Heifetz and Fritz Kreisler, and by pianist/composer Rachmaninoff. There were performances by legendary ballerina Anna Pavlova and dancer/choreographer Vaslav Nijinsky.

The actors and actresses that played in the theater are too many to list, but include Al Jolson, Otis Skinner, Sarah Bernhardt, and Ethel Barrymore.[6] Local theater groups, chiefly the Maylon Players, gave regular performances, often starring Will Maylon.

By the '30s, the glory of the Auditorium was being replaced by movie theaters. After the Fox theater opened in 1931, out of town artists appeared more frequently at the newer theater, though some stage productions were still given in the Auditorium. In 1930, a "Stock Company (Guild Players)" presented "a Hollywood stage success" called "Chicken Legs" at the Auditorium. All seats were 35¢.[7] In some of its last days "a burlesque troupe played briefly, wrestling matches were held frequently, and there was a walkathon for several weeks, twenty-four hours a day." The final presentation on April 24, 1933, was "Hamlet," given by a traveling drama company and starring nationally famous actor Walter Hampden.[8]

The Auditorium was torn down in 1934. Lillian Sperry recalls that her uncle, Thomas McCart, was able to obtain one of the stained glass windows from the building; it was installed in an apartment building he owned. His daughter, Mrs. Bruce Hay, lived in the apartment soon after she married and through her life. The window may be the cut glass rosette window; it remains in the building in Browne's Addition on West Riverside.

When the Auditorium was demolished, the theater was showing its age, unappreciated, and unfashionable. One cannot help but think about "what might have been" if it had been restored.

MOVIE THEATERS

THEATER EXTERIORS

Dazzling white lightbulbs turned on and off giving a sparkling effect around some of the brilliantly lighted marquees of the movie theaters in the '30s and '40s. Under the marquees on exterior walls and on those leading to the doors, enclosed in glass, were 25 to 30 black-and-white 8 X 10 glossy photographs of stars in scenes from the movie, along with poster sized drawings in color. Fans would linger over these on their way in and out of the theater.

Box offices were aptly named as they were tiny cubicles that were often completely detached from the rest of the building, placed near the sidewalk and away from the entrance. This type, which isolated the ticket seller, was eliminated in later years because of security. Some box offices were centered between two entrances and were part of the building.

Going to movies with no regard for the starting time was common in those days. Because of this strange habit, lines forming outside of a theater did not mean that a feature was about to begin. People were allowed to go inside in twos and threes as others came out; patrons were coming and going throughout the show and stayed as long as they wanted. I remember reading in a travel guidebook around that time that Europeans went to movies at the beginning of a film.

PRICES OF MOVIES

Newspaper advertising of prices was sporadic, but according to some that did appear, they ranged from 10¢ to 25¢ for matinees in the early '30s through the mid-'40s, with most theaters charging 15¢. The *Egyptian* theater advertised its prices as "15¢ ANY TIME" in 1930. Evening prices in the theaters ranged from 25¢ to a surprisingly high amount of 50¢ at the *Orpheum* in 1932. Also in 1932, the *Fox* advertised "25¢ 'til one, 35¢ 'til 6," but did not give a price for after six o'clock. The *Empress* advertised "Always 10¢ and 15¢" in 1933.

Several theaters advertised "Children 10¢, anytime." In 1944, the *Post Street* theater advertised: "Hey Kids. Bring a Ralston Box Top Saturday morning at 10:45 a.m. Free Admission." Around the mid-'40s, prices were not often seen in the ads. Sue Nikotich Weipert, who worked at the *Fox* theater then, remembers: 50¢ for adults, 75¢ for a loge seat, and 12¢ for children.

ALL OF THIS FOR 35¢

When we went to a "show" in those days, (locally we didn't speak of going to movies, we spoke of going to shows) we saw much more than a single feature film and a preview. Also shown were a cartoon, a second companion picture (usually a "Grade B" movie), sometimes a "short" (a ten to fifteen minute story, usually amusing), and a newsreel, many times made by Fox Movietone News that featured Lowell Thomas, or possibly a newsreel by another company, such as Pathe-RKO. These were films of relatively current news, though it might be a week or more old. We did not have TV news then. Many of the newsreels began with a short, fast piece of stirring music; a short phrase of the music ended the newsreel. It was so dramatic that its memory almost makes me laugh. One frequently seen ending showed a movie camera coming toward the audience with these words printed across the screen: "The EYES and the EARS of the world!" Some newsreels ended with the picture and sound of a white rooster crowing.

CHANGES—SILENT TO SOUND

A major change in theaters, from silent to sound films, had begun before 1930 and was still in progress. In 1930, some movies were advertised as "All Talking," some as "Silent," and others did not say. An ad in a January, 1930 newspaper tells that Joan Crawford is playing in "Untamed,...Her First All Talking Picture," at the *Orpheum* theater. On the same page the *Empress* theater advertises another Joan Crawford picture, presumably a silent film. One film is advertised as "All-Talking! All-Singing! All-Dancing!" In the same paper, the *Egyptian* theater calls itself "The House of 'Silents'—No Talkies!" This ad also says: "Organ synchronization," meaning that an organist watched the screen and played music that was in the spirit and mood of the film.

Sources on downtown Spokane theaters of those days speak of pipe organs in all theaters except two. There is no mention of an organ in either the *Unique* or the rather small *Lyric* theater. Lufkin's *Spokane Spectacle* refers to the use of a piano in the *Lyric* in its early days.

Every one of the other theaters had a pipe organ and somewhere in the building 500 to several times that many pipes had to be concealed. If the organ was a large one, the pipes were under the floor, under part of the stage, above the ceiling, or in a basement area. The huge organ at the *State* theater had over 3,000 pipes that were above the stage and below the projection room.[9] In most theaters, the console of the organ, where the organist sat, was in view of the audience. If the organ was a very small one, many of the pipes could be seen by the theater's patrons. In the *Egyptian/Bandbox* theater, for ex-

ample, pipes were behind the organ, which sat on the diagonal to the left of the screen. This made it necessary for the organist to look in a mirror to see the screen.[10]

The *Granada* theater had the smallest of the downtown theater organs, the only one with a single manual (keyboard). Most of Spokane's downtown theater organs had two manuals, some had three, and one had four.

Theater organs have a sound of their own. Extra wind pressure in the pipes helps compensate for their having fewer rows of pipes than classical pipe organs. The result is a powerful and exhilarating rush of sound unlike any other. A tremolo (vibrato effect) adds to the alluring and exciting tone quality.[11]

In the early '30s, the organs were still being used fairly often, even in theaters in which sound equipment had been installed. The curtain would close, lights would come up, and the thrilling organ sound would fill the theater. There was uncertainty, however, about the future of theater organs. When the *Fox* theater was built in 1931, a three manual organ was installed that was small for the size of the theater, probably indicating doubt about how much it would be used. The organ was removed after only a few years.[12]

As sound films became common, and as the Depression deepened, theaters began to sell their organs. Some were sold to churches, some to roller rinks, some to individuals. As time went on, the few that were left in theaters sat mostly unnoticed and voiceless. An exception was the organ at the *Orpheum*, which stayed in the theater through the late '40s and was used for children's plays, Saturday movies, and special performances.

CHANGES—VAUDEVILLE ENDS

The other major change that happened in this era was that vaudeville gradually disappeared. At the beginning of 1930, the *Music Box* theater had vaudeville acts along with films. Though the *Fox* theater did not do much with vaudeville, there were some stage shows there in the early '30s. In March, 1932, it advertised "Spokane's only Stage Revue," Fanchon & Marco's 'Five Races'...a diversified vaudeville production personally staged by Fanchon." In 1933, the *Fox* advertised a "FASHION REVUE On the Stage."

Vaudeville was a tradition at the *Orpheum* theater, as the building had been constructed specifically for it. On January 1, 1930, the *RKO-Orpheum* began the new decade by advertising what appears to be a five-act show with a variety of acts that included: "Stuart & Lash with their Cavaliers," and "Charles Derickson and Burton Brown, Dramatic Tenor and Concert Pianist." Vaudeville was dropped from the *Orpheum* for awhile, but returned in 1933. On April 4, 1933, we find the *Orpheum* advertising: "Big-Time Vaudeville RETURNS TO SPOKANE'S FAVORITE VAUDEVILLE THEATER. It'll be the talk of the town! Starts WEDNESDAY. Five big acts, every act a feature."

In 1934, the *Orpheum* used innovative spelling when it advertised: "VODVIL...A new treat in entertainment for Spokane." In 1938, "On the stage, All New! Major Bowes...Revue! 10 big acts, 20 people..." In 1940, "World's Fair Follies, 30 Gorgeous Girls, 25 Big Scenes." In 1941, Ted Mack "and his famous 'Rhythmic Revue,' A Road Show with 25 Stars—Breaking All Records in Entertainment and Crowds!" was advertised. As late as 1947, at the *Orpheum*, "On our stage in person, 'Sugar Chile' Robinson Boogie Woogie Wonder Boy and his own All Star Stage Revue."

Vaudeville performances were routine at the *Post Street* theater also. In April, 1933, the theater advertised: "Starts TODAY. Another Big Happiness Show—With Al. Franks, His GIRLS and the Original New York BURLESQUE. Come Early Stay late." In 1938, "Five Big Time Acts..." were advertised that included "Little Patsy O'Conner of Screen and Stage Fame" and other names that are generally unknown today. In October, 1945, "In Person! On Stage! MANDRAKE the MAGICIAN and Princess Narda." In October, 1946, "On the STAGE, Mysterious MATHEW The "Spookologist...He's Baffling! He's Sensational! Hollywood's most beautiful ghosts."

CHANGES—BLACK AND WHITE TO COLOR

It should be mentioned that most films were made in black and white at the beginning of this period. For three years beginning in 1932, Walt Disney had exclusive rights to Technicolor, the trademark for a widely used color process. Many movies were made in color by the end of the '40s, often advertised as being "In Technicolor!"[13]

INDIVIDUAL THEATERS

Called the Music Box for a short time in 1930, the **Avalon** was located on the east side of Howard near First Avenue. This theater, designed by Preusse and Zittel, had opened in 1906. For most of its existence called the Hippodrome, the theater presented traveling musical and stock productions at times, but usually showed motion pictures and vaudeville acts. The audience sat in a large, wide area that seated 1,434. The theater closed in 1933.[14]

On the south side of Sprague near Post was the rather tiny **Bandbox** theater. It had a seating capacity of 450, and a "mite-size balcony" which would seat "not more than 25 people."[15] This theater was originally called the Clem, for its owners, the Clemmer family, and in the early '30s, was called the Egyptian. The theater closed, the organ was sold and then the house re-opened in 1933 as The Bandbox, a newsreel theater. After a few months the theater changed the format and started twenty years of successful showing of second and third-run products from major studios.[16]

The **Empress** was on the south side of Riverside in the West 200 block. With a seating capacity of 1,200, the floor of the Empress had a steep pitch, giving every seat a good view of the stage and screen. When the theater opened as the Washington in 1905, it was in a reputable part of the city. As time went on, the area became more and more rundown. Yet, in 1933, an article in the newspaper praised the Empress for putting in the most up to date sound equipment, undoubtedly the first sound equipment in the theater.[17]

In 1937, the Empress was holding talent contests along with movies, and they advertised, "On Our Stage, ALL THE WINNERS OF OUR TALENT 'CONTESTS,' SPOKANE'S BEST ALL IN ONE SHOW." An article on the same page tells: "Winners...will compete for the grand prizes. The program will include two dance teams, acrobats, singers, a whistler and an accordionist."[18] By the '40s, it was definitely in the skid row area and its age and location had taken a heavy toll on the Empress. Some of its ads stated: "Open All Night," a further indication of problems.

We were proud of our art deco **Fox** theater, with its glitzy lobby and indirect lighting, like Spokane's own Radio City Music Hall. Its large seating capacity of 2,300, plush loge seats, immense balcony, and large stage made it a wonderful place not only for movies, but for some high school graduations, and for productions that came from out of town, such as Community Concerts, operas, and plays.

The Fox was part of a theater chain known as Fox West Coast Theaters, then as Fox West Coast Evergreen Theaters, and finally simply as

The Empress Theater. (*Eastern Washington State Historical Society, Spokane, Washington, Detail of photo L87-1.50593-46*)

the Evergreen theaters. By the mid '30s, the chain would own four theaters in Spokane—the Fox, State, Orpheum, and Liberty theaters.

Generally, theaters were the first places to be air conditioned, and in the summers they often advertised "COOL INSIDE." When the Fox theater was built in 1931, air conditioning was still an innovation, though the Audian (State) was cooled with ice, and The Davenport Hotel had an air cooling system.

Even the term "air conditioning" was not generally used in 1931. Many details about the system in the Fox theater were published in the newspaper. *The Spokesman-Review*, calling "the ventilating machine...one of the largest in the west," gave the purchase price as $43,000, a very large sum of money in those days.[19] This was such a novelty that "the ventilator" was put on display in a large two-level area, glassed-in, so that passersby could look in and watch the interesting machinery in operation. I can remember as a child standing outside the building next to the First Avenue exit and looking at this massive machine.

Sue Nikotich Weipert began working at the Fox in 1940 as an usherette, and worked there for seven years, eventually becoming Head Usherette: "It was a very pleasant place to work. Everything was kept in first class condition. The seats were re-upholstered and rugs replaced when they were somewhat worn, and everything was very clean." She remembers that Oscar Nyberg, "a very fine man," was the manager of the theater who "was very protective of the young girls that worked there."

Weipert recalls that the usherettes' uniforms were individually made for each person. She said one basic uniform was wide-legged black pants with a white satin blouse with puffed sleeves. Another uniform used a crisp weight gabardine in dusty pink for wide-legged pants, and a darker pink flowered top that had puffy sleeves and a band around the waist. For the movie "Bathing Beauty," starring Esther Williams, special uniforms were worn. These had pleated shorts, white blouses, and a wide band saying "Bathing Beauty" across from one shoulder to the opposite hip. Sue was photographed in this outfit on the stairway of the Fox for newspaper publicity for the film. The caption of the picture also promoted "KORET Trikshorts," and "a grand selection of [the] Trikshorts" that could be purchased at the Palace.

The Fox is much as it was in the '30s and '40s, though it is divided into three theaters. The once spacious balcony is separated down the center into two parts and a wall runs across the edge of the balcony. With no view from the balcony, it is difficult to see the art deco figures at balcony level on either side of the stage. They must now be viewed from the main floor and lighting is poor, but one can still make out two stylized eagles standing on the backs of turtles.

Much of what was in the theater is unchanged and in remarkably good shape. Though we can no longer see the air conditioner through windows from the outside of the building, it is clear where these windows were as concrete blocks have replaced them.

On the south side of Riverside, near Lincoln, was the **Granada** theater. The interior was almost square, and the floor flat. It had a seating capacity of 700, which included a small loge section in a balcony.

On the north side of Riverside, just west of the Crescent, was the **Liberty** theater. On either side of the foyer of the theater were large concrete stairways with brass railings that led up to a balcony.[20] Pictures of the interior indicate that this balcony extended across the back and wrapped around each side of the theater all the way to the stage. The Liberty had a seating capacity of 1,000. Norm Thue was the organist at the theater in the late '20s and early '30s. The pipe organ was removed later in the 1930s, taken to Seattle, and put in the basement of a roller skating rink, where it was soon destroyed by a fire.[21]

The **Lyric**, which opened in 1910, had a seating capacity of 250. It was located on the east side of Washington between Riverside and Sprague under the center wing of the Lindelle Building.[22] The Lyric had no marquee and, to my knowledge, was the only theater without one. After a fire in 1931, the theater was closed.[23]

The **Rex** or **New-Rex**, the **Rainbo**, the **Ritz**, and the **Unique** did not enjoy much in the way of status, at least by the '40s. All bordered on or were in the skid row area. I was never in any of them except the Ritz, when for a short time in the '70s it was an "arts" theater named the Cinema Fine Arts.

An art deco design with eagles, turtles, plants and a sunburst adorns each side of the stage in the Fox theater. (*Eastern Washington State Historical Society, Spokane, Washington, L94-24.45*)

The **New-Rex** theater was located on the north side of Riverside, west of Washington street. Seating 250, it had a long, narrow interior. The building, constructed in 1908, was a small gem. Hyslop describes the outside as being rococo-classic white plaster on brick, with elaborate broken entablature and column caps.[24] In a 1983 remodeling, a false ceiling was removed in the lobby, and a series of five arches, each wired for 15 light bulbs, was uncovered. At that time, many Beaux Arts plaster decorations in the lobby and auditorium were restored and the theater reopened as the Palace.[25] The eighty-two-year-old Rex, when torn down in 1990, was the oldest building in Spokane that had been built as a theater.[26] When razed, the outside of the building was as originally built except for minor changes.

The **Orpheum** was located on the east side of Howard, midway between Riverside and Main. This large theater had a seating capacity of 1,375.[27] The theater had been built by Pericles "Alexander" Pantages who, in the '20s, built and owned thirty theaters and controlled forty-two

Usherettes, each with a new Chevrolet, stand in front of the Liberty theater in 1940. *(Eastern Washington State Historical Society, Spokane, Washington, L87-1.18857-40)*

others. He booked top theater acts and seemed to be a genius at knowing what audiences wanted to see. Eventually he sold all of the theaters to Radio-Keith-Orpheum for twenty-four million dollars.[28]

The interior of the Orpheum was ornate. A floral design decorated the proscenium arch and parts of the ceiling. Boxes were placed like steps going down toward the stage. Completely redecorated in 1926, the theater was described in the newspaper as "a beautiful atmosphere that is suggestive of the romance of Spain and Italy in bygone days...The walls have been transformed into Travertine stone. The process gives the appearance of walls built up with old Italian stone, honeycomed with decay. They are overglazed in a soft, mellow richness that creates a...background for the ensemble of Italian and Spanish color draperies and mural decorations."[29]

One hundred new wrought bronze and iron light fixtures set with glass, mica and jewels were to be installed in the foyer, under the balcony, and under the boxes. The dome of the theater was decorated with a "resplendent medallion... [like a] jewel aglow with color...[and] painted against a gold leaf background." New draperies and curtains were installed at the time, along with a number of new "drops," which were used for background curtains for the vaudeville acts.

When the Robert Marten organ was installed, *The Spokesman-Review* described it in lofty terms as "a three manual unit organ [plus] pedal organ...Equivalent to 25-piece Orchestra With Amplified Tone...[with] a 49-note marimba harp, a 37-note orchestra bell and a 37-note xylophone with drums, castanets, tomtoms, wood block, tambourines and bass and snare drums."[30] The sounds

111

The Rex or New-Rex theater in early days. (*Northwest Room, Spokane Public Library*)

The facade of the Orpheum theater was made of white terra cotta. The words "Pantages Theater" were in a frieze at the top of the six tall pilasters. (*Eastern Washington State Historical Society, Spokane, Washington, L97.1-385*)

of the drums, the tomtoms, and other effects were not produced electronically as might be done today. The organist sat at the organ console and adjusted "stops," then played the organ, which in turn, played an actual snare drum or xylophone or other instruments that were located (in this case) in a room behind the pit and in the basement.

While in high school I played the organ at the Orpheum during intermission and before some children's plays. It was great fun to be in command of this large instrument, though saying I was in command is an exaggeration. I was primarily a pianist, but had had a few organ lessons and experience in playing for church services. Still, I remember the organ's lush, romantic sound, and the thrill of experimenting with the variety of effects when I was practicing.

When a teenager in the '40s, Jim M. White worked at the Orpheum. He remembers that he and other teenaged boys would come to

work early on Saturday mornings to do such things as scrape gum off the bottoms of the seats. While working, they entertained themselves by turning on the organ and getting it to repeat the sound of the snare drum. Jim thinks they may have worn a hole through the drum head by doing this.

The *Spokane Chronicle* sponsored a Tilakum Krazy Kat Klub matinee on Saturday mornings for children twelve and under at the Orpheum from at least 1937 through around 1943. Admission was 10¢. An article in the *Chronicle*, May 14, 1937, tells that on the following Saturday there would be two feature films, a cartoon, the fourth chapter in the Klub's serial of Dick Tracy, and "Excursions in Science." Beginning at 9:15 a.m., metal Dick Tracy badges were to be issued at the box office. Also there was to be a song and dance review on the stage following the "'Kiddies' Amateur Kontest." "The matinee will open with Carol Babcock's organ songfest. Every boy and girl attending the matinee will be presented with

The generous boxes of the Orpheum theater were faced with plaster of paris scrolls, flowers, and other designs. *(Courtesy of Spokane Children's Theatre)*

an ice cream 'Scooter' and a novelty water gun."[31] (This sounds like a recipe for disaster.) Norm Thue recalls that he played the organ for some of the Orpheum Tilakum presentations.

White remembers that Major Bowes was one of the vaudeville performers that came to the Orpheum while he worked there. White worked first as a page boy, which meant simply doing odd jobs that were necessary. At times the box office would run out of change and White would go to a bank to get cash; but on Saturday nights when no banks were open, Jim recalls: "I would carry a bank bag of $50 or $100 and walk along Main or Trent toward Division, stopping at different restaurants and taverns to get rolls of nickels, dimes, and quarters. I wouldn't think of doing that now!" Jim would also take a newsreel or other film to one of the railroad stations and put it on a train that would take it to nearby smaller towns' theaters. He also worked as doorman, taking tickets at the entrance.

The **Post Street** theater was located near Post and Trent (Spokane Falls Boulevard). Sometime around 1930, the entrance was moved from Trent to Post, and the name changed from American theater to Post Street. The lobby was of marble and mahogany.[32] This large theater had a seating capacity of 1,650.

The interior of the Post Street theater had ornate plaster ceiling and wall decorations that incorporated numerous scrolls and floral designs. Several rectangular areas of the ceiling were edged with scrolls alternating with a smaller floral pattern. Large plaster columns on each side

of the stage had Ionic capitals. Between the scrolls on these, smiling faces looked down toward the floor. Just below this were several bunches of grapes, or perhaps bunches of flowers. More plaster decorative work was exhibited on boxes on either side of the stage at the first and second levels, and on the edges of the balconies.

The theater had a large stage, which made it suitable for all kinds of productions. After the Spokane Symphony's first season in 1945-46 when its concerts were given in the Masonic Temple, the orchestra moved its programs to the Post Street theater. It performed there for 22 seasons before moving to the Fox in 1968.[33] After six seasons at the Fox, the symphony moved to the new Opera House in 1974.

The Post Street was one of the last theaters in Spokane to have vaudeville performances. My sister and I were not allowed to go to vaudeville performances as they were considered somewhat risqué. However, when I was 11 or 12 years old, an older and bolder female cousin marched me into the Post Street against my protests. I sat guiltily enjoying the show, as a comedian performed, dancers danced, and musicians played. A few things shocked me a little, but by today's standards it was very mild.

The **Rainbo** theater, seating 500, was located on the east side of Washington Street between Riverside and Main and just north of the alley. Though there was a pipe organ in this theater in earlier days, it was removed in the early '30s.[34] The Rainbo had a neon spray of colors in a modified rainbow design over each side of its marquee.

An interior picture of the Post Street theater taken from the stage. Some of the seats on the second balcony were wooden benches. *(Eastern Washington State Historical Society, Spokane, Washington, L87-1.41284-30)*

Looking west on Main, the "Unique Theatre" can be seen on the far left, the Ritz theater on the far right. *(Eastern Washington State Historical Society, Spokane, Washington, Detail of photo L86-219.186)*

The **Ritz**, a theater that seated 550, was located on the north side of Main, a little east of Howard Street. Lufkin's book says it is Italian Renaissance in design, but Hyslop's book describes the facade as having a Spanish flavor. After closing it was remodeled and became a Jay Jacobs shop in the 1980s, but today is the Rocky Rococo restaurant. The charming facade still shows the Italian/Spanish influence.

The **State** theater, on the southwest corner of Sprague and Lincoln, had a seating capacity of 928 in the '30s and '40s. The theater has been beautifully restored as the Met. The lovely domed rotunda area that serves as part of the foyer today was part of the outside entrance in earlier days and open to the street along the north side. A box office was located in one back corner and a wall with three pairs of doors gave access to a foyer on the south side of the rotunda.

The State had a large four manual (four keyboard) Kimball pipe organ. It was a combination theater and classical organ, though it was mostly classical. It was one of the largest organs in Spokane at the time. Nationally known concert organists presented concerts on the organ at times.[35] In 1937, the organ was removed by Balcom and Vaughan of Seattle, who rebuild organs for churches, and the organ was installed in St. John's Cathedral where it was used for over twenty years.[36]

Because the State was built as the Clemmer and called that for many years, there was a large "C" over the center of the proscenium arch all through this period, though the theater had long been renamed. For over ten years, from mid '30s to mid '40s, the State usually had single features. We were used to double features in the other theaters, so we sometimes avoided the State as we felt a bit cheated there.

In the early '30s, the Tilakums' Krazy Kat Klub shows were held at the State theater. In May, 1934, during the Depression, an ad for a free movie stated: "Hey, Kiddies—Big FREE SHOWS at the State Saturday, 9:30 A.M. and 11:30 A.M., COMPLETE TILAKUMS' KRAZY KAT Klub Show. Admission: One Complete Label From a Tall Can of PET MILK. (Ask your grocer) Come down early...Bring Your Label."

The **Unique**, a theater seating 300 people, had a strange arrangement in that the auditorium was hidden in the middle of the block. The entrance to the theater was at 509 West Main on the south side of the street. Inside, a long narrow hallway ended at the ticket office near the seating area. Hyslop says: It "had a front so narrow as to deny its existence, except for its sign over the sidewalk and show bills beside (and on) the doors."[37] A small semicircle above the door served as a marquee. Lufkin says: "On each side of the entrance were four full-length mirrors, each making a person looking in them appear to be unusually tall and slender or short and fat, or...terribly distorted."[38]

RADIO AND RADIO STUDIOS

It's a Saturday night in 1938. You and a friend hurry along the street to Post and Sprague where you enter the Radio Central Building. You don't want to be late because there might be too big a crowd for you to get in. You tell the elevator operator, "Seven, please." When you get out of the elevator you go into the large radio studio at *KHQ*. You've come to see "The Old Time Party," one of the programs that draws a goodsized audience for its show each Saturday night. You heave a sigh of relief as there are still seats left.

You and your friend might have chosen other programs to view, especially in the '30s. Radio stations of those days were so different from those of today that it is almost hard to imagine them now. Most of the stations had studios with large audience seating areas and stages on which small orchestras, bands, choruses, and soloists performed.

What a variety of programs we heard! The stations, all located downtown, produced homemaker shows for women, programs about public affairs and farming, and shows featuring music performed live by musicians employed by the stations. Several stations had music libraries with enormous amounts of printed music that could be used on a moment's notice. Spokane stations gave us the music of Bing Crosby, Bob Crosby, and probably Patrice Munsel before they were heard nationally. There was even a local quiz show, and during World War II, broadcasts were made to help the war effort. Most of the programs were sponsored by local businesses. An announcer would intone: "Sponsored by George R. Dodson," or by "Sartori—Master Craftsmen in Jewelry." The sound of a bell introduced a noontime music program known as "The Bell Furniture Hour."

Among the names of radio pioneers in Spokane are Arthur L. Smith of *KFIO*, Thomas V.

Symons of *KFPY* (later *KXLY*), and Louis A. Wasmer, who owned five radio stations in Spokane at various times. These broadcast leaders established stations here in the '20s, and were active in radio as it grew from infancy to its golden years in the late '30s and '40s. Spokane had four stations that were broadcasting in 1930. These four, *KFIO*, *KFPY* (*KXLY*), *KGA*, and *KHQ*, continued through 1949. In the late '40s, two other stations entered the picture—*KREM* and *KNEW*.

Though many station employees remained at one studio for long periods, there was a fair amount of movement from one station to another. Also, because *KGA* and *KHQ* had the same owner and were located in the same building, many employees worked at both stations.

INDIVIDUAL RADIO STATIONS
KFIO, EARLY YEARS

KFIO began operating in 1922, only a year after the first radio license was issued in the country. KFIO was at first owned by and located at North Central High School, its first transmitters having been built by students under the direction of physics teacher, Arthur L. Smith.[1] KFIO was sold by North Central to Smith in 1929. It moved to the downtown area where it was in a couple of locations before settling in 1936 on the third floor of the Ziegler Building. Its transmitting tower was on top of the taller Sherwood Building next door. In the Ziegler location, KFIO had two theaters seating 350 each, and another studio that seated 50 persons.[2]

One of the North Central students, D. Winsor Hunt, was an announcer in KFIO's school location, where, he recalls, they read directly from the newspapers for their news programs. He continued announcing at the station in the '30s. Hunt also wrote advertising scripts and directed a weekly program sponsored by Dr. David Cowen's

RADIO STUDIOS

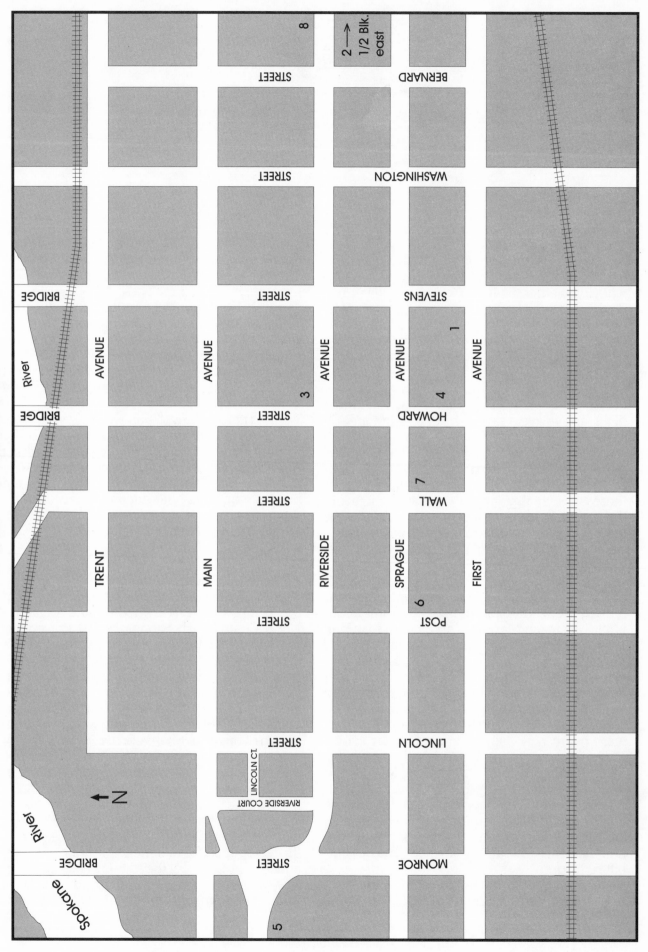

1. KFIO, 1930 and 1931
2. KFIO, 1932 to 1935, (Pedicord Hotel)
3. KFIO, 1936 through 1949 and beyond, (3rd floor, Ziegler Building)
4. KFPY/KXLY, (2nd floor, Symons Building) KFPY, 1930 to 1946; then call letters changed to KXLY, 1947 through 1949 and beyond
5. KGA, 1930 to 1933, (Sun Life Assurance Building)
6. KGA, 1934 to 1946, (7th floor, Radio Central Building)
6. KGA, 1947 through 1949 and beyond, (6th floor, Radio Central Building)
6. KHQ, 1930 through 1949 and beyond, (7th floor, Radio Central Building)
7. KNEW, 1947 through 1949 and beyond, Cowen Building
8. KREM, 1947 through 1949 and beyond, (2nd floor, Realty Building)

KHQ staff (musicians in tuxedos, announcers, and office staff) ca. 1933. Row one, second from left, Cecil Underwood, announcer who went on to NBC; Row two, third from left, Mrs. Wasmer No. 1; fifth from left, Mrs. Wasmer No. 2; Row three, second from right, Harry Lantry, well-known announcer; Row four, far left, Fred Hartley; far right, Louis Wasmer, station owner. *(Courtesy of Gerald S. Hartley)*

Peerless Dentists called "The Happy Gang." Hunt was master of ceremonies and was known as "Swenson."

Hunt writes that The Happy Gang program featured Sammy Mossuto as "the star"; [Mossuto was] "the sex interest—he crooned, 'Just Friends,' 'Always,' 'Miss Otis Regrets' and laid them in the aisles." Another singer "with a wonderful voice" was 12 year old Baby Jean Miller. Several banjo and accordian players and a singing trio also performed regularly. "We became so famous that we began appearing at grange halls, churches, rodeos, basket socials etc.—for free...as long as...the Peerless credit manager could make a sales pitch."[3]

KFPY/KXLY, EARLY YEARS

Like KFIO, **KFPY,** called briefly KFDC, began operating in 1922 when Tom Symons hired 18-year-old Ed Craney, an offspring of North Central's radio club, to build a transmitter and to talk on the station each night.[4] At the time they were operating on only 10 watts of power.[5] The station gradually increased its wattage, so that by 1930 it was using 1,000 watts and was also affiliated with the CBS network. The call letters were changed from **KFPY** to **KXLY** in 1947 because of being part of a chain of "XL" stations.

The **KFPY/KXLY** studio was located in the Symons Building, on the east side of Howard, between Sprague and First Avenues. It was owned by the family of Tom Symons, Spokane pioneers who consecutively built three Symons buildings on that site. (The first one was destroyed by the Spokane Fire.) KFPY was Spokane's first commercial radio station.[6]

D. Winsor Hunt did double duty by working at both KFPY and KFIO in the early '30s. At KFPY he wrote and read advertising scripts during the Depression for Cowen's Peerless Dentists. Hunt believes that the Peerless Dentist's accounts were largely responsible for keeping local radio stations in business at that time.[7]

Two KFPY programs from the '30s, "Meet Your Neighbor" and "Male Chorus Parade," received national recognition. In 1935, KFPY installed a full pipe organ, the first station on the West Coast to do so. The following year, wattage was again increased, this time to 5,000. In 1937, the station began the earliest regular farm program in the Northwest.[8]

In 1934, pianist Arthur Zepp played informally over KGA radio in his first performance in Spokane. Before long he began playing regularly at KFPY, while continuing to play on The Davenport mezzanine. At KFPY, Zepp played a program that was sponsored by Hollenback Piano Company called "Portraits in Black and White." His theme song was "Midnight Bells," from the Opera Ball by Heuberger. Zepp was paid $3.50 for each fifteen minute program; this led to his full time employment in radio.

KHQ

Louis Wasmer began operating **KHQ** in Seattle on 10 watts of power in 1920.[9] In October 1925, Wasmer moved KHQ and its equipment to Spokane (some say on a three-wheeled motorcycle, others say in a Model T Ford) where a two-room studio was set up in The Davenport Hotel. A radio tower was put on top of the building to accommodate the 500 watt station. In 1928 the station was moved to the Standard Stock Exchange Building, on the southwest corner of Sprague and Post. Around 1935, Wasmer changed the name of that building to the Radio Central Building. KHQ's studio seated 100 people.[10]

During the Depression, The Davenport Hotel and KHQ both needed musicians. In 1932, they jointly hired a 10-piece orchestra, directed by Fran Morton, paying them to play in both places. In the mornings the group would play light music on the radio. For part of the afternoon they would rehearse with other musicians for a radio variety show. At night they played from six to midnight, with a one hour break, in the Italian Gardens at the Davenport.[11]

Norm Thue played the organ at KHQ in the '30s and remembers that "Fred Hartley was the studio orchestra director, Dutch Groshoff played banjo and guitar, and a woman named Marian Boyle played the piano." Paul Corbin was a newscaster at KHQ around 1930 and gave Spokane "The Monitor Views the News." Chet Huntley, who went on to NBC, worked briefly at KHQ in the mid-thirties.

We could tune in to "The Old Time Party," a program featuring an orchestra directed by Fred Hartley that broadcast every Saturday night for 25 years, including this entire two-decade period. They played ragtime and other popular music from the '20s and '30s and were sponsored by the Peerless Dentists. Gerald Hartley, son of Fred, played regularly on this program. He recalls that there were full capacity audiences at the broadcasts in earlier years, but that later the number

Musicians of "The Old Time Party" in action, 1945. Left to right: Fern Hutchins, piano; Unidentified vocalist; Paul Frick, Bass; Ruth Harris, Cello; Harold Treadwell, Trombone; Paige Davis, Violin; "Pete" Peterson, Clarinet; Unidentified flute player; Fred Hartley, Drums and Leader. *(Courtesy of Gerald S. Hartley)*

would vary a lot from one week to another, though there was always some audience.

KGA

KGA began operating in 1926. In 1930, it was located in the Sun Life Assurance Building, later the Chancery Building, at W. 1023 Riverside. Owned then by A.E. Pierce of Seattle, the station was purchased by NBC in 1931.[12] Louis Wasmer owned and managed both KGA and KHQ by the mid-thirties. In 1934, KGA joined KHQ on the seventh floor of the Standard Stock Exchange Building (Radio Central Building). The two stations were known by then as "sister stations" and each was affiliated with NBC—KHQ on the "red" network chain and KGA on the "blue" network chain.[13] In 1938, the seating capacity of KGA's studio was 100; the two stations probably shared this studio. KGA moved to the sixth floor of the building in 1947.

Performers on KGA included singers Margel Peters Ayars, Phil Wacker, Anthony Pinsky,

Donna Rees, pianist Marilyn McGuire Stanton, and violinist Rita Lorraine. A singing trio with Don Eagle on guitar played regularly on both KHQ and KGA. Sometimes they would add an outside instrumental soloist to the group. Other music programs on the station were "Studio Parade" and "The Band Wagon."

In the war years, those of us who were in elementary school listened during school to KGA each Friday and heard a program called "The Spokane Rangers." On the program we were urged to help the war by collecting such things as scrap metal, rubber, and aluminum foil, or "tin foil" from gum and cigarette wrappers. We painstakingly separated the foil from thin paper to which it was fused, then formed the foil into balls before turning it in. We were encouraged to buy defense stamps at school. Each cost 10¢ and had a light red picture of a minuteman on it. We licked the stamps and put them in a special little booklet. When we had accumulated enough of them, $20 worth as I recall, we could turn them in for a War Bond.

"Serenade in the Night" was sponsored by the First National Bank. Left to right: Hartley Sater, announcer; Al Lowery, staff organist; Shirley Curtis Hawkins, mezzo soprano; Tom Skeffington, tenor; Marilyn McGuire Stanton, pianist. *(Courtesy of Shirley Curtis Hawkins)*

During the Spokane Rangers program, secret messages were given which we deciphered later with the "Ranger Code," a copy of which I have carefully copied into the back of a sixth grade school notebook. A contest was held among the listeners for both an emblem design and a song for the Rangers. After the winners were chosen, we were each given a red, white, and blue oil cloth arm band to wear. I can still sing the Spokane Rangers' song which had a rousing tune and the following words:

We are the Spokane Rangers,
Fighting for victory,
We gather scrap and rubber,
To make the Axis flee,
The stars and stripes are flying,
Keep them flying high,
KEEP THEM FLYING HIGH!
KEEP THEM FLYING HIGH!
HIGH FOR VIC-TO-RY!

We also heard the "Story Lady," a children's program originated by Mrs. George Crampton, on KGA. In the early '40s the voice of Harry Lantry may have been the most familiar local radio voice. On KGA he gave us farm reports and special events. We recognized the sounds of news commentator Captain Robin Flynn, newscaster Ken Hutcheson, sportscaster Del Cody, and Susan Allen and Barbara Dale, who gave us "women's interests." These could all be heard on both KGA and KHQ.[14] In 1948, KGA increased its power from 10,000 watts to 50,000 watts.[15]

Remote broadcasts, programs done outside of the studio, were fairly common throughout the period. In the '30s, music without announcements was aired regularly from the Garden ballroom. Around 1946, KHQ did a national program over NBC from the Post Street theater. Francis Baxter, music director at Lewis and Clark

As staff organist, Norm Thue did a regular program called "Tunes by Thue". *(Northwest Room, Spokane Public Library)*

Arthur Zepp accompanies Janice Zimmerman at KFPY, ca. 1945. *(Family Collection)*

High School, directed an orchestra which featured Byron Swanson as vocal soloist. In April of 1949, Bing Crosby and the Gonzaga Glee Club did a program over KGA from the Fox theater that was aired nationally. In the late '40s, I participated in two music broadcasts that were done from the lobby of The Davenport Hotel, one on KGA.

In its 1949-1950 season, the Spokane Philharmonic orchestra played on national radio over NBC on the "Pioneers of Music" series. A different orchestra was featured each week on this program. This would be comparable to playing on national television today, and to the orchestra members and to director Harold Paul Whelan, it was a major honor to have been asked. NBC specified that the orchestra was to play the Richard Strauss tone poem "Don Juan."

KFPY/KXLY, LATER YEARS

In the late '30s, Arthur Zepp became Music Director at **KFPY**. Around the same time, Norm Thue, who had worked for twelve years at KHQ, began a twelve year period at KFPY.

Thue and Zepp often played together on two grand pianos that were in the studio. Sometimes Zepp would play on the piano while Thue played on the organ. At one time this well known team was hired by Emry's, a clothing store for men, to play at one of the minstrel shows (a yearly parent show) at Lewis and Clark High School. For this performance they played on two concert grands, wore tails and top hats, and were called "The Two Toppers."

Zepp recalls that as music director of KFPY he directed a little orchestra. Sometimes this would simply be a few players, perhaps a violin, cello, and Zepp on the piano. At other times the group would be augmented with other performers, perhaps a flute or clarinet. Occasionally more musicians would be added. KFPY claimed to have over 10,000 arrangements and orchestrations in its music library in 1948.[16]

Edna Storms was heard on KFPY with a fifteen minute daily program called "This Woman's World." KFPY brought us "Spokane Speaks," a program which gave an individual a chance to come to the studio and give his or her views on many subjects. Guests might be candidates for public office, the president of a local college, a group of newspaper reporters, or an informed citizen who asked to speak on a particular subject.[17]

In the '40s, "Forward Spokane" featured

soloist Barbara Duanne, singing songs in tribute to various businesses and firms that had done something for the betterment of the community of Spokane. A quiz show called "Playground," with questions about the Pacific Northwest, was produced locally by KFPY.[18] Newscasters in the early '40s at KFPY were John Mallow and Ed Butherus. George McGowan gave the farm news.[19]

We listened also to "Good Morning Neighbor," in which requests could be made of Thue playing the organ, and Del Yandon on the piano. Zepp remembers Yandon as being a very talented pianist who played both by ear and by reading music. He had a casual approach to doing a radio program. He seemed unable to think of things to play and would come to Zepp before his program was to be aired and ask him for help in deciding what to play. Zepp would help him make a list of pieces, and Yandon would go into the studio and do the program without rehearsal. Yandon would become Music Director of the studio in the late '40s after Zepp left the station.[20]

During the war, there was "Take-Off," an Army Air Corps Band program. We listened weekly to a mixed choir of forty voices, organized and directed by C. Robert Zimmerman, called the "Serenaders." This radio choir, formed in 1943, sang in the style of the nationally known Fred Waring group, which was very popular at the time. While singing with this radio group, my sister Marianna met another singer who would become her husband. He was Gene Stensager, a sergeant stationed at Galena, who also played in the Army Air Corps Band mentioned above.

Many talented musicians were stationed at nearby bases during World War II, according to Arthur Zepp. One of the young singers who came to Spokane at the time and remained here was baritone Phil Crosby. Another gifted musician was Perry Lafferty, a pianist who had worked in radio in New York City. After Lafferty began working at KFPY, he began bringing other young musicians with him from Galena and Geiger.

Lafferty got permission to use some scripts written by Norman Corwin of New York. With these, a series of broadcasts was created called "Between Americans." Zepp remembers: "The program was very important to the war effort in Spokane as it was used to raise money for War Bonds." Zepp, who played organ for this show, recalls that Lafferty would give descriptive directions for short musical phrases called for in the script. Here "a flowing melody," here "rising

"Rita Lorraine and her Magic Violin," accompanied here by Dorothy Ross, was heard on KFPY in the '40s.*(Family Collection)*

chords and a big crescendo," here "a happy theme," or "a shock chord," meaning a dissonance. Zepp would then improvise the desired music interludes. Lafferty would later produce and/or direct TV programs on all three major networks.[21] Other musicians that both Zepp and Thue recall from those days at KFPY were singers Byron Swanson and Tom Skeffington, and violinist, Jimmy Clark, who was Music Director before Zepp.

KFPY changed ownership in 1945. One of its former owners, Arthur Bright, acquired control of KHQ. Zepp was appointed Music Director there, and many programs that had been established at KFPY were continued at KHQ, among them, the "Serenaders."

By 1948, **KFPY** was called **KXLY**. The station boasted that year that its main studio, a handsome area called "The Golden Concert Studio," seated almost 300 people.[22] But in a listing of Washington stations dated 1940-41, KFPY had listed its "Golden Concert Studio" as seating 400, and in the same publication dated 1938-39, the capacity was given as 500.[23] I remember this studio fairly well, and it seems to me that all of these

"The Serenaders": Left to right, Row one: Unknown, Evelyn Brooks Webster, Marian Hanennberg, Betty Bell Reinertson, Unknown, Unknown, Pat Rule Zimmerman, Unknown, Marianna Hage Stensager, Sylvia Newton Shepherd; Row two: Betty Sampson, June Anderson Holman, Unknown, Erma Thorstensen, Shirley Gaucher, Beverly Koester Gilger, Unknown, Earline Victor, Shirley Curtis Hawkins, Donna Peelgren; Row three: Unknown, Unknown, Keith Parker, Eugene Vanderhoff, Eugene Stensager, Unknown, James McEvers, Eugene Fink, Edwin Mason, Chuck Mason; Row four: Tom Mason, Edgar Mason, Arthur Lysell, Unknown, Ray Van Hees, Conductor C. Robert Zimmerman, James Scott, Unknown, Arthur Lien, Will Riggen, Garth Ruckhaber. *(Family Collection)*

are inflated figures, though it might possibly have seated "almost 300." A picture of the studio from a 1948 brochure shows folding chairs so perhaps the capacity depended on how tightly the chairs were crammed into the area.[24]

It was a pleasant and impressive facility. Audiences faced a curtained stage on which the console for the pipe organ sat. Nearby were the two grand pianos. Along the wall to the left side of the audience hung a large purple curtain with the letters KXLY emblazoned across it. In the '40s, the KXLY studio had the most modern radio equipment available, according to their promotional brochure of 1948.

KFPY/KXLY was generous in lending its large studio when it was not in use. Student recitals were often given there. An acknowledgment in a Spokane Philharmonic Orchestra pro-

gram from the 1946-47 season is as follows: "The Philharmonic appreciates the splendid civic attitude of Mr. McGowan and Station KFPY in the offer of their main studio for rehearsal space for the orchestra." Adjudications for the string division of the Spokane Music Festival were held there in 1948. The Spokane Junior Symphony held its rehearsals there in the 1949-50 season.

KFIO, LATER YEARS

"**KFIO**, although a station of lesser power than most, enjoyed a comparable broadcast signal strength due to its strategic location of transmitter and tower smack in the middle of the business district of Spokane," writes Ed Antosyn, Chief Engineer at KFIO in the mid-'40s. "It provided its audience with a full fare of broadcast news, en-

The foyer and reception lounge at KFPY, ca. 1945. The entrance to the studio was at the top of this staircase. *(Northwest Room, Spokane Public Library)*

tertainment, sports, and public service programming." By the '40s, it was an affiliate of the Mutual Don Lee Broadcasting System. National news came from United Press or Associated Press on teletype machines, was torn off and read verbatim over the air.

By the mid-'40s, most stations were playing a lot of recorded music. Antosyn recalls that a program in the after school hours was called Penny Serenade; it was hosted by the main disk jockey at KFIO, Frosty Fowler. Listeners sent in penny postcards, a postcard only cost a penny then, and made requests for particular recordings.

KFIO broadcast a number of local religious programs through the week. The Radio Church of the Air was done each weekday morning, and on Sundays a remote program of the service from the Westminster Congregational Church was aired.

Though most remote broadcasts came by telephone line then, KFIO's location on busy Howard and Riverside made a "Man on the Street" program feasible. A microphone was dangled out the window and an interviewer would ask questions of people going by. Variety shows and organ programs were also done from the nearby Orpheum theater by running a cable over the rooftops to the theater.

In the '40s, KFIO became a training place for some of the young journalism graduates from Washington State College. A popular KFIO program that was associated with the public library was "The Story Lady." KFIO also joined the Chamber of Commerce lunch each week, particularly to broadcast their speaker. Late at night, a sonorous-voiced poet known as Rex King read poetry accompanied by music. KFIO also broadcast many late evening classical music programs from recorded albums.

In late 1947, KFIO lost Mutual Don Lee Broadcasting to KNEW, but this allowed a more flexible schedule making more sports programming possible. Among the sportcasters were Frank Herron, Herb Hunter, Del Jones, and Loyd Salt. The station did reports from Playfair Race Track along with a broadcast of "The Race of the Day."

CHANGES IN OWNERSHIP

After the war, changes occurred in the ownership of several stations. Tom Symons died in the early '40s and after his death, KFPY was owned jointly by his widow, Frances Symons and Arthur L. Bright. In 1945, KIRO of Seattle paid $150,000 for Bright's one/third portion of the

Ed Antosyn at KFIO in the Ziegler Building, ca. 1946. (*Courtesy of Ed Antosyn*)

KFPY stock. The rest was purchased by E. B. Craney of Butte, Montana, who as a young 18-year-old had been hired by Symons to build KFPY's first transmitter when the station was getting started.[25]

KHQ, Inc., a newly formed corporation owned by the *Spokane Daily Chronicle* and Arthur Bright, purchased KHQ from Louis Wasmer for $850,000. Eighty-five per cent of KHQ, Inc. was owned by the the *Spokane Daily Chronicle*; Bright owned the remaining 15 per cent.[26] Newspaper accounts reported that Louis Wasmer then bought the northwest corner of Sprague and Monroe as a site for FM and for television broadcasting, neither of which was in our region yet.[27] For some reason, Wasmer did not go ahead with the venture, but he did purchase KFIO in 1950, changing the call letters to KSPO and the frequency from 1230 to 1340 kilocycles.

CHANGES IN BROADCASTING

The late '40s was a pivotal time in radio broadcasting. Tape recordings and vinyl rather than shellac records were improving the quality of recorded music dramatically. Stations could subscribe to music services of transcriptions on large 16-inch phonograph records. Scripts were provided with these so that entire programs, usually 15 minutes in length, were ready for broadcasting. Staffs were curtailed; script writers weren't needed for this new kind of broadcasting. The days of live orchestras in radio studios were numbered. Radio's future was also uncertain with TV on the way. Still, Spokane saw the birth of two new radio stations in 1947—KREM and KNEW.

NEW STATIONS

KREM

KREM is first listed in *The Spokesman-Review* under "Radio Programs on the Air Today," on January 18, 1947. Its station was located on the second floor of the Realty Building at W. 242 Riverside. Cole Wylie was owner and manager at KREM in its early days. Wylie recognized the new trends in broadcasting and established KREM as the first record station in town. Instead of musicians, disk jockeys were hired who worked in relatively small studios. Large audience capacities were no longer needed.

Wally Nelskog, who was an engineer at the station, was also a popular disk jockey doing remote programs from downtown store front windows. Another of KREM's well-known disk jockeys was Ed Mosley, or "Silver City Ed," who played country music and had a telephone request program. One of the remote programs that was broadcast each evening around dinner time was a half hour of organ music from the Chef O'Malley restaurant. Announcements for the program were made from the studio.

KNEW

In the late '40s, Arthur Smith applied to the FCC for use of 5,000 watts of power for KFIO. This would have boosted the station from a local to a regional category. By the time the FCC was ready to approve this, the aging Smith was no longer interested. Other broadcasters picked up the option, and **KNEW** came into being. Consequently, KFIO lost Mutual Don Lee Broadcasting to KNEW.

KNEW's studios were on the southeast corner of Sprague and Wall. The station began operating on Labor Day in 1947. The network praised Spokane throughout KNEW's first day: [It is]..."the major transportation center between the Twin Cities and the Pacific tidewater. It is served by five of the eight transcontinental railroads that

KNEW's studio was on the second floor of the newly remodeled and renamed Cowen Building (formerly the Idaho Block). *(Eastern Washington State Historical Society, Spokane, Washington, L87-1.57293-48)*

cover the western United States, and it is the hub of more railroad mileage than any city west of Omaha. It is served by two major air lines, by motor bus systems, and is the center of a vast network of improved highways." Also, Spokane was called "The Friendly City, the Capital of the Inland Empire" and "gateway to Grand Coulee Dam—eighth wonder of the world."[28]

The manager of the new station was Harry Lantry, who had been active at KHQ and KGA. John R. Fahey was news editor, and Anthony Pinsky, music librarian. Chief Engineer was C.W. (Bill) Evans, and Program Director was Paul M. Crain. Other staff members included Bill Rhodes, Budd Bankson, Hilary McPherson, James Agustino, James Scott, and Fred Stanton.[29]

At first, the management at KNEW expected the station would follow in the footsteps of Spokane's older, larger stations, with live music and good-sized staffs. But it became apparent that those days were gone. KNEW not only had to rely on recorded music, it became the most popular disk jockey station in town according to Ed Antosyn. KNEW would become KJRB.

NETWORK PROGRAMMING

Through our local stations we received memorable nationally produced programs. We listened to newscasters and commentators such as H.V. Kaltenborn, Lowell Thomas, and staccato-voiced Walter Winchell. We heard Washington state's own Edward R. Murrow with his reports before and during World War II that began: "THIS—is LONDON!" We heard Allen Funt with

"Candid Microphone" long before "Candid Camera" appeared on television, fireside chats with Franklin Delano Roosevelt and national Democratic and Republican party conventions.

In the late '30s we began to get quiz shows. One program called "The $64 Question" gave the contestant a dollar or two for a first question, then doubled the money for each correct answer until the final grand prize of $64! We also were sometimes engrossed in dramas that kept us not only close to, but actually staring at the radio. These included "Lux Radio Theater," "First Nighter," and "The Little Theater off Times Square." "Oxydol's Own *Ma Perkins*," was first broadcast in 1933. This and other fifteen minute daytime serials, often sponsored by soap manufacturers, were soon dubbed "Soap Operas." I remember hurrying home from school each day at Christmas time in order to hear "The Cinnamon Bear." Others remember listening to "Let's Pretend" on Saturdays, and "The Shadow," or "Tom Mix."

We heard the NBC Symphony with Toscanini conducting; gravel voiced Jimmy Durante; Fannie Brice as Baby Snooks; "Fred Waring and the Pennsylvanians"; "Inner Sanctum"; "Fibber McGee and Molly"; "Hit Parade," Big Band music; ventriloquist Edgar Bergen with Charlie McCarthy; Joe Louis prize fights; "Jack Armstrong, the ALL-AMERICAN BOY!" and its theme song: "Have you *TRIED* Wheaties? The best breakfast food in the land"; "Blondie," ("Ah, ah, ah! Don't touch that dial! YOU'VE got a date with BLONDIE!"); and "Little Orphan Annie";my sister can still sing all of the words to the theme song that began: "Who's that little chatterbox, The one with all those curly locks? Who could it be? It's Little Orphan Annie—" Ovaltine sponsored it and later the popular "Captain Midnight," action adventure program. They were one of the first companies to offer badges, secret code rings, and decoders, so we all drank Ovaltine in order to get the required premiums.

Our imaginations were stimulated, we could "see" a gorgeous costume, visualize a horrible face, or envision the loveliest place! With no limits to the imagination, the illusions surpassed anything that could be made for television, and we didn't have to adjust the color. Our imaginations worked so well that we used to *listen* to people tap dance on the radio! My how that kid could dance! We could tell by the rhythmic clickity-clack, clickity-clack of his feet. What a wonderful world it was.

On warm summer evenings in the '30s, music wafted from the open windows above the Central Market on Main and Howard in the heart of downtown. We could hear it echoing down the street to Riverside Avenue, sometimes lively and exciting, sometimes waltzing, sometimes sweet and slow. These enticing sounds came from eleven different public ballrooms downtown in the years 1930 to 1949, though there were never more than five of them open at one time.[1] In an article recalling those days Spokane was called "one of the dancingest towns in the country."[2]

"Tripping the light fantastic" may be remembered especially at cherished places such as Natatorium Park, Liberty Lake, and Lareida's on East Sprague, but downtown there were many places to dance. The Italian Gardens in The Davenport Hotel, the Silver Grill in the Spokane Hotel, the Roundup Room in the Desert Hotel, private clubs, and the public ballrooms...all had dance floors.

When I asked a group of people who were young adults in the '30s and '40s, "Do you remember any particular place to dance downtown at that time?" an almost startling chorus of "**The Garden**" came back to me. The most popular of the dance places, The Garden, was at W. 333 Sprague Avenue. It is remembered as "the best in town," "a high class place," "had good music," and "attractive interior with special seating areas." The Garden had opened in 1919 as Whitehead's Dancing Palace, but its name was changed to the Garden Dancing Palace, Inc. in 1923. It remained open until 1942. In its last year it was called **The Brook**. As remembered in the *Spokane Daily Chronicle*, it was "a large ballroom, [that] often had 1,200 and more dancers on hand for name bands and other attractions. A feature was its loges, enclosed with railings that enabled parties of several couples to sit together between dances."[3]

"Live music" was all that was used in the ballrooms, partly because of tradition, but mostly because sound systems were of only fair quality until later. Don Eagle, who played at the Garden in the '30s, recalled that the bands would range from about seven to twelve people, and averaged around ten, plus a vocalist. He said, "The Garden had its band stand in the middle of the floor and the dancers would dance around the band moving counter clock-wise. That was common in many places, but became old-fashioned. The members of the band wanted to modernize by moving out of the center of the room. We made a deal with the manager, who agreed to pay for the materials. Several band members who were pretty good at carpentry built a new band stand in one corner and added a shell behind it to throw out the sound."

In 1932, the Garden advertised that prices had been cut. Gentleman, 50¢ ; Ladies, 15¢ . This "includes Checking [coats] and Dancing. Finest of Music by the New Garden Troubadours." Prices were sometimes "by the dance." Eagle recalled that dance tickets were sold from a roll, one dance being allowed per ticket. Nickel dances, or twenty tickets for $1 was the going price. Each dance lasted about three minutes. Eagle remembered: "At one time, the Garden had a system of roping off the dancers with long velvet ropes. After playing only a chorus and a half, which they called two dances, the dancers were pulled to one side so that they would have to pay again before continuing." After a lot of protests from customers this was stopped. Imagine the discomfort and stress of being jostled into a crowd of bodies being hauled to one side in this way, let alone the problem of the price. No wonder people complained.

Dancing lessons were also taught at the Garden. Several of the other ballrooms doubled as dance studios in the daytime. After the Garden closed as a dance hall it was converted into a

BALLROOMS

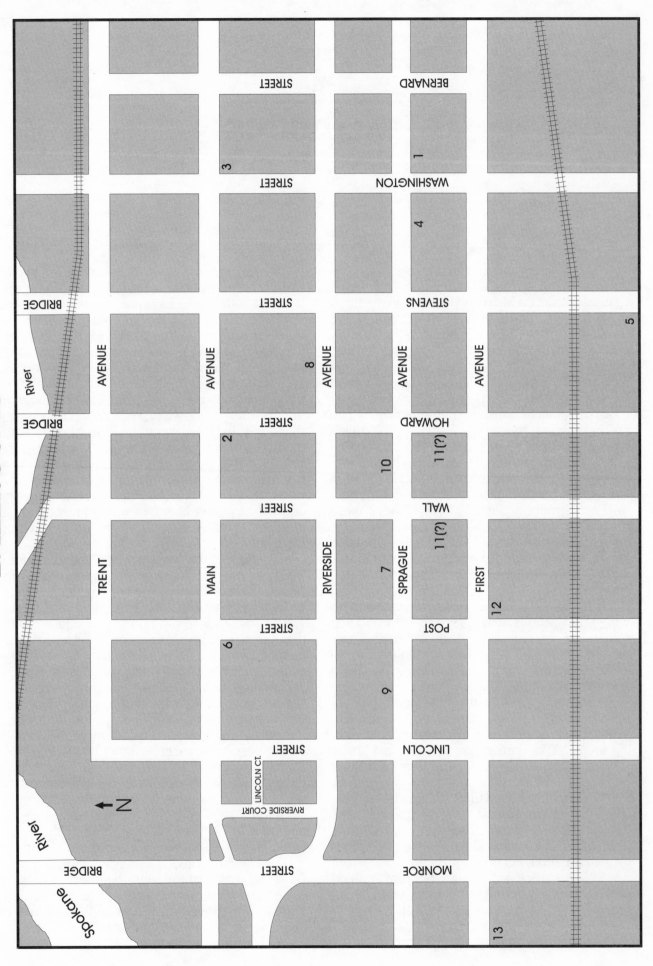

The interior of the Garden in 1923, showing a mezzanine along one wall, and the band stand on the far right. (*Eastern Washington State Historical Society, Spokane, Washington, L93-74.71*)

1. Garden Dancing Palace, 1923 through 1941; Brook, 1942
2. Crystal Ball Room (over Central Market) 1930; Metronome Ball Room, 1931 - 1947
3. Washington Hall (over Washington Market) 1930; Bluebird Dance Hall, 1935 through 1940; Rainbow Ballroom, 1941 to 1946
4. Ramp Dance, 1930; Odean Dance Hall, 1933 through 1935; New Dreamland Dance Hall, 1936; Ramp Dance Hall, 1938 and 1939
5. Dreamland Dance Hall, 1932 to 1935
6. Melody Heaven Ball Room (over Westlake Market) 1932 to 1936
7. Trianon Ball Room (over Model Cafe) 1934; Metronome Dance, 1949
8. Roseland Cabaret, 1945 to 1947
9. Dance-In Ball Room, 1933
10. Cinderella Ballroom, 1931
11. Hi-Nite (first location) somewhere on South Wall or on South Howard (Very brief time)
12. Hi-Nite (second location) Roundup Room, Desert Hotel
13. Hi-Nite (third location) 1944 to 1951; Hi-Spot Dance, 1952 to 1956; Metronome, 1950 to 1953

This 1935 picture taken in front of the Garden and labeled "Garden School of Dancing" presumably shows the teachers and staff from that school. *(Eastern Washington State Historical Society, Spokane, Washington, L87-1.6000-35)*

bowling alley, becoming Garden Lanes Sports Center, and it remained one until the '60s.[4]

The City Directory at the time listed the ballrooms under "Dance Halls and Pavilions." **Metronome Dance**, the one that was located above the Central Market on Howard and Main, had its entrance almost at the alley at 123 N. Howard, across from the Orpheum theater. Called the **Crystal Ball Room** in early 1930, it became the **Metronome Ball Room** later that year. A late 1930 ad ended with "Note—The 'Metronome' has been completely remodeled and is now under Garden management." The Metronome was also the home of Calvert's School of Dance.[5] It remained in the location until 1948; in 1949, the Metronome is listed in the City Directory at W. 718 Sprague, above the Model Cafe. In 1950 it moved to W. 1015 First Avenue in the I.O.O.F. building, where it remained until 1953. The year 1953 is apparently the end of adult public ballroom dancing in the downtown area.

The stair entrance to the second floor ballroom at N. 120 Washington (Main and Washington), was immediately north of the Rainbo theater. A total of 13 years of operation made **Washington Hall** (1930 and earlier), **Bluebird Dance Hall** (1935-1940), and **Rainbow Ballroom** (1941-1943 or 1944), the third most popular ballroom of those days. I was told by one senior citizen that when it was called Washington Hall, "it was a wild one—a really rough place."

People who went to the public dance places have assured me that generally they were considered nice places to go. Edith Meeker remembers that single girls would go to the Garden. Don Eagle also recalled that there was no stigma attached to going to the ballrooms without a date, and added that "the ballrooms were well run, and checked frequently by the police for problems." Minors were welcome in them during at least some of the years.

Rough and wild may have been typical at times in some of the dance halls. In 1936, a Spokane policewoman told how she had spent her time during 1935. Perhaps she was over zealous in her work, but she showed more time spent on items listed under "Dance Halls" than any other category. This included checking dance halls 1,289 times, finding minors in them 121 times, sending 43 minors home, arresting 58 for disorderly conduct, and "Boys spoken to" 107 times, dealing with "Drinking and Drunks," 209 times, and "turning up the lights," 5 times.[6]

Imagination and a little fantasy went into naming most of the dance places. The **Crystal Ball Room**, **Dreamland Dance**, **Bluebird Dance**, and the **Cinderella Ballroom** were glamourous and illusionary names. **Roseland Cabaret** and the **Trianon Ball Room** were named for more famous ballrooms with similar names back east. The seemingly unexciting name **Ramp Dance** was near the almost new and handsome City Ramp Garage. **Melody Heaven** could invoke a celestial place with beautiful music, but names can have surprising effects on some people. My mother's uncle, a missionary to China, was offended while visiting here when he saw a sign saying "Melody Heaven Ball Room." He thought it was wrong to use the word "heaven" in a name for a wicked place such as a dance hall.

HI-NITE

Hi-Nite was the name of a place for high school students to dance in the '40s. During World War II, Edith and Chet Meeker had neighbors who did not want their teenage daughters to date servicemen. Meeker was a member of the Active Club, a service club composed of young men. Meeker began talking to other Active Club members about organizing something that would be for local teenagers. Meeker's father was active in the Odd Fellows lodge, and the younger Meeker enlisted his father to get that organization interested in the project also. The result was Hi-Nite.

All of this probably took place in the spring of 1943, as a summer article in a newspaper of that year tells that letters had been received from all over the country asking about the high school dance organization.[7] Here another and perhaps coinciding reason for organizing Hi-Nite is told: Students came from each high school to discuss a plan to head off vandalism, and they said "a sort of club where they could have dances...would help."

For a short time the Hi-Nite dances met in "an old Benewah market," that was on south Wall, or possibly on Howard Street, according to Mrs. Meeker, but she is not certain where it was located. The Roundup Room, in the basement of the Desert Hotel, was Hi-Nite's next home, where the second dance of the fall season was to be held on Aug. 13, 1943, after the Active club had spent $1,000 getting the project going there.[8] The Meekers would sometimes chaperone the dances. Music was provided by small bands and combos, at first from Lewis and Clark, directed by Johnny Powell, and later from North Central and probably from the other high schools. Sometimes arrangements from "the big bands" were played, Mrs. Meeker recalls. She remembers being impressed by how good these groups sounded.

In the fall of 1944, Hi-Nite moved to its final location in the I.O.O.F. hall, at W. 1015 First Avenue. Edith Meeker recalls that the Odd Fellows spent $25,000 renovating the room that Hi-Nite would use. This included adding a soda fountain, a snack bar, new tables and chairs; the room had been newly decorated in green and chocolate brown, according to *The Spokesman-Review*.[9] The first dance had students "from every part of Spokane. Set behind flashy blue and silver stands were the members of Sid Schulein's orchestra, who 'gave out' with everything from sleepy-time waltzes to pipin' hot jive." A membership in the club cost 50¢ and was good for a year's admission on weekday afternoons from 3 to 6 o'clock. Evening dances with music "by an orchestra of student choice" were planned for every Friday evening.

At the opening night of the 1948 season of Hi-Nite, *The Spokesman-Review* reported that there were 500 students.[10] Nancy Gale Compau remembers in the '50s that "the girls danced with each other in the middle of the room while the boys stood around the outside and watched. The boys cut in when they saw someone they wanted to dance with."

Sometime in the late '40s, high school students began to refer to their dance place as "**The Spot**."[11] Apparently the name was officially changed as the Polk City Directory lists a **Hi-Spot** Dance Hall at the address from 1952 to 1956. This building had to be shared with the I.O.O.F. and with Metronome Dance, which was in the building from 1950 to 1953. The building was either large enough to accommodate several groups at once, or these organizations used it at different hours.

An undated picture of a streetcar in front of the Review Building. *(Eastern Washington State Historical Society, Spokane, Washington, L83-113.63)*

8

STREET RAILWAYS

What a romantic idea to think of riding streetcars on the street railways through our city! My husband John, who grew up in Pullman, remembers coming to town with his father several times when he was a boy and staying at The Davenport Hotel. Two things made him know he was "in the big city,"...one was the sound of the newsboys calling in the streets and the other was hearing the "Ding, Ding, Ding" of the streetcars warning people to move out of the way, and the humming "Roar—r" as they started. The thought of having this turn of the century mode of transportation available seems intriguing today so it is hard to believe that we were excited when the street railways were replaced by busses.

In earlier days several different power sources were used for our street railways. Spokane's first street railway line, built in 1889, was powered by horses. A number of lines and owners followed. The lines included a steam tram which generated sparks that at times set clothing on fire, and sometimes turned over on hills because of high speeds needed for the climb. An early electric line operated at a loss. Two cable car lines, well suited to the hills, used power from a water wheel that was located under the Monroe Street bridge. Most lines were built by developers to get prospective buyers to house sites. The Cable Addition was named because cable cars were used to get there. Our Cable Add bus line is the offspring of this early line.

Finally, and before the turn of the century, the electric trolley system was installed. Power for the streetcars came from electric wires suspended over the streets. The power was conducted to the cars through the trolley, a pole which stretched from the top of the car to the wires. By 1900 the Washington Water Power Company owned most of the street railway lines. There was a final merger in 1922 between Spokane Traction Company and the Washington

Water Power Company forming the Spokane United Railways, or SUR. Washington Water Power then owned them all.

At the beginning of the '30s, numerous streetcars could be seen and heard in all of the central area as there were street railways, tracks and suspended wires on all major downtown streets. They ran the length of Riverside from Division to Monroe and beyond, on Sprague from Washington to Lincoln, on Main from beyond Division to Lincoln, and on Trent from beyond Division to Post. They ran also on most north/south streets from Post to Washington in the above areas.[1]

Not only the downtown area, but the entire city was veined with a network of these lines. "There were 66 miles of streetcar routes and 110 miles of track, served by 120 cars. The principal downtown intersection where all car lines met was Howard and Riverside Avenue."[2] Many people did not have cars in the Depression years so street railways allowed people to work and play in all parts of the city. They could have a job far from home, go to ball games, to parks such as Natatorium Park, to visit friends in another corner of the city and, of course, go downtown.

Street railways were gone by the end of 1936 when I was a small child. Perhaps I wouldn't remember them at all except for the fact that, until around that time, we lived at the end of the East Nora line. That line was not only the last street railway line to be installed, but was one of the last to be converted to a bus line.[3]

The streetcar sat many times a day near our house waiting for the time to return to town. I have dim memories of the dark green and yellow on the cars' exteriors. Gold leaf was used for letters and numbers on the outsides of the cars.[4] What I remember most is the seats made of natural-colored, narrow-gauge, woven rattan that was shellacked or painted making the rattan rigid. So-

Until I was five years old, we lived on Greene Street at the end of the East Nora line. Our house was hidden behind the streetcar in this 1935 photograph. *(Eastern Washington State Historical Society, Spokane, Washington, L88-408.556)*

called "walk-over seats" allowed passengers to slide the back of the seat over the seat from one edge to the other so that people could sit facing either forward or backward. In this way, a small group of people could sit facing each other.

I recall that the conductor walked through the car at the end of the line and, with arms outstretched, pushed all of the seat backs so that they would be facing forward when the trip to town began. The seats were constructed this way because at one time there was no way to turn the streetcars around at the ends of some of the lines. This meant that the streetcar needed to be "double-ended," or designed so it could be run from either end.

Spokane had both "double-ended" cars and cars that would operate only in one direction. Originally, most of the cars here were "double-ended" and had two trolleys on top. At the end of the line, the trolley at one end of the streetcar was tied down, while the one at the other end was raised and placed on the wire. With this method the car did not have to turn around. The conductor simply moved to the other end of the car for the return trip. Later, cars that were controlled from a single end were used. These had open-air, rear standing platforms. This sort of car required either a Y turn-around, or a loop at the end of the line.[5]

Not all of the streetcars had rattan seats. In 1979, then 91 year old Charles S. Adam, a former trolley driver in Spokane, was interviewed by a staff writer of *The Spokesman-Review*. Mr. Adam stated that "some [streetcars] had red velvet upholstery and observation platforms. Really grand."[6]

There were several disadvantages to street railways. First, there was the inflexibility of routes after track had been laid. It was not so simple as with busses to move the route a few blocks. A second problem was the cumbersome necessity of having the electric lines for the cars above the streets. And third, written by Lois Valliant Ryker, "Everytime a streetcar in the center of the street stopped for passengers to board or alight, automobiles were forced to wait until the motorman tapped the warning bell...to signal...that his streetcar was moving once more."[7] Busses did not disturb the traffic this way.

It became apparent that motor vehicles could be run more profitably than street railways, and busses began gradually to replace them in 1931 in Spokane. On August 1, 1936, streetcars ran for the last time.[8]

A sad ending awaited the streetcars of Spokane. After converting to busses the Washington Water Power Company needed space in its car barns. Jay J. Kalez wrote: "Immediately

Part of the parade of streetcars and busses downtown on August 31, 1936. Car No. 202, shown here on Main moving west, was draped in black, had flowers on the front, and a sign which read: "Doomed! this will be cremated at the Nat tonight The end of 1,625,789 miles of faithful service." *(Northwest Room, Spokane Public Library)*

the...streetcars took on the status of used razor blades. What to do with some 60 street cars to make way for as many busses?"[9] The streetcars were offered for sale. Some of the cars were bought and moved to lakes to be used as cabins. Others were purchased for diners and taverns, while some were auctioned off at "give-away prices," put on trucks, and carted off to unknown destinations. Still, there were streetcars left.

A month after the last streetcar had run, a drastic step was taken. It was decided that the remaining cars should be burned, the first one, ceremoniously, at Natatorium Park. This car, "luxurious car No. 202," was to burn on the night of August 31, 1936.

That afternoon, a parade of the streetcars and of some of "the most ancient of North American transport devices, including Indian travois and [a] stage coach," passed through the down-

town streets, according to the *Spokane Daily Chronicle*. Several streetcars carried city officials and Spokane United Railway officers. Others carried "old time employees" of the street railway company. Pioneers of the city rode in two of the largest streetcars and led the parade.[10]

The final streetcar was Car No. 202. Charles Adam recalled that car No. 202 was "paraded around town draped in a black ribbon."[11] A long procession of new busses followed the streetcars. That night, car No. 202 was burned. As described by Jay. J. Kalez in the *Spokane Daily Chronicle*:

> Spokane would be treated to a burning ceremony that would challenge Nero's Rome spectacle, even to the fiddle-playing. The United system did itself proud in its effort. The event was advertised in

newspapers and on radio. The old turn-around track loop at Natatorium Park was to be the scene. The victim would be trolley car 202, which from 1910 to 1936 had tallied up more than a million miles on its Hillyard run.

By dark on the big night the hillside was jammed with people. WWP manager J.E.E. Royer delivered the eulogy to Old 202. The car [was] stuffed with baled straw. A battery of fire trucks stood by. Then, with due sedatedness, the torch was applied. Old 202 leaped into flames. As the black skies stained crimson, a lone fiddle sounded above the crackling flame tongues. 'Should old acquaintance be forgotten' was the vocal accompaniment. The days of the old electric trolley were over.[12]

Kalez went on to say that he watched Old 202 burn from the hillside with a lump in his throat. Men who had worked on the streetcars also watched mournfully. Charles Adam revealed when interviewed years later that he would never forget it. "It broke my heart. A lot of the old fellows just stood on the hill and cried that night. A man named Doc Davis played the fiddle while the car burned."[13]

A picture of the burning of car 202 was shown in *The Spokesman-Review* with this caption: "Burning Car Signals Progress in Transportation." The blaze was then described as the climax of "a day of civic celebration of the last day of street cars in the city."[14] The burning foretold the fate of the other streetcars. Somewhere "east of town," a crane put them into a pile, kerosene was poured on them, and they too were burned. The metal was sold to the Alaska Junk Company.[15]

At least one of the streetcars, Spokane United Railways Trolley No. 140, is still in existence, and is under restoration at this writing. The car was located by the Inland Empire Railway Historical Society some forty miles north of Spokane, in Chewelah, Washington. In the summer of 1979, the car was moved by the railway society back to Spokane. While in Chewelah it had been used as both a restaurant and as a floral shop.[16] Time had taken a heavy toll on this old streetcar, which had been built in 1886.

The railway society has spent the years since bringing the car "home" trying to bring it back to its original splendor. With no directions or plans to follow, it has been like putting together a puzzle from the past. Rotted and rusted parts

have been replaced. The interior walls and some of the windows have been restored. One entire end of the car was missing and had to be rebuilt. The car has been painted in what are believed to be the original colors on the exterior—a dark green with orange trim.

Original rattan seats that had been donated to a church in northern Idaho were located and purchased. The seat backs can still be moved from back to front, allowing people to face either direction. The seats are supported by cast iron legs and an ornate plate on the side with a floral design and the words "J.G. Brill Company, Philadelphia, U.S.A.," manufacturer of the car. SUR Trolley No. 140 will be shown at Spokane Interstate Fairs after a track has been laid to take it outside.[17]

The Washington Water Power Company retained the word "railways" in the name of the system even after the entire fleet became busses, continuing to call it the Spokane United Railways. The company operated the busses until 1945, when it sold the system.[18]

Street railway track can still be seen in several areas of town at this writing. Two blocks of tracks are on South Madison between 14th and 16th Avenues. About a half block of track is still visible at the south end of Manito Park on Manito Place just west of Grand Avenue. On the north side, there are tracks beginning on the West 2500 block on Broadway at Cochran, running north for two blocks to Dean, then turning and running west from the 2500 block through the 2800 block. Along with car No. 140, it would seem valuable to save these last bits of street railway history for our city.

CHAPTER
9

SPECIAL EVENTS AND CELEBRATIONS

DEDICATION OF THE LINCOLN STATUE, 1930

It was a dreary gray day, but despite this a huge throng of people crowded the area at Main and Monroe, and more of Spokane's citizens jammed the nearby streets for blocks.[1] It was Armistice Day, November 11, 1930, and the Lincoln statue was about to be dedicated. The figure was draped with two large American flags; other flags hung over Main Avenue. An abundance of flowers decorated the base of the monument.

Before the dedication, there was a ceremony recognizing the end of "the World War" just twelve years earlier. The armistice had taken place at the eleventh hour, of the eleventh day, of the eleventh month. In keeping with this, taps sounded at eleven o'clock "calling the living" to come closer. A roll of drums was followed by bugle calls and then a two-minute commemoration honoring those who had died during that war.

Though it was some sixty-five years since the end of the Civil War, the Lincoln memorial was to be dedicated to the Grand Army of the Republic. In 1912, the Daughters of the Grand Army of the Republic had first conceived the idea of putting a memorial at Main and Monroe, but it was not until 1922 that a Lincoln Memorial Association was formed, and Seattle sculptor Victor Alonzo Lewis was commissioned to do the work.[2] An early conception for the statue envisioned Lincoln holding a stovepipe hat in his right hand, the other clasping his coat near the waist. A drawing of this version was published in the *The Spokesman-Review* on October 1, 1922. Children of Spokane brought dimes, nickels and pennies to school to contribute to the statue.[3] Other contributions were added and the first $6,000 was given to Lewis to start the project.

By 1923 a clay model was ready to be sent to New York to be cast in bronze.[4] The 10 feet tall base of the statue was put in place and dedicated that year, but Spokane's citizens were slow in raising the remainder of the money. Several fund drives were held in the late '20s for the project. Spokanites were told that they should not disappoint the school children, that the memorial would distinguish Spokane, that it would be a great embarrassment if the statue were to go to some other city.[5] Door to door solicitations were made, at least one benefit was given, and the additional $22,000 that was needed was finally raised.[6]

Now the day had arrived to dedicate the statue and many proud citizens of the city were there. At one o'clock a small group of gray-haired veterans of the Civil War sat in a reviewing stand north of the sculpture. Behind the statue sat the sculptor, along with the speakers of the day. The crowd was held back from the center of the area by a human wall of soldiers wearing khaki uniforms and white gloves, carrying muskets over their shoulders.

The ceremony began with the combined bands from North Central and Lewis and Clark high schools playing "America." Excitement was high as people checked their watches for a countdown to 1:05 p.m. Senator C. C. Dill read a telegram from President Hoover: "The thought of Abraham Lincoln instinctively recurs on every occasion when the conception of healing peace following conflict is in our mind. It is most fitting, therefore, that you should dedicate this statue on this day consecrated to those whose sacrifices in the World war led the way to enduring peace."[7]

Then came a flash over a Western Union wire. President Hoover had pressed a gold telegraph key in Washington, D.C. which released a large balloon holding the flags veiling the statue. The balloon soared into the air pulling the flags with it. As the crowd got its first glimpse of the brooding bronze figure, planes roared overhead

The new Lincoln statue is draped in two flags before its unveiling, November 11, 1930. (*Eastern Washington State Historical Society, Spokane, Washington, L94-9.30*)

dropping red, white, and blue streamers, color guards dipped their colors, soldiers came to attention, and the band began to play the national anthem. (It is not clear what was played, because The Star Spangled-Banner did not officially become the national anthem until May, 1931.)

The sound of the music "united the crowding throngs in a wave of emotion that put tears into many eyes and hearts into throats...They silently gazed upon this man of the ages done in bronze and felt his brooding spirit. Thousands of persons, but not a sound except airplanes droning above in wide circles."

Samuel P. Weaver, president of the Lincoln Memorial association, spoke briefly at the ceremony about the twelve feet tall figure of Lincoln. He stated that this work was "unique among the Lincolnia [sic] of the world. It is the only one representing Lincoln as the commander in chief of the Union forces." Lewis had sculpted Lincoln, now with both hands down and his hat in his left hand, as though reviewing his men on some battlefront. An army coat hung over one shoulder, and, according to Weaver, "in its features and in its bearing are revealed the dignity, the strength, the power and the kindly sympathy that make

Lincoln, like King Arthur, the idolized hero of a great Anglo-Saxon nation." Senator Dill said he was gratified "that the statue should be placed in the heart of the city's busy life rather than in a park, so that it...[might] be an inspiration to the working people for whom Lincoln lived, worked and died."

Dr. E.O. Holland, president of Washington State College, was the main speaker of the day. He presented an address that reviewed Lincoln's life, giving special emphasis to Lincoln's principles and to the idea of the "spiritual miracle that brought a leader, prophet and savior out of a heritage of poverty and penury."[8]

The monument to Abraham Lincoln stood on this spot facing directly east for thirty-seven years. Then in October of 1967, because of changes in the pattern of the streets around it, the statue was moved about thirty feet north and northwest, turned slightly north, and put on an enlarged island of grass.[9]

SPOKANE'S GOLDEN JUBILEES

Spokane held two Golden Jubilees during the thirties. The first was in 1931, fifty years after the city's incorporation in 1881. A second golden jubilee was held in 1939 to celebrate, along with the entire state, the fiftieth anniversary of Washington statehood. It was also the fiftieth anniversary of the Spokane Fire of 1889.

THE GOLDEN JUBILEE OF 1931

Spokane held its first Golden Jubilee on September 3rd, 4th, and 5th, 1931. What a birthday party for Spokane! *The Spokesman-Review* reported before the event that it was to be "the biggest celebration in Spokane's history." Fifty blocks of downtown were to be "garbed with large golden balls, blue and gold drapes, and thousands of flags." The event was marked by a parade each day, by style shows, street dances, a carnival, and the opening of two new downtown buildings.[10]

When the first day of celebrating came, a parade opened the festivities. It featured honored guests, Wiley Post and Harold Gatty. Just two months before this date, these two aviators had flown around the world in Post's plane, the Winnie Mae, in record-breaking time—eight days, fifteen hours, and fifty-one minutes! They arrived in Spokane for the Golden Jubilee in the Winnie Mae on the morning of the first parade.[11] In July, 1933, Wiley Post would make the first solo round-the-world flight in the Winnie Mae.

Special fall style show windows "with elaborate displays...and creations from New York, Paris, and Hollywood, and the world's style centers" were unveiled at downtown stores at the time the parade started. A luncheon for Post and Gatty in the Marie Antoinette room at The Davenport followed the parade. Simultaneously, a luncheon in the Crescent auditorium was given for "visiting ladies." That afternoon, a street carnival, sponsored by 30 of Spokane's fraternal and civic organizations, began. It took place on Sprague Avenue from Howard to Lincoln, and the street was "literally bathed in myriad colored lights." At the same time, displays and exhibits of agriculture, fine arts, and flowers were opened. The Isabella Room in The Davenport was the setting for an afternoon tea.[12]

THE FOX THEATER OPENING

In the evening there was another parade heralding the formal public opening of the new Fox theater, which had been designed by Seattle architect, Robert C. Reamer.[13] The opening of the theater was hailed by *The Spokesman-Review* as a red letter event of the Golden Jubilee. It was, the paper said, "a historic milestone in the annals of Spokane's development as the theatrical center of the Inland Empire...The Fox theater hopes to and should attract thousands of Inland Empire residents as regular patrons. Good roads in all directions and automobiles will be factors in attaining this result."[14]

On opening night, hundreds of powerful lights searched the sky, and crowds of people packed the area in front of the theater. As reported in the next morning's paper:

Spokane had its first taste of a Hollywood premiere last night when the Fox Theater, Spokane's new play house, was dedicated before an audience that filled the 2500 seats and before a huge crowd outside the theater. Stars from Hollywood...Fox executives from Los Angeles, and civic representatives participated in the gala opening.

The crowd outside the theater gathered long before the doors opened at 7 o'clock. A band kept them entertained while squads of policemen patrolled Monroe and Sprague around the outdoor stage and kept roped-off areas clear for ticket holders and guests. Spotlights glared, flashlights boomed [camera flash powder] and motion picture cameras clicked.

Cheers greeted the picture stars Anita Page, Mitzi Green, Victor McLaglen, El Brendel and George O'Brien—as they left their cars and walked over to the stage at Sprague and Monroe. There Oscar Kanterner, merchandising manager of the Fox West Coast Theaters, acted as master of ceremonies and introduced the stars over the radio and over a loud speaking system. Each star responded briefly with good wishes before entering the theater for the main show.[15]

Inside, the eager theater patrons first entered a large foyer that was described as a "veritable fairyland of chased glass, gold, and silver" with ebony railings and a balustrade with panels of etched aluminum and glass. The "exquisite metal doors" were described, and above them "great aluminum sunbursts" on the ceiling.[16]

Before the opening, newspaper reporter Wilbur W. Hindley said patrons should save their gasps of amazement for the thrill of the sheer beauty when they would get their first glimpses of the interior of the theater and its unusual decor. After the audience had found its seats, they found themselves looking up at another fanlike "gigantic sunburst" on the ceiling that was also "studded with silver stars."[17]

Master of ceremonies Jules Buffano led a twelve-piece orchestra and then introduced Eric Johnston, president of the Spokane Chamber of Commerce, who gave an address of dedication. Johnston would later become one of the city's nationally recognized citizens as president of the United States Chamber of Commerce for an unprecedented four years, and then president of the Motion Picture Producers and Distributors of America. In these roles he became a good-will ambassador, visiting many heads of government and taking part in numerous conferences with other internationally known figures.

The first Fox theater program was a full one. The main attraction was entertainment by Fanchon and Marco, nationally known producers of stage presentations. Following this, two comedians, billed as "America's foremost blackface harmonica team" were presented, then "Max and his gang of five trained fox terriers," plus Ben Dova, (love that name) "the convivial inebriate," and Paul Olson, who offered burlesque with his partner, "Miss Clara Bow-zo." Finally there was "Joe Pasco, world's champion endurance and fancy bag puncher, and the 12 versatile Sunkist Beauties." All of this and a movie, "Merely Mary Ann," starring Janet Gaynor and Charles Farrell, a Laurel and Hardy comedy, movietone news, and an "all-color sequence," called "Honeymoonland." What an opening!

Afterward, a "Golden Jubilee Frolic" was held in the Italian Gardens at The Davenport, beginning at 11:00 p.m. Spokane was not going to bed early that night!

THE SPOKANE AND EASTERN TRUST BUILDING OPENS

The new Spokane and Eastern Trust Building had its formal opening on Saturday. Bank officials estimated that about 33,000 people visited the building in six hours that day. So many flower arrangements were sent to the building that "several truckloads had to be deposited in the old quarters of the bank across the street." Each guest was given an American Beauty rose and the bank passed out ten thousand cigars. Visitors marveled at the "departure from the old-time cages, [and] low glass partitions trimmed in nickel-silver affording the customer easy contact...with the banking officials."[18]

CARNIVAL, CANTALOUPES, AND FASHION

The carnival continued through the week, and several teas were given in The Davenport Hotel.[19] "Thousands of Hearts of Gold cantaloupes raised in Spokane valley were given away at the agricultural show." The Heart of Gold variety of cantaloupe was considered unusually delicious and was grown mainly in this area. At night a continuous fall style show was held on a decorated stage on Post between Sprague and Riverside. It featured thirty-six men and women models and a 24-piece band.

MARDI GRAS PARADE

On Saturday night there was a Mardi Gras Parade.[20] Hundreds in costumes, a dozen bands, many floats from businesses and lodges participated. A description of part of the parade from *The Spokesman-Review* said: "The Wells Chevrolet company used horses to advertise their 'economical transportation' and Willy Wiley, (sic) Spokane's well-known wild man, was there ballyhooing the Orpheum [theater] with a 1904 Reo [car] and his pair of trunks." Willie Willey, (a family member has confirmed this spelling), was Spokane's nature boy. He used to appear in various places around town. We would stop everything and run to look when some other kid would come by and tell us excitedly, "Willie Willey's in the park." It was my understanding as a child that he lived in his run-down truck with several animals.

The newspaper continues: "Probably the most spotless float in the huge exhibit was that one entirely in white of the fuel dealers of the city depicting Jack Frost or King Boris, followed by a lot of grimy fellows carrying coal shovels. Just after this float emerged from the line of march it burst into flames (quite an ad for hot coal) and fire engines came racing down the street to add to the entertainment. A man fell off a truck and was kicked in the head by a horse, calling out the patrol wagon, with accompanying siren. Otherwise there were no casualties." The Floral association float was called "a radiant thing in white." Another, by "hostess cakes," was done entirely in pink, and had "a girl perched atop its splendor tossing kisses to the crowd." After the parade,

Willie Willey attracted onlookers because he wore a pair of shorts and sandals, but no shirt, in summer and winter. *(Courtesy of Gerald Numbers)*

there was dancing on Post Street. So many people tried to take part that dancing was nearly impossible. What a gala celebration it was, and how proud Spokane's citizens must have been of their city.

THE GOLDEN JUBILEE OF 1939

Spokane's second Golden Jubilee, commemorating the statehood of Washington, was held in 1939. Washington State had an "invite a million" campaign, with an effort to attract a million tourists during the year.[21]

During this celebration, Spokane tried to capture the spirit of the pioneer period of the city, and in many ways to re-live it. People wore period costumes, local history was emphasized in the schools, and placards were placed at his-

toric sites throughout the city. These signs marked locations of places that had been in the little village of Spokane Falls—the first school, the first stores, homes, churches, bridges, fire department, ferry, theaters, the place at which the first newspaper was published, and so forth. The historical markers were to be made permanent markers, but that idea wasn't accomplished.[22]

PAGEANTS PLANNED

Early in the year, the Spokane Chamber of Commerce began making elaborate plans to sponsor the major event of the celebration, an "Historical Spectacle" that would be held in August. Described in a letter to prospective committee members, this pageant would show "the book of history of Spokane and the Inland Empire from

One of many downtown businesses that had workers who wore period costumes during the Golden Jubilee, over seventy of the Spokesman-Review employees posed in old fashioned clothing on July 6, 1939. *(Spokesman-Review)*

the time of the fur traders down to the present...in a series of dramatic chapters, each one presenting a thrilling, exciting episode." It was to be produced by Jerome H. Cargill and associates of New York.[23]

School District #81 planned a Golden Jubilee pageant of its own that was held during Boys' and Girls' week in May of 1939 at Gonzaga University stadium.[24] Five thousand students sang and danced in a symbolic presentation. The life of native Americans of the Spokane area was interpreted, followed by scenes about Lewis and Clark's journey, about missionaries to the region, about Spokane's first school building, and about military leaders in Spokane's history.

The program's climax, according to the *Spokane Daily Chronicle*, was a great ballet that symbolized the historic Spokane Fire of 1889. "All the excitement and terror of that famous incident...[was recaptured] for the crowd by the dancing children."[25] Hundreds of girls from 12 elementary schools took part in the dance. My sister, Marianna, was one of them. I remember that she and many others wore costumes with orange and yellow crepe paper streamers at-

tached to them to simulate the fire. She recalls that it was so hot on that May day that some of the participants fainted.

Meanwhile, the Spokane Chamber of Commerce continued planning its extravaganza which was to be held in August. Hundreds of names had been submitted for the historical pageant. "The Columbia Cavalcade" was the final selection because the "mighty Columbia has directed the history and the romance, and holds sway over the future of the great Pacific northwest."[26]

Excitement was growing in the city as the time for the presentation of the Cavalcade came closer. On July 1, the morning paper declared, "There is a feeling of expectancy in the air today. Flags are aflutter in the downtown streets. Everywhere are mementoes of 50 years ago; in the show windows of shops and stores are treasured relics of another generation; in the dress of men and women is seen the garb of frontier days, and all about is sensed the approach of something significant and outstanding in the history of the Inland Empire."

Curly Jim is pictured on this version of the wooden nickels used during the Golden Jubilee of 1939. The "tail" side was the same on each of them according to *The Spokesman-Review*. Shown actual size. (*Northwest Room, Spokane Public Library*)

OLD FASHIONED CLOTHING
AND WOODEN NICKELS

Many of Spokane's citizens were wearing old-time clothing on the streets of downtown. Organdy sunbonnets and long calico print dresses with crinolines were sold to the women. Men bought frock coats, very wide ties, fancy vests, top hats, canes, and derbies. When these outfits were offered for sale the stores sold out in two days and were placing rush orders in the east for more. All of Montgomery Ward's employees "from the highest official to the lowliest stock boy" were shown in two pictures in the paper wearing these fashions.[27] It seemed that it would be a fun idea if my father would grow a beard, as other men were wearing them around town, so I tried to talk my father into growing one.

On the morning of July 6, 1939, souvenir wooden nickels began to appear. These flat, 2½ inch round disks were first sold at a public auction on a corner of Howard and Riverside, and proceeds were used to "help boost the Cavalcade."[28] From that time through the Columbia Cavalcade celebration, the "nickels" could be used for any purchase. By mid-July, the first 25,000 had been sold, and an additional 12,000 were put on sale.[29]

Three styles of nickels were available. One pictured James Glover, calling him "Father of Spokane"; the second pictured Grand Coulee Dam; the third pictured a Native American in a tall feathered headpiece who was well known among the city's pioneers—"Curly Jim." Curly Jim was a town character; by 1939 he was considered an emblem of Spokane's frontier past. A member of the Spokane tribe, he lived in a teepee at Indian Canyon, but could be found on most winter days inside the Sprague Avenue entrance to John W. Graham, and on summer days on the stone steps of the Cushing Building, headquarters for the Spokane and Eastern Bank, then at Sprague and Howard. Curly Jim died in 1917.

AUDITIONS, COSTUMES, & REHEARSALS

In July, a call went out to the people of the city to audition for the pageant. Men and women who could do speaking parts were especially urged to come. Larry Doyle, production director, noted that 400 men were needed for all kinds of roles, and said, "We want men who can ride horses, with saddles or bareback. We want men who can drive a team or drive a carriage. We need bicycle riders."[30] Rehearsals were to be every night, but each scene would have only three rehearsals, including one in costume.

Costumes were furnished and ordered from New York. They ranged from silks and satins for women, to rough clothing worn by trappers, prospectors, and stagecoach drivers. Requests were made for a variety of authentic stage props and among items promised by mid-July were a rawhide sidesaddle, a huge black walnut chest, music boxes, a medical kit from pioneer days, a pack-train, fire engines, military, prospecting, and railroad clothing, iron kettles, all types of old furniture, a stagecoach, an ox team, brass kettles, and spinning wheels.[31]

Though the extravaganza would be staged out of doors, rehearsals were held in the auditorium in the basement of the Civic Building, (Chamber of Commerce) at W. 1020 Riverside. The indoor setting was cramped compared to the area that would actually be used. In practicing for the Spokane Fire of 1889, more than 200 people crowded onto the floor of the rehearsal area. "Since the old fire engines can not be used inside, a large coat rack is substituted in the rehearsals. Instead of the fire buckets, coat hangers are passed from man to man in the fighting line...Tonight more than 100 horsemen will rehearse the Steptoe Butte attack, but there will be no horses to ride."[32]

By July 21, all of the costumes had arrived from New York. Next came the immense task of individual fittings of the outfits. A huge array of fancy clothes included dancing dresses for "Floradora girls," and redcoats of the British troops.[33]

PARADE

On Tuesday, August 1, a huge parade with both historic and military sections was held downtown. Spectators were urged to wear pioneer clothing. Governor Clarence D. Martin and Mayor Frank G. Sutherlin led the two-hour long parade. The historical section featured hundreds of characters from the cast of the Cavalcade program, and many of the "props" such as stage coaches and covered wagons.

A number of floats and fifteen balloons about twelve feet tall in the shapes of Mickey Mouse, Ferdinand the Bull, and other characters were in the parade.[34] The military section included the Fourth infantry and band, the 161st infantry, the Washington National Guard and band, Battery D, 148th Field Artillery, the Idaho National Guard, and the 14th Battalion United States Marine Corps Reserve. Overhead, planes from the 116th Observation Squadron and the 41st Division Aviation were in flight.

THE CAVALCADE

The Columbia Cavalcade drama was ready for the first of its five presentations on August 1, 1939. Given at the old fairgrounds, there were 1,200 people in the cast, a mammoth stage with a frontage of 300 feet (the length of a football field), plus "elaborate electrical equipment to produce brilliant light effects."[35] The old fairgrounds referred to were located directly west of the Playfair Race Track on Regal and Front and were be-

---

The cover for the program for the Columbia Cavalcade (opposite page). *(Northwest Room, Spokane Public Library)*

"COLUMBIA CAVALCADE"

Spokane

FAIRGROUNDS
AUGUST
1·2·3·4·5
15¢

ing called the "old" fairgrounds at the time as they had not been used for several years.

The newspaper reported that, although the initial performance had been excellent, the second performance "was presented with all of the verve and snap of trained troupers, the...colorful episodes moving across the vast outdoor stage with the precision of clockwork. The actors and audience seemed to join forces in making the Columbia Cavalcade a pageant of surpassing beauty."[36]

The 23 scenes of the program told the history of the Pacific Northwest beginning with the ship of Captain Robert Gray arriving at the mouth of the Columbia river and continuing through such scenes as the Steptoe Butte battle, which brought the crowd to its feet. "To see those wagon trains race across the stage, drawn by mule teams at a dead run, is to witness a sight seldom seen outside of the movies."[37] Troops of cavalry and of Indian bareback riders were recruited to provide this dramatic scene.

The arrival of the first train in Spokane was another colorful episode. The whistle of the locomotive as it chugged its way across the stage brought cheers. Another excellent scene was the realistic fire of 1889 which razed the pioneer city of Spokane Falls. Real flames leapt hungrily at the stagework of the buildings which collapsed as the fire spread.

The final setting was of Grand Coulee Dam during construction and at completion. "At its base danced a chorus of ballet dancers carrying sparklers, while over the crest of the dam [poured] a waterfall of liquid fire."[38]

After the pageant, the Spokane Little Theater presented shows which were held in a stockade at the fairgrounds.[39] These productions, in imitation of dramas that might have been held in the Falls City Opera House of earlier times, were reminiscent of the old music hall of the gay nineties. The shortlived Falls City Opera House, built in 1887, was a three story building on the southwest corner of Riverside and Post that was destroyed in the 1889 fire. Its theater was on a third floor which had a high ceiling with a balcony bordering it.

Included in the 1939 productions were melodramas such as "Only a Farmer's Daughter," and "Every Inch a Sailor." In an effort to recreate the atmosphere of the past, sawdust covered the floor and old-fashioned gas lights were used.[40] Old time dancing followed the plays each night.[41]

TRAGEDY

The programs at the fairgrounds in August, 1939, marked the culmination of the Golden Jubilee. Unfortunately, one of the performances ended in a disastrous fire. On Thursday night, during the third of the five performances, five of the ballet dancers in the finale became human torches when their white fluffy gauze gowns caught fire from the sparklers as they entered the stage.[42] In the grandstands, 7,500 stunned spectators watched as the screaming girls' dresses became masses of flames. I remember hearing at the time that at least one of the dancers had tried to run from the fire, which simply fanned the flames. Three men were burned on their hands and arms as they tried to extinguish the fire.

The five girls were hospitalized, four with critical burns. Two of the teenagers, ages 13 and 15, died within four days.[43] Another victim spent around three weeks in the hospital recovering.[44] Still another was given a "50-50 chance" to live, had many skin grafts, and spent nearly seven months in the hospital before going home.[45]

The night of the fire, in traditional "show must go on" fashion, the program continued to its finish. For the fourth and fifth performances of the Cavalcade, no sparklers were used.[46]

FIRST LILAC FESTIVAL, 1938

Spokane's first Lilac Festival was held May 17th to 24th, 1938, with a parade on May 17th. The focus was truly on the beautiful lilacs of the city. It was announced a week before the festival that displays of blooms could be entered and would be judged at the Civic Building during the week.[47] The Crescent planned to feature lilacs in its displays. Women's clubs were asked to use lilacs in their decorations. People were urged to take lilacs to those who were ill or in the hospital.[48]

From the *Spokane Daily Chronicle* the day of the parade:

> Beautiful lilacs are on display everywhere. They're at their best at the city's many fine parks and gardens. There are huge bouquets of choice blooms in scores of stores. The Davenport hotel lobby is a bower of lilacs. Lilac-decorated automobiles paraded the downtown streets at noon. And best of all is the lilac show at the Spokane Art Center, N. 106 Monroe, where

hundreds of blossoms were on display. There were French lilacs, pure white in a cluster more than a foot wide; tall waving plumes of lavender, more than 15 inches tall on one stem; persian lilacs of red-purple with blossoms measuring an inch across each petal, and the lovely feathery Japanese variety of pale pink.

Heavy showers just before noon did nothing but freshen the flowers piled thousands upon thousands on an elaborate float heading the lilac parade. Lilacs of every hue and shade were included, presenting a colorful picture as the downtown streets were traversed. Following the float were automobiles, also bedecked with lilacs to show what Spokane can do in the city's first lilac festival, one which it is expected will be made an annual affair.

The Davenport hotel fountain, dressed in lilacs for the day, has the deep purples at the base shading up to the big circle of white about the central figure. Every vase and jardiniere that make the lobby nation-famed is filled with the beautiful blossoms, and guests from far places are carrying away an unforgettable picture of Spokane's first lilac festival.[49]

THE LILAC FESTIVAL 1939 to 1949

The next year, 1939, the parade still had only one float.[50] That year the American Legion drill team presented lilacs to passengers on arriving trains and busses. The first year in which there was a Lilac Festival Queen was 1940, but through all of the '40s (until 1958) the contest was open only to women 18 years and older. High school bands were first used in the parade in 1940.

During the war years, there was little Lilac Festival activity, though there were flower shows, and lilacs were given to soldiers going through Spokane on troop trains. After the war, the Spokane Lilac Festival Association was formed. The Association members decided to focus on having a beautiful parade and lilac show, decorating the city, and holding a contest for a queen. By 1948, the parade had 40 bands and 30 floats. Until 1949, the phrase used by the garden clubs for the festival was "Spokane's Best When Lilac Drest." It was replaced at that time by "Spokane, the Lilac City."[51]

It was not until the mid-'50s that the Armed Forces Day parade and the Lilac Festival Parade merged.

THE FREEDOM TRAIN, 1948

On April 14, 1948, Spokane was visited by the Freedom Train, which traveled to 330 American cities, carrying 137 historic documents in three railroad cars. Documents came from the National Archives, the Library of Congress, historical societies and private collections.[52] Spokane's citizens had to raise $7,500 to pay its share of the train's expenses.

Schools were closed for the day to give as many children as possible an opportunity to view the documents. The red, white and blue train with gold seals was waiting at the Great Northern freight loading area in downtown Spokane early in the day. At least one person had waited all night to be at the beginning of the line, and by 5 a.m. a crowd of several hundred people was there. An estimated 8,000 people were in line by 8:30, though the exhibit didn't open to the general public until 10 a.m. The train was guarded by an honor guard of marines assisted by local police and fire department personnel and a squad of air force personnel.[53]

Fragile and priceless documents were exhibited in air-conditioned compartments. Among the papers shown were: a 13th century copy of the Magna Carta, a letter written by Christopher Columbus describing his voyage to America, Thomas Jefferson's rough draft of the Declaration of Independence, a manuscript copy of the Declaration of Independence, Washington's copy of the Constitution of the United States with corrections by Washington, the original of Washington's Farewell Address, a copy of the Bill of Rights, the manuscript copy held by Lincoln while giving the Gettysburg address, the original manuscript of Paul Revere's commission as an official messenger, the original manuscript of The Star Spangled Banner, an early copy of the Emancipation Proclamation, the surrender papers from World War II, and the United Nations charter.[54]

"Freedom flags" were also shown. These included the flag that was raised at Iwo Jima, General Eisenhower's personal flag, and a flag that flew on the U.S.S. Missouri when the Japanese signed the surrender ending World War II. There were 30 war documents, 25 from World War II and several from the American Revolution.

Most people spent several hours waiting in a line that wound in a long wide serpentine between Washington and Division. Twelve area bands with 650 musicians presented a continuous program of patriotic and concert music to the people who waited in the chilly April air.[55] Most viewers were in the train about 25 minutes. After seeing the final documents, people were given an opportunity to sign a pledge to help maintain freedom. Patriotism was high in the country as World War II had been over only 2 years and eight months. Seeing the documents had reminded people that the rights that go with freedom should not be taken for granted. Most of the 10,188 people who went through the train that day signed this pledge. I was one.

In 1975, in celebration of the Bicentennial of the United States, a similar Freedom Train traveled to all 48 contiguous states. In this, a more high-tech exhibit, viewers traveled through the train in 20 minutes on a conveyer belt. In addition to ten cars containing archival historical documents, there were fifteen other cars, each with a different theme, showing such things as sports memorabilia, fine arts, and pictures of famous people.[56]

10

WORLD WAR II YEARS

They came from the midwest, the south, the west, and north—small town boys, boys just off the farm, big city boys. At first they came in small numbers, but later they swarmed into downtown Spokane, almost taking it over. They were the soldiers, sailors, army air corpsmen, and a few marines who were stationed nearby during World War II. Sometimes a group of them with caps at a jaunty angle would walk together in a line that stretched nearly across the sidewalk. Some servicemen walked across a street when the light was red...an audacious act at that time in Spokane! Public places were jammed with men in uniform. At times, lines at the larger theaters reached completely around the block.

Soon after America was in the war, a flurry of war supporting activities of all kinds began. Patriotism may not have been felt more strongly at any time in our history. As a popular song of the time said, there was "a job to be done, to be done," and "a war to be won, to be won." Unless you remember those days, it may be hard to realize how people mobilized to work for the war effort.

IMMEDIATE REACTIONS

During the first days of the war changes came rapidly. Stunned that the Japanese reached Hawaii without being noticed, people feared that mainland U.S.A. might be attacked. Hurried preparations were made for our defense.

Spokane's radio stations were ordered to be off the air by 7 p.m. on December 8th and 9th, 1941, the two successive nights after the attack on Pearl Harbor. It was feared that approaching enemy planes could follow radio beams to target the city. On December 8th, the stations reported over and over that there would be a blackout that night, only to announce just before

going off the air that the blackout was only for cities on the coast. Later it was said that because of fog it had not been necessary. The stations were flooded with calls all evening as Spokanites tried to find out what was happening. People even went to the studios to find out, many remaining for some time to sit and talk. Spokane's radio stations were requested by the Army and Navy to make no further weather broadcasts in case enemy planes were listening and making plans to attack.[1]

By December 10th KHQ was designated as the key station of the Inland Empire which, if given orders not to broadcast, was to transmit these orders to other stations. In the event that there wasn't time to transmit the orders, "all stations must go off the air the moment the key station...[stopped] broadcasting."[2]

Since work had to be done after dark, the Review Building covered its windows with a heavy material on December 10th so that it would be ready if there was a blackout.[3] Businesses and homes received information on preparing for blackouts and in early 1942 were ready. The Davenport Hotel covered its skylight with black tar for blackout purposes. It was not uncovered until 1993, more than 50 years later.

Spokane's young men immediately began volunteering for duty in the services. Forty-seven men left by train on the night of December 11th. In one 24-hour period, the Navy office in the Federal Building/Post Office, interviewed several hundred, examined 23 and accepted 15 recruits. The Coast Guard in the same building accepted 11 tentatively, waiting for investigations and references. The Army office in the Ziegler Building had several hundred applicants of whom formal applications were accepted from 60, while of 36 who were given physical examinations, 30 were accepted for enlistment. The Marine office in the Rookery Building "tentatively accepted six out of 15 applicants."[4] Local hospitals soon expanded their nursing training schools in anticipation of the need, and young women, eager to help, enrolled.

During that first week, Spokane's citizens scrambled to support the war monetarily by buying Defense Bonds—later called War Bonds. A spokesperson from the Spokane and Eastern bank reported that it was swamped with orders. Albert E. Reid of the First National Bank announced they were having trouble keeping enough bonds on hand and the Old National had to increase staff to handle the bond sales. Fred Stanton of the Washington Trust Bank said "it was inspirational to witness the rush to buy bonds and the patriotic fervor aroused by the entry of the United States into war."[5]

Six months later, one of the Hollywood stars traveling around the country selling War Bonds was Lana Turner. She sold thousands of dollars worth of bonds at a street rally in front of the Desert Hotel and at a luncheon afterward sponsored by the Spokane Athletic Round Table in the Hotel's Roundup Room. Henry A. Pierce, president of the Inland Empire Press club, bought the first bond for $5,000. Some 150 bond subscriptions were printed in the newspaper the next day that ranged from individual pledges for $25 to a high of $30,000 from the Peerless Dentists. By July, 1942, Spokane citizens had purchased more than a million dollars worth of war bonds.[6]

SERVICEMEN AND WOMEN STATIONED NEARBY

Because it was a railroad center and had a protected inland location, Spokane was a choice place for the construction of wartime facilities. It is astonishing to look back at the number of important military installations that were in the area. Fort Wright and Felts Field had been established for some time. To these were added Geiger, Galena, Farragut, Baxter Hospital, and the Velox Naval Supply Depot. All involved military people.

Few actual figures are available about numbers of service people stationed in the greater Spokane area during the war. The numbers were classified at the time and are unattainable now; however, the numbers were huge. T.O. Hoagland, head of the health and welfare office of Defense for the Northwest, made the following statement in 1942 when he was in Spokane to help plan and set up a U.S.O. here. "We are facing the problem of providing recreation and beds for an amaz-

ing number of military men, both army and navy, who will be in Spokane on week-ends...I am not allowed to quote figures, but by fall there will be a stupendous number."[7]

Certainly there were some tens of thousands of military personnel stationed near Spokane during much of the war. Nearly all of them were men, though there were WAACs stationed at Galena and Fort Wright, Army nurses at Baxter Hospital, and a few WAVES in the area. When the war started, 5,000 military people were already stationed at Geiger, Fort Wright, and Felts Field.[8]

Though the numbers were classified, some projected figures slipped into the newspapers. It was stated in early 1941 that at Geiger, "6000 or more men may be stationed at the field.[9] In 1943 at Galena, "there are 1100 solders there now, a number which will be increased to 3500 later."[10] Geiger would one day become our airport, Galena would become Fairchild Air Force Base.

No figures seem to surface for Felts Field or for Fort Wright. Support forces were located at Felts Field, but they were small in number. As for Fort Wright, it is known that basic training for both regular and reserve army units took place there, and that from 1941 to 1943, it was the headquarters for the Second Air Force and for the Army Air Corps in the area. Specialties such as counter intelligence and protection against chemical warfare were taught there.[11] A hospital at the Fort served nearby army personnel for general medical problems and wounded men later. Fort Wright was continually expanding during the war.[12]

Baxter Hospital, located in northwest Spokane for the care of the wounded, had a staff of several hundred—enough to handle 1,500 beds.[13] It also had housing for personnel, a theater, restaurant, chapel, post exchange and library. It was a large complex that is hard to visualize today with the Veterans Hospital, Albi Stadium, and the sports complex now on the site. Velox Naval Supply Depot in the Valley had 100 to 130 Marine and Navy men guarding the facility at all times.[14] It became the Spokane Industrial Park after the war. All of the above nearby service areas surely had over 10,000 people at the height of the war.

However, it is the number at Farragut, located at Bayview, Idaho, on Pend Oreille Lake, that assures us that tens of thousands of military people were in the area. The second largest naval training center in the country, Farragut was

A Women's Army Corps detachment from Baxter General Hospital marches east on Sprague past the Perry Block on July 4, 1944. *(Eastern Washington State Historical Society, Spokane, Washington, L89-137.5)*

built for a population of more than 45,000. Most were recruits, about 30,000 at peak, in boot camp training for six to thirteen weeks. A personnel group of around 5,000, another 5,000 sailors in more advanced training schools, and an outgoing group of 3,000 brought the total to around 43,000.[15] When Farragut opened, the influx of tens of thousands of men caused a temporary shortage of milk, butter, and eggs in the Spokane area.

WHERE TO GO ON LIBERTY?

When off duty, a natural destination for the service people was the heart of Spokane. Except for Farragut, all of the military facilities were very close. A short ride in a bus or car got military personnel to the downtown area in a few minutes. Farragut was some 50 miles away, but

bus routes, among them the Green Hornet Bus Line, were set up nearly round the clock for the 50 minute ride to town.[16] Later, three *trainloads* a day made scheduled round trips to Spokane, each trip taking one and a half hours.[17]

Busses and trains spilled their eager passengers into depots. They flowed out onto the streets, some slowly searching their way if it was their first time in town. Others surged down the sidewalks. Many felt they had to grab life while they could because it might be short. They hurried to try to be first in line at the theaters, raced to get on a city bus to go to see a girl friend, rushed to buy a bottle and begin drinking in an attempt to ease homesickness, boredom, and fear. Some went to one of the two or three ballrooms that were in business then. Some were merely glad to have a leisurely walk, get time to relax, or go to a

Servicemen sleeping in the lobby of The Davenport Hotel. *(Peter Stackpole, Life Magazine, © Time Inc.)*

service center to play pool or write a letter home. A day or night on the town seemed priceless. Time was precious.

Servicemen wanted to stay away from the confinement of their bases as long as possible, so when night came they would try to find other places to stay until they absolutely had to return. Downtown hotels, from first class to tiny lower class places, allowed uniformed men to sleep on sofas, chairs, and floors. The Davenport Hotel also allowed servicemen to sleep on the carpeted stairways. A cameraman from the newspaper took pictures in The Desert, The Coeur d'Alene, The Davenport and others hotels on a Saturday night in 1943; he estimated later that he had seen nearly 1,000 sleeping servicemen during a two hour tour.[18] As one former sailor said when he recalled sleeping at The Davenport, "Where were you going to go at three o'clock in the morning?"

Gilbert Heggemeier, a recruit from Nashville, remembers the times he came from Farragut to Spokane. He would come into town and go to a movie or bowling. While he was not a drinker, he remembers that many of the recruits' idea of a good time was to get a bottle and get drunk. On weekends after the first weeks of training, the sailors did not have to be back to the base until 8:00 a.m. on Monday morning and "some of them barely made it and were still drunk when 8 o'clock rolled around."

Servicemen were easy to identify because they were required to be in uniform. New trainees, or "Boots," on Liberty from boot camp at Farragut were easy to spot because they all wore tan laced leggings.

As the military people walked around, we became accustomed to seeing lots of saluting. Even when off duty, enlisted personnel had to salute all officers, whether or not they were in the same branch of the service, so this small ritual was performed over and over on our streets.

USOs AND OTHER SERVICE CENTERS

With the mass of military people in the area, a number of places for their entertainment and support were needed. By 1943, servicemen and women crowded into three different USO clubs and several other service centers downtown. One was the **USO Lutheran Service Center** at N. 106 Monroe, the former location of the WPA Spokane Art Center.

The USO Club was located on the southeast corner of Third and Monroe in the building that had been headquarters for the WPA, and before that the location of the Federal Land Bank. The WPA moved out in July, 1942, and the USO began operating in the fall of that year. Bands played for dances several times a week. During 1943 and 1944, the facility registered over 645,000 soldiers and sailors each year.[19] Three thousand junior hostesses were listed at the USO Club in 1944.[20] They served snacks, were available for bridge and other card games, and gave the men someone with whom to talk and to dance. Many of the songs that were danced to, such as "I'll Be Seeing You," "Saturday Night is the Loneliest Night in the Week," "Don't Sit Under the Apple Tree with Anyone Else but Me, (—'til I come marching home"), and "Harbor Lights," ("When the lights come on again, all over the world"), were about longing for the ending of the war or separation from a loved one.

Activities available at the USO Club were letter writing, ping pong, and pool. Servicemen could take showers, shave, record messages to be sent home, take classes in such things as woodburning, soap carving, painting, and drawing. One could read, get a shoe shine, play bridge, rent a camera, hear a concert, see lists of commercial entertainment, get free snack food, make and receive telephone calls, develop photos in a darkroom with chemicals provided, and meet and dance with girls.[21]

Women were available to sew the stripes and insignias on uniforms. Mothers were urged to make and donate cakes to the USO, which would in turn reimburse the donors with sugar which was rationed. By 1947, when the USO closed its doors, it reportedly had served 1,955,403 service men and women.[22]

The third USO was the **George Washington Carver Club**, a USO for black servicemen. The services were not integrated at that time, and the USO clubs weren't either. This club was at S. 101 Division, the southeast corner of First and Division. Special features were a spacious dance floor, reading rooms, showers, a game room, and an outdoor lawn area with a barbecue pit.[23] During 1944, 86,460 used the George Washington Carver Club.[24]

The **Soldier Service Center**, later known as the **Service Men's Center** at W. 820 Sprague, was similar to the USO clubs. It was sponsored by the Victory Shop, with aid from the Community Chest, the Council of Church Women, and several downtown businessmen's clubs. The Center provided recreation, along with information about

Floral arrangements and formal gowns suggest a special occasion at the George Washington Carver Club USO. *(Eastern Washington State Historical Society, L96-1.11)*

homes that would entertain service men. Stationery and magazines were available and a mammoth cookie jar filled with anywhere from 75 to 125 *dozen* cookies a day. In 1946, it was reported that a "home away from home" had been provided for 1,400,000 during the five year existence of this Spokane service center.[25]

An **Inter-church Service Center** was located at W. 908 Sprague and a **Service Men's Welcome House** at W. 313 Riverside.[26] In addition, clubrooms in the basement of the **Cathedral of St. John** offered similar services, entertainment, and dances to live music. Arrangements could also be made to have dinner in a Spokane home. The **YWCA**, the **YMCA**, the **Woman's Club** and other groups held dances for the men in uniform where hundreds of Spo-

kane girls volunteered for hostess duty.

Members of families, often those who had a loved one in the service stationed elsewhere, went to the bus depot and train stations and invited service people to their homes for dinner or a place to relax. The servicemen stationed near Spokane did not lack for a place to go.

MANY DOWNTOWN BUILDINGS USED

During the planning and building of Galena, officially known as the Spokane Army Air Depot, administrative headquarters were at first established in the Hutton Building, on the east side of Washington between Sprague and First. As planning accelerated, that building was outgrown and a move was made to 1011 W. First.[27]

Walking west on Sprague, units from Farragut march in a parade in 1943. *(Eastern Washington State Historical Society, Spokane, Washington, L93-18.76)*

By mid-1942 these offices were also not sufficient and, while retaining two floors at that address, the major portion of the command was moved to the newly closed Kemp and Hebert department store building. The Air Corps occupied the entire building with executive offices. Betty Fogelquist Schnabel recalls: "There were a lot of women hired as secretaries and typists working in the building. I worked for a safety officer and sometimes we went to the Galena site—it was just an empty flat field—and I took dictation there as plans for the base were laid out."

Though an army air corps base, Galena's main function was to be an aircraft repair facility. Classes for training the civilian workers were established and carried out on a 24-hour basis in 44 different buildings in Spokane. By 1943 when Galena was ready for occupancy, approximately 7,000 workers were fully trained. When the Service Area Command vacated the Kemp and Hebert Building, training of workers continued in the building.

THE DEFENSE INDUSTRY— WORK FOR CIVILIANS

The war brought jobs for many of Spokane's people, affecting all of the city, and ultimately downtown. Large construction crews were used to build the new military facilities. Both Farragut and Velox were planned by the Spokane architectural firm of Whitehouse and Price who worked with the Navy on these huge projects. At Farragut, 30,000 people, many from Spokane, were used in construction in 1942.[28] In early 1941, 100 buildings, mostly barracks, were erected at Geiger in only 29 working days.[29] It took a year to build the 262 buildings at Galena. The construction work force was over 2,500 at its height. The Trentwood aluminum plant was built with a construction crew working seven days a week, 24 hours a day, for about a year. They produced what was then the largest building under one roof west of the Mississippi.[30]

After construction, huge numbers of people worked in these places, some leaving other

New women bus drivers pose in front of a city bus. The bus advertises "S.U.RYS. CLASSIFIED AS AN ESSENTIAL WAR JOB." *(Eastern Washington State Historical Society, Spokane, Washington, L93-18.75)*

jobs because of better pay. Ten thousand civilians worked at Galena by the summer of 1943 and another 5,000 civilians were employed at Geiger and at Fort Wright by the middle of the war.[31]

The plants at Mead and at Trentwood made aluminum for the bodies of fighter planes, for propellers, and for Quonset huts. Trentwood had close to 7,000 employees, and there were several thousand more at Mead. These plants operated in three shifts and worked 24 hours a day.[32]

As people assumed wartime roles, a shortage of workers was inevitable. The Naval Supply Depot was a holding and shipping area for staggering amounts of navy equipment and supplies. In 1944, the Depot needed 1,500 more employees than the approximate 500 already working there. The work force was strained to the limit. Workers were recruited from farm districts, and sailors (presumably from Farragut) were brought in to help at critical times.[33]

Because of the need for workers, many women began working for the first time. By 1943, five percent of jobs in Spokane that had been held by men were being filled by women.[34] Twenty-five percent of those that worked at Galena were women.[35] They were trained to do carpentry, radio repair, parachute packing, and welding. A number of women worked at Mead and Trentwood.[36] Women worked also at Brown Industries making parts for Boeing planes.

Wherever workers were needed, women did their share. Women began to drive city bus-

ses for the first time in 1943. Until the war years, married women teachers in Spokane could work only as substitutes. Getting married meant the end of a teaching career, but by 1942 married women were allowed to hold permanent classroom teaching positions.

With the shortage of workers, very young people were sometimes issued special work permits by the state. John Reed got such a permit in 1942 while he was in the seventh grade so that he could work as a busboy in the Italian Gardens at The Davenport. Later in life he would work at the hotel as a bellman; he is still employed by the hotel. In 1943 a city ordinance was passed establishing a 10 p.m. curfew for children under age sixteen.[37] After that, it was necessary to show a work permit late at night.

Until the war, hours at most stores downtown had been 9:40 a.m. to 5:30 p.m., Monday through Saturday. In order to accommodate working women, stores and shops began remaining open until 9:00 p.m. on Mondays, and in turn accommodated their own employees by not opening until noon that day.

War time activities were the major reason for an increase in the population in Spokane during the '40s. The population grew from 122,001 in 1940, to 161,721 in 1950, the largest increase in any decade except 1900 to 1910.[38]

Business was good during war time; the economy everywhere was stimulated by the special needs of war. There were large numbers of people traveling, high employment, and service-

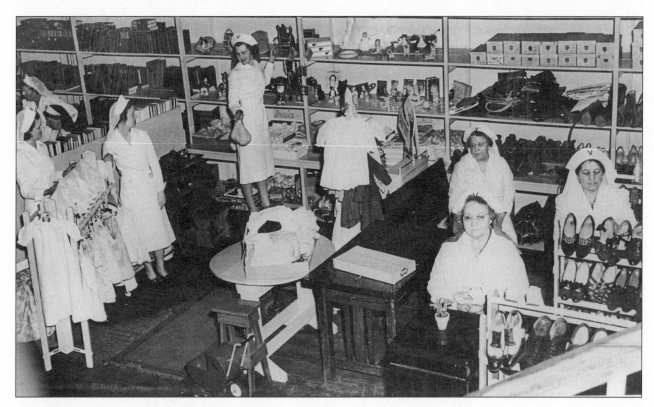

Regular workers at the Victory Shop, pictured working there in 1942, wore white or dark uniforms and nurse-like caps, each with a letter "V" in the center and an attached veil at the back. *(Spokesman-Review)*

men spending money. America pulled out of the Depression.

SPOKANE VOLUNTEERS

Spokane citizens found countless ways to help in the war effort. Before America was in the war, a thrift shop at W. 926 Riverside, across from the Review Building, sponsored Bundles for Britain. It was run by volunteers and called the Superfluities shop.[39] After our country was involved, hundreds of women volunteers worked there and it was known as the **Victory Shop**. These volunteers collected reusable clothing, old jewelry, and household items, and after necessary repairs were made, the merchandise was priced and resold.

The operation was so large that some women were assigned to permanent positions as heads of departments, such as receiving, jewelry, china and glassware, infant, shoes, kitchenware, window trimmings, and millinery. One popular sales item was wedding rings, which sold for 25¢ to $1. [40]

By the end of the war the Victory Shop had raised thousands of dollars and given it to the American Red Cross, French relief, Geiger Field and Fort Wright. A Red Cross canteen wagon was purchased and equipped with some of the money raised. *The Spokesman-Review* reported: "Thousands of dollars went to Bundles for America to buy yarns. Many of our boys on ships and stationed in cold countries have received warm knitted garments through the Victory Shop...Merchants have been liberal in their contributions and a most generous Spokane citizen has contributed the use of the room ever since the shop opened."[41]

The Inland Empire Navy Mothers' Club was located almost across the street from the Victory Shop, at 919 West Riverside. Here the Navy Mothers had a sewing center where they made clothes for the men from the Navy, Marines, and Coast Guard.[42] By October, 1942, they had made many regulation Navy garments, including eighty turtleneck sweaters, 90 watchcaps, 60 sleeveless sweaters, 128 pairs of socks, and 24 pairs of mittens.

Alterations were made on surgical gowns and jackets for the hospital at Farragut and, in addition, a monthly quota of 100 mittens and 100 sleeveless sweaters was filled for that naval training station. A large order from Alaska requested sweaters, socks and balaklava helmets (knitted coverings for the head and neck that have openings for nose and eyes).[43]

The **Red Cross** also had busy volunteers. In both the Paulsen Building and the Hutton Building, wool was distributed to hundreds of women to knit and sew. Sewing centers were set up at fire stations where volunteers worked on surgical dressings and other items needed. A *Spokesman-Review* article reported: "Many women have regular days at these centers and congenial groups meet together. They wear white uniforms and Red Cross head-dresses. They work up material faster than it can be secured...and occasionally must shut down because of lack of materials. Their produced items run into the thousands. Mrs. August Paulsen, chairman of volunteer services for the Red Cross, reported in a single month the production of 7,440 garments, ready for service."[44]

At the **Armory**, besides the draft registration boards, three companies of the new Home Guard, about 350 men, met regularly for drill beginning in 1942. This uniformed, volunteer group was ready for home guard work throughout the state if it became necessary. A Civil Air Patrol of private pilots and ground crews drilled at headquarters in the Armory. Nearly 5,000 workers prepared at the Armory to serve as air raid wardens. The Civilian Defense program, centered in the Welch Building, was training "more than 5,000 men to serve as auxiliary police and fire department workers. They worked regular shifts guarding all bridges and utilities in the city."[45]

DOWNTOWN SUPPORTS THE WAR EFFORT

Spokane's stores showed their support for the war with patriotic displays, posters, and signs. **The Crescent** encouraged the sale of war bonds in a display on the first floor stairwell. A framed spotlighted poster showed a soldier getting ready to throw a hand grenade, and the words: "LET 'EM HAVE IT." In large letters at the bottom of the sign the viewer was told: "BUY EXTRA BONDS."[46]

In 1942, **Payless Drug** employees did their share by making the following offer: "FREE CIGARETTES to Our Boys Overseas when You buy a carton of 200 CAMEL Cigarettes for only $1.53, regular price...3 regular packages of

Five smiling service people, an Army Air Corpsman, a soldier, a Navy nurse, a sailor, and a marine, walk arm in arm in a drawing displayed in the Old National Bank. A sign below it reads: "BUY U.S. SAVINGS BONDS." *(Eastern Washington State Historical Society, Spokane, Washington, L87-1.24097-42)*

CAMELS...will be forwarded to the War Department for FREE distribution to our Overseas Forces. Sponsored without profit by Payless Drug Employees!" This offer was advertised in a full window display complete with cardboard cutouts of uniformed servicemen.[47]

These patriotic posters and signs continued to appear throughout the war; all of Spokane wanted to sell the effort to win. Many stores' window displays included posters with pictures of servicemen and captions to purchase war bonds, such as: "If you can't go across, Come across. BUY WAR BONDS." Near the end of the war, a sign across the front of the **Exchange Building** stated: "IT ISN'T OVER YET... BUY WAR BONDS."[48]

Honor Rolls were hung in many of the larger stores. These were lists of names of employees who had left to serve the country. The **Washington Water Power Company** had a list in the lobby area of its building on Main and Lincoln. Many businesses also displayed a banner with a wide red border, a white field, and a blue

Around sixty names were recorded on this World War II Memorial when it was dedicated in 1943. By the war's end the list numbered over 400. *(Spokesman-Review)*

star for each employee that was in military service. **The Crescent** had one of these above the first floor elevators. Homes with family members in the military displayed service flags in their front windows, too. In time, some of the blue stars were replaced by gold ones, a poignant reminder that people were dying in the war.

On Memorial Day, 1943, the American Legion placed a monument behind the Lincoln statue. On this wooden memorial were the names of Spokanites who died in the war and these words by Lincoln: "We here highly resolve that these dead shall not have died in vain." Intended as a temporary monument, by the early '50s it was in need of paint and considered an eyesore. The All-Veterans' council had it removed, with the intention of putting up a permanent list.[49] Later a Memorial Park at the northeast end of the Monroe Street Bridge was dedicated to World War II Veterans, but individual names are not listed.

SHORTAGES OF NYLONS, COFFEE, AND DISHES

Silk stockings and the rather new "nylons" were almost impossible to get. Long lines would form at store counters if the word got out that either was being sold. Several of our downtown stores had women employees whose job was fixing "runs" in stockings. This service was available for years before the war at The Crescent, the Palace, Kress, and at other stores. The stocking was stretched over a small drinking glass, and a small tool was used to re-hook the threads of the run. The women who did this became very skilled, and could punch the hooking device up and down quickly to make the "run" disappear like magic. The business flourished during the war when hosiery became scarce. "Why stand in line for HOSIERY?", an ad from Kress read in 1945. "It's patriotic to repair 'em. Average run, 35¢ ."

Repairing runs did not solve the problem of the shortage, however, and before long, leg paint was devised to simulate stockings. It came in a small bottle and could be purchased at dime stores and department stores. The paint was applied by pouring the liquid into the palm of the hand and rubbing it over the leg. My sister informs me that the leg paint would last for two days. Stockings had seams in those days, and a special pencil could be purchased to draw the seam on the back of the leg!

Restaurants were affected by shortages and by rationing. We did not see such foods as bacon or whipping cream for many months. Butter, sugar, and coffee were rationed. The newspaper told of local restaurants posting signs regarding coffee rationing in 1942. One sign in a Sprague Avenue cafe read, "Due to Government Rationing of COFFEE, It will be necessary to discontinue warm-ups and refills."[50] I remember hearing adults talk about re-using coffee grounds several times before discarding them. Restaurants also had to be extra careful not to break dishes as they could not get replacements.[51]

THE END OF THE WAR

By late 1944, it was obvious when we listened to radio news and read the papers that we were winning the war. In April, 1945, the Germans surrendered, and efforts turned toward ending the war in the Pacific. On August 14, 1945, at 4:00 p.m. Pacific War Time, radios announced that World War II was over. Over KFPY, Bob Trout, of CBS, dramatically reported it this way: "The Japanese have accepted our terms *fully*! That's the word we have just received from the White House in Washington. This, ladies and gentlemen, is the *end* of the Second World War! The united nations, on land, on the sea, in the air, and to the four corners of the earth, are united, and are victorious!"[52]

Within minutes, hundreds of people poured into the streets of downtown Spokane. At first they were quiet; they seemed stunned. Then people in cars began sounding their horns, the fire department blew sirens, and the crowds went wild. Emotions were high, some people openly crying, others cheering and yelling. Servicemen grabbed and kissed women whether they knew them or not. The next day's newspaper described the reaction:

Automobile horns began to blow. In a few moments their blasts became a solid wave of sound in downtown streets. Their noise drowned out the shouting, and even the noise of the siren atop city hall. A storm of confetti swirled down from windows of high buildings as office workers gave vent to their joy.

Torn paper blanketed sidewalks within a matter of minutes. And still more came down. Thousands upon thousands of Americans, deliriously happy after the long, bitter years of war, gave way to their emotions openly and unashamedly. It was no uncommon sight to see people crying, but smiling happily at the same time, on the streets. The long-awaited end of fighting had come—it was official at last...Downtown streets, which had been comparatively free of automobile traffic, became packed with cars less than half an hour after the news broke. And every driver, it seemed, leaned on his horn.

Patrons in many downtown theaters, not notified of what had happened, sat calmly viewing the screen until they became aware of the noise outside. They, too, then joined the celebration, pouring from theater entrances...Among the first to spread the glad news in the downtown area were scores of newsboys who raced from The Spokesman-Review plant into the streets, shouting: "It's all over! The war's over!"...Sidewalks were crowded with men and women and children of all ages. Their faces were a study of emotion. Some merely stood, gazing up at the shower of torn paper drifting down from office windows. Others laughed and shouted, or talked animatedly...Workers coming home from war plants in the Spokane area swelled the throng...By 5 o'clock noise in downtown Spokane had reached bedlam dimensions. People were really getting into the spirit of the celebration...When the news of the war's end reached Comstock pool, several hundred children who had been splashing about climbed from the pool and solemnly sang "God Bless America," it was reported.

In a way the spontaneous celebration was like a gathering storm. It started slowly, with a few cheers and a few bits of paper fluttering down. One woman, pushing a baby carriage, stood weeping in the middle of the sidewalk, blocking passers-by. A stranger went up to comfort her. Everybody was everybody's friend. Men in uniform in the downtown streets were often the subjects of impromptu ovations. They were slapped on the back, and shaken by the hand. "Well, boy, you'll be out of that uniform soon," strangers shouted.

The snake dance, a traditional part of American jubilation, was missing at first. But at approximately 5:15 p.m. a group of young people formed a line and snake-danced down the middle of Sprague. The line split up and portions of it weaved through various office buildings. One section, totaling 35 boys too young for the army, girls and a few soldiers, tramped through The Spokesman-Review newsroom, shouting: "Have you heard? It's all over!"...Showing his joy in the most expressive way he knew was an army sergeant riding in one of the cars which formed the endless tooting parade downtown. His head was out the window, he was shouting loudly—and wildly waving his pants out of the side of the car.[53]

My father had witnessed a lot of this from his fifth floor office window. My sister, who had been working on West Riverside, also came home and told about it. Later that day my parents and I went downtown to see and hear the commotion. By the time we got there no one was attempting to drive on Riverside. People were wandering all over the street and it was thick with paper. Though some of the chaos had died down, it was still exciting to see.

What a wonderful time it was! Families could be reunited and the world was finally at peace, but it was a time for reflection, too. Thoughts of sorrow were mixed with thoughts of joy. Heartache for families who would never again see a son, a brother, a young husband or father could not be forgotten easily. Nearly everyone knew more than one person who would not be coming home.

Following World War II, service people that returned to Spokane gradually found work. Economically, the country was booming, but places to live were difficult to find and veterans and their families lived in cramped apartments or bought trailers and put them in someone's back yard, or lived with parents. New housing developments sprang up in many parts of town.

Downtown was as bustling as ever for awhile. As returning veterans began earning more money, they sought recreation. Some joined private clubs where they could buy mixed drinks and where slot machines had been available since the early '30s. The American Legion and Veterans of Foreign War posts, the Marine Club, the Eagles lodge, the Moose Club, the Elks lodge, the Press Club, the Athletic Round Table, the Greek American club, the Early Birds, the University Club, the Spokane Club and a number of other downtown clubs flourished. "One armed bandits" weren't allowed in taverns, cigar stores, confectioneries, restaurants and other public places, but pinball machines were permitted.[54]

The City Council banished both slot machines and pinball machines for a brief period in 1947.[55] In 1949 slot machines were outlawed in the entire state.[56] That same year, the state began allowing mixed drinks to be served in public places. The decisions must have been a blow to private clubs; much of their income came from drinking and gambling. State and city taxes from slot machines were also lost. Appeals to keep slot machines continued in the state supreme court until 1952 when the court decided the machines were unconstitutional because the state constitution prohibited all lotteries. The city of Spokane had received $143,229 from the machines in 1951, and $94,166 by the time of the ruling in 1952; slot machine revenue was not planned for in the 1953 budget as the decision to ban the machines was anticipated.[57]

After World War II our city followed a pattern of decentralization that was happening all over the country. Changes in transportation were a major factor in altering our central area. More people than ever owned cars. They were not so dependent on city busses and could go anywhere to shop. In the '50s, the Eisenhower Administration decided to improve the nation's highways and new freeways rather than to revitalize the railway system with high speed trains. Consequently, freight by truck increased, automobile travel grew even more, and railroads were used less. Railroads were further weakened as air travel became more common. In the already blighted areas of our train stations, more deterioration occurred.

As people traveled more by car, additional motels began to appear. Motels were built conveniently near highways, and parking was always available and near one's room. Dress could be very casual. Downtown hotels found it difficult to compete.

Theaters were also affected by the increased number of cars. The Garland theater opened in November, 1945, with an adjacent parking lot; and several drive-in theaters appeared in outlying areas in the late '40's. Until that time, only the Rialto in Hillyard and the Dishman theater had been out of the central core. People were drawn away from downtown theaters to the new ones. When TV arrived in Spokane in the early '50s, people could be entertained at home. Five of Spokane's downtown theaters closed in the '50s.

Spokane's first shopping mall opened with eight stores at Northtown in December, 1954. Twenty-six more stores were planned at that time for the mall, most to open in 1955.[58] Shadle Park, University City, then Manito Shopping Centers followed, along with expansion of Five Mile and Lincoln Heights Centers. Neighborhood banks and small office buildings began popping up near the shopping centers and elsewhere. Before long, downtown office buildings had many empty spaces. A number of the buildings had to close above the first floor. Others were torn down for such things as parking areas, new banks, or drive-in banks.

Those of us who lived here in the '30s and '40s remember the active, busy downtown. It has been sad to see the changes taking place over the years with urban sprawl and moves from downtown shopping to many malls. We are, however, heartened by the recent determination of city officials and downtown property owners to bring back some of that earlier vitality to the core area. It is nostalgic to look back; let's hope for a better and more active downtown in the future.

NOTES

INTRODUCTION. The Depression in Spokane

1. William Stimson, *A View of the Falls, An Illustrated History of Spokane*, Northridge, CA., Windsor Publications, 1985, p.64.
2. Orville C. Pratt, *Story of Spokane*, Original unpublished manuscript, 1948, p.228, Northwest Room, Spokane Public Library.
3. Ibid., p. 219.
4. Ibid., p. 237.
5. Ibid., pp. 243, 244.
6. Ibid., p. 223.
7. Ibid., pp. 226, 239, 240.
8. Ibid., p. 245; *Spokane Daily Chronicle*, J.J. Kalez, Dec. 25, 1970, p. 40.
9. Pratt, p. 240.
10. Ibid., p. 234.
11. *Spokesman-Review*, M.B., Dec. 8, 1940, Magazine Section, p.1, 6.
12. *Spokane Daily Chronicle*, J.J. Kalez, Dec. 25, 1970, p. 40.
13. WPA Art School Bulletins, Vertical Files, Northwest Room, Spokane Public Library.
14. Pratt, p. 223.
15. *Spokane Daily Chronicle*, June 19, 1939, p.6.
16. *Spokesman-Review*, June 27, 1937, Special Section, unpaginated.
17. Pratt, pp., 244, 245.
18. Ibid., p. 246.
19. Ibid., p. 222.
20. Ibid., p. 230.
21. Cheney Cowles Museum picture, *(L87-1.1614-32)*
22. Pratt, p. 224.
23. Ibid., p.226.
24. Ibid.
25. Robert B. Hyslop, *Spokane's Building Blocks*, Spokane, Privately published, Standard Blueprint Co., 1983, p.261.
26. Pratt, p. 232.
27. Interview with Edith Meeker.
28. Pratt, p. 231.
29. Claude A. Campbell, *The Old National Bank of Spokane*, Reprinted from *Research Studies of The State College of Washington*, Vol. XVII (1949), p. 154.
30. Ibid., p. 166.
31. Oral History Interview by Nancy Gale Compau, Canterbury Court, Dec. 1990, Northwest Room, Spokane Public Library.
32. Ibid.
33. Ibid.
34. Interview with Harry Jones.
35. John A. Guthrie, *Wartime Changes In Spokane's Labor Forces*, Bulletin No. 1, Pullman, Wa., The State College of Washington, Bureau of Economic and Business Research, June, 1944, p.3.
36. Pratt, p. 273.
37. *Spokesman-Review*, Jan 22, 1936.
38. John Luppert, "The Glory Days of the Davenport Hotel," *The Pacific Northwesterner*, Vol. 35, No. 1, 1991, p.4.
39. *Spokesman-Review*, July 23, 1942, p.1.
40. *Spokane Daily Chronicle*, Feb. 7, 1973, p.3.

CHAPTER ONE. Street Images

1. Orville C. Pratt, *Story of Spokane*, Original unpublished manuscript, 1948, p. 253, Northwest Room, Spokane Public Library.
2. *Spokesman-Review*, Aug. 4, 1939.
3. Ibid., Nov. 12, 1939.
4. "Traffic Signals," Newspaper clipping, card file, Northwest Room, Spokane public Library
5. Nov. 3, 1929, Vertical Files, Northwest Room, Spokane Public Library.
6. Pratt, p. 232.
7. *Spokesman-Review*, Jan. 2, 1942.
8. Interview with Jim Read, former policeman.
9. *Spokesman-Review*, M.B., Magazine Section, (Pacific Parade), Mar. 2, 1945, p.5.
10. George L. Lufkin, *Spokane Spectacle*, Shelton, Wa., Privately published, 1984, p.36.
11. Picture Files, Northwest Room, Spokane Public Library.
12. "Stoical Indian Newsmen's Pal," Vertical Files, Northwest Room Room, Spokane Public Library
13. Pratt, p. 216.
14. Pratt, p. 242.
15. Robert B. Hyslop, *Spokane's Building Blocks*, Spokane, Standard Blueprint Co., 1983, p. 73.
16. Ibid., p. 366.

CHAPTER TWO. Stores, Shops, and Markets

1. Robert B. Hyslop, *Spokane's Building Blocks*, Spokane, Standard Blueprint Co., 1983, p.74.
2. Ibid., p. 163.
3. Ibid., p.253.
4. Orville C. Pratt, *Story of Spokane*, Original unpublished manuscript, 1948, p 269, Northwest Room, Spokane Public Library.
5. *Spokesman-Review*, Oct. 26, 1947, p.6.
6. Ibid., Sept. 11, 1937, p.6.
7. Gustav Pehrson Scrapbook, Northwest Room, Spokane Public Library.
8. *Spokesman-Review*, Sept. 11, 1948, p.6.
9. Ibid., Mar. 19, 1950, p.6.
10. Cheney Cowles Museum, Parade picture, Cresent Float.
11. Hyslop, p.196.
12. Ibid., p.164.
13. Pratt, p.218.
14. Hyslop, p. 331.
15. Pehrson Scrapbook.
16. Cheney Cowles Museum picture, Riverside-West-600 (Howard to Wall)
17. Interview with Earl Rogers of Glen Dow Academy of Hair Design.
18. "Newest Jewelry Store is Ready," Sept. 27, 1936, Pehrson Scrapbook.
19. *Spokesman-Review*, Oct. 17, 1965.
20. *Spokane Daily Chronicle*, Oct. 10, 1972, p.1.
21. *Spokesman-Review*, July 27, 1938.
22. Ibid., Aug. 16, 1957, p.1.
23. "New Fur Store Throng Magnet," Aug. 22, 1939, Pehrson Scrapbook.
24. *Spokane Daily Chronicle*, Nov. 15, 1969, p.3.; Dec. 3, 1933, Pehrson Scrapbook.
25. Pehrson Scrapbook.
26. Ibid.

CHAPTER THREE. Buildings

1. Robert B. Hyslop, *Spokane's Building Blocks*, Spokane, Standard Blueprint Co., 1983, p.13.
2. *Spokane Daily Chronicle*, Dec. 6, 1933, p.7.
3. Ibid., April 16, 1937.
4. Hyslop, p.223.
5. Ibid., p.68.
6. Ibid., p.82.
7. Ibid., p.92.
8. *Spokane Daily Chronicle*, Nov. 6, 1971, p.13.
9. Hyslop, p.97.
10. *Spokesman-Review*, Jan. 6, 1949, p.9.
11. Hyslop, p.153,154.
12. Picture, Spokane City Directory, 1905, p.92.
13. *Spokane Daily Chronicle*, Jan 1, 1977, p.21.
14. Hyslop, p.155.
15. Ibid., p.157.
16. Ibid., p.161.
17. Ibid., p.165.
18. Ibid., pp.171,202.
19. Ibid., pp.178,179.
20. Polk City Directory, 1932.
21. Hyslop, p.188; Polk City Directory
22. Hyslop, p.203.
23. Cheney Cowles Museum picture, Riverside-West-400 (Washington to Stevens); Descriptions from Harry Jones.
24. "Move Federal Bank Into Old National," Aug. 26, 1933; "Federal Reserve at Old National," Oct. 19, 1933, Gustav Pehrson Scrapbook, Northwest Room, Spokane Public Library.
25. Interview with Harry Jones.
26. Hyslop, pp.221-223; Orville C. Pratt, *Story of Spokane*, Original unpublished manuscript, 1948, p.218, Northwest Room, Spokane Pubic Library.
27. Ibid., pp.225,226.
28. Ibid., pp.87,88.
29. *Spokane Daily Chronicle*, Mar. 10, 1976, p.15.
30. Hyslop, p.254.
31. *Spokesman-Review*, Aug. 30, 1931, B, p.2.
32. Ibid., Sunday Magazine, Aug. 18, 1968, p.27.
33. Cheney Cowles Museum picture, Riverside-West-600 (Howard to Wall)
34. Ibid.
35. M.B., "Presenting...Joel Ferris," "Joel E. Ferris has Full Life," and excerpt from "Race Against Time; the story of salvage archaeology," Vertical Files, Northwest Room, Spokane Public Library.
36. Hyslop, pp.273,274.
37. Ibid., p.285.

38. Ibid., pp.340,341.
39. *Spokane Daily Chronicle*, Aug. 11, 1972, p.5.
40. Hyslop, pp. 132,133.
41. Ibid., p.192.
42. Ibid., p.305.
43. *Spokane Daily Chronicle*, Oct. 11, 1972, p.50.
44. Hyslop, pp. 56,57.
45. Ibid. p.57.
46. Henry Matthews, "A Wedding of Function and Fantasy," *Columbia*, V, 1991, p.5.
47. Louis Davenport, "The Pride of an Empire," condensed from a book, (no name given), Spokane, Originally published by E.J. Boxer, 1915, pp. 4,5. Northwest Room, Spokane Public Library.
48. Ibid.
49. Dorothy Powers, "Davenport's 'Silver John' outwitted federal agents—with raw egg, of all things!" *Spokane Daily Chronicle*, Feb. 10, 1987, p.A-11.
50. There were a half-dozen fish tanks in the hotel: John Luppert, "The Glory Days of the Davenport Hotel," *The Pacific Northwesterner*, Vol. 35, No. 1, 1991, p.1.
51. Cheney Cowles Museum picture, Sprague- West- 800-(Post to Lincoln) Davenport Hotel Interior.
52. *Davenport Hotel, U.S.A.*, c. 1928, p.17.
53. Cheney Cowles Museum picture, Sprague-West-800-(Post to Lincoln) Davenport Hotel Interior.
54. Interview with Arthur Zepp.
55. Luppert, *The Pacific Northwesterner*, Vol. 35, No.1, 1991, p.1.
56. Interview with John Luppert.
57. Interview with Sophia Gerkensmeyer, who worked at the Davenport candy factory; through her niece, Carol Measel.
58. Luppert, *The Pacific Northwesterner*, Vol. 35, No.1, 1991, p.6.
59. Interview with John Luppert, (source on windows).
60. Polk City Directory.
61. *Spokesman-Review*, Feb. 3, 1985, p.3.; *Spokesman-Review*, Mar. 17, 1996, p.E-3; Christopher S. Brookes-Miller, *Davenport, Creation Damnation and Problems of Resurrection, 1890-1990*, Master's Thesis, Washington State University, 1990, p.45; Dorothy Powers, *Spokane Daily Chronicle*, June 27, 1985, p.A-19; *Spokane Daily Chronicle*, Jan. 22, 1974; Luppert, *The Pacific Northwesterner*, Vol. 35, No.1, p.11; Jim Kershner, *Spokesman-Review*, Mar. 10, 1996, p. E-1, E-7; Ibid., Mar. 17, 1996, p. E-1.
62. *Spokane Daily Chronicle*, Jan. 22, 1974.
63. "Davenport Hotel to Spend $35,000," ca. 1930, Gustav Pehrson Scrapbook, Northwest Room, Spokane Public Library.
64. Cheney Cowles Museum picture, Sprague-West-800-(Post to Lincoln)
65. Interview with John Luppert.
66. *Spokesman-Review*, Oct. 15, 1939, p.1.
67. "Early Birds to Share Davenport Remodeling," Sept. 19, 1939, Pehrson Scrapbook.
68. Ibid., July 6, 1940.
69. Ibid., Oct. 12, 1940.
70. Brookes-Miller, *Davenport, Creation Damnation and Problems of Resurrection, 1890-1990*, pp.47-55.
71. Interview with John Luppert.
72. Margaret Bean, *Spokesman-Review*, Magazine Section, Feb. 13, 1949, p.8; Unicorns on wallpaper and crystal chandeliers are evident in picture in Davenport Hotel collection.
73. Ibid. (Margaret Bean).
74. Hyslop, pp.215,216.
75. "New Rooms to Be Artistic," July 30, 1933; "Dessert Offers New Food Place," Sept. 10, 1933, Pehrson Scrapbook.
76. "Prevue is Given New Night Club," Nov. 19, 1934; "Newspaper and Radio Men Dine in New Roundup Room," undated, Ibid.
77. Interview with Edith Meeker.
78. "Dessert to be Air Conditioned," Aug. 8, 1936, Pehrson Scrapbook.
79. Hyslop, pp.215,216
80. Ibid. pp.283,284.
81. Cheney Cowles Museum picture, First-west-500-(Stevens to Howard) Spokane Hotel.
82. "Spokane Hotel Improvements Should Please Most Fastidious of Patrons," July 7, 1942; "Spokane Hotel Spends $35,000," Oct. 15, 1941, Pehrson Scrapbook.
83. Hyslop, pp.246,247.
84. *Spokesman-Review*, Extra Edition, Mar. 1, 1950, p.1.
85. Hyslop, p.310.
86. Pratt, p.274.
87. Interviews with Jeanette Carlsen and Edith Meeker.
88. Hyslop, pp. 45,46; *Spokesman-Review*, Nov. 18, 1968, pp. 6,16; "Spokane Landmark," Bob Cubbage, *Spokane Today* Feature Magzine, Mar., 1986, Vertical Files, Northwest Room, Spokane Public Library.
89. Interview with Jim Read, former policeman.
90. Interview with Jim Delegans, Jr., renovator of the old City Hall.
91. Hyslop, pp.106-107.
92. *Spokesman-Review*, Sunday Magazine, Oct. 11, 1992, p.4.
93. "Spokane Golden Jubilee Festival of Music and Dance," printed program, May 7-14, 1939, personal collection.
94. Interview with Robert Armstrong.
95. Hyslop, pp.260,261.
96. Ibid., pp.334,335.
97. Ibid., pp.337,338.
98. Ibid., pp.257,258
99. Ibid., p.13.
100. *Spokesman-Review*, Dec. 14, 1941, p.6.

101. Ibid., May 10, 1936, p.1.
102. Hyslop, pp.169,170.
103. Polk City Directories, 1964 to 1980.
104. "Industrial Revival Seen in Opening of New Brewery!," Industries—Breweries Vertical File, Northwest Room, Spokane Public Library.
105.Claire Bishop, Al Kiefer, Sara Patton, "The Schade Brewery," Spokane County Historic Preservation Project, Spokane, Industries—Breweries Vertical File, Northwest Room, Spokane Public Library.
106. Wilfred P. Schoenberg, S.J., *Gonzaga University, Seventy-five Years, 1887-1962*, Gonzaga University, Spokane, 1963, pp.277 to 282.
107. Ibid.
108. *Spokesman-Review*, Sept. 30, 1938, p.11.
Note: *Historic Landmark Survey, Spokane*, 1979, Consultants Moritz Kundig, Patsy M.Garrett, Harvey S. Rice, was used for some styles, and names of architects of certain buildings.

CHAPTER FOUR. Restaurants

1. Duncan Hines, *Adventures in Good Eating*, New York, Duncan Hines Inc., 1947, p.286.
2. Ibid., 1938 edition.
3. The Polk City Directory was used to calculate these figures. Many places listed under "Confectionary and Ice Cream," and under "Restaurants" had soda fountains. To these were added an estimate from listings for "Drug Stores," bearing in mind that neighborhood drug stores usually had soda fountains, but most downtown drug stores did not. To these were added soda fountains in the downtown area that would not have been under the above listings, such as those in dime stores and in The Crescent department store. Spokane has approximately five soda fountains in the mid-'90s, but some are simply "for show" and are not working soda fountains.
4. Cheney Cowles Museum picture, First Street looking west, 1948, First-West-600-(Howard to Wall)
5. Hines, *Adventures In Good Eating*, 1949.
6. Interview with Darlene Pappas Compton.
7. Interview with Jim Haynes, former policeman.
8. Interview with Carole Cooke Jones.
9. Interview with Robert Peters, former owner of Peters and Sons.
10. Interview with Helen Turner.
11. Cheney Cowles Museum picture, Charles A. Libby Studio, 1945, Sprague-West-700-(Wall to Post)
12. Robert B. Hyslop, *Spokane's Building Blocks*, Spokane, Standard Blueprint Co., 1983, p.168.
13. Cheney Cowles Museum picture, Wallace Gamble Collection, Sprague-West 500-(Stevens to Howard)
14. *Spokane Daily Chronicle*, May 30, 1968, p.20.
15. Travo family scrapbooks and interview with Della Travo.
16. The Isabella Room is listed as "main dining room" in several publications from early years. Though prices in the Hines book seem terribly low for such elegant dining, when comparing them to restaurants listed in the New York area in the same editions, we find the Waldorf-Astoria Sert Room dinner listed as $2 and up, other restaurants up to $3.75, and some simply "prices are not low."
17. *Spokesman-Review*, Dec. 9, 1945, p.8.
18. Luppert, *The Pacific Northwesterner*, Vol. 35, No. 1, 1991, p.7.
19. Menu, Gerald S. Hartley collection.
20. Interview with John Luppert.
21. Menu, Northwest Room, Spokane Public Library.
22. Interview with John Luppert.
23. The room was newly redecorated in 1927 and was still called the Orange Bower at that time. It is called the Apple Bower in several sources from the mid-'30s.
24. Interview with John Luppert.
25. Dorothy Powers, "Idaho readers offer ideas for Davenport restoration," *Spokane Daily Chronicle*, Feb. 4, 1986, p.A-13.
26. Cheney Cowles Museum picture, Sprague-West-800-(Post to Lincoln) Davenport Hotel Interior
27. Interview with John Luppert.
28. Cheney Cowles Museum picture, Sprague-West-800-(Post to Lincoln) Davenport Hotel Interior
29. "Davenport Hotel, Spokane, U.S.A.," C.W. Hill Printing Co., Spokane, ca. 1928; Duncan Hines, *Adventures in Good Eating*, NewYork, Duncan Hines Inc., 1938, '45, '47, '50.
30. John Luppert, *The Pacific Northwesterner*, Vol. 35, No. 1, 1991, pp. 4, 8.
31. Henry Matthews, "The Davenport Hotel, A Year of Hopes and Fears," *Arcade*, Feb./Mar., 1991, p.10.
32. Interview with John Luppert.
33. Ibid.
34. Ibid.
35. Gustav A. Pehrson Scrapbook, Northwest Room, Spokane Public Library.
36. Ibid.
37. Hyslop, p. 215. In 1951, the Desert Hotel owners opened the Desert Caravan Inn on the sunset hill on the southwest side of the city. For ten years they operated this and the older downtown hotel, but in 1961, closed the mid-city business.
38. *Spokesman-Review*, Jan. 24, 1943, p.8.
39. Hyslop, pp.283,284.
40. *Spokesman-Review*, Oct. 19, 1958, Magazine Section, p.9.
41. Hines, *Adventures in Good Eating*, 1947.
42. Hyslop, pp.283,284.
43. *Spokesman-Review*, Dec. 26, 1961.
44. Hyslop, pp.283,284.
45. Information from Ridpath Hotel employees.

CHAPTER FIVE. Theaters

1. George L. Lufkin, *Spokane Spectacle*, A Study of Spokane, Washington Theaters Between 1883 and 1983, Shelton, Wa., Privately
   published, 1984, p.8; Cheney Cowles Museum picture, dated 1930, Post-North -200 (Main to Spokane Falls Boulevard)
2. Descriptions of the Auditorium theater are from Lufkin book pp.7-23 unless otherwise indicated.
3. Robert B. Hyslop, *Spokane's Building Blocks*, Spokane, Standard Blueprint Co., 1983, p.14.
4. Lufkin, p.8.
5. Hyslop, p.14.
6. Jay J. Kalez, "Spokane Theaters Big After Turn of Century," *Spokane Daily Chronicle*, Oct. 25, 1967; Lufkin, p.9.
7. Auditorium theater advertisement, *Spokesman-Review*, Nov. 11, 1930, p.5.
8. Lufkin, p.9.
9. Interview with Michael Smith, Manager of Met.
10. Lufkin, p.60.
11. Interview with Fran Reamer, organist; interview with Jim Wallrabenstein, member of the American Theater Organ Society.
12. Interview with Jim Wallrabenstein.
13. E & T, "Color added gradually as film-making evolved," *Spokesman-Review*, Dec. 12, 1993, p.15.
14. Lufkin, pp. 33, 34.
15. Ibid., p.59.
16. Ibid., p.61.
17. *Spokesman-Review*, Sept. 10, 1933, p.A-8.
18. *Spokane Daily Chronicle*, May 14, 1937, p.12.
19. *Spokesman-Review*, June 7, 1931, p.5.
20. Lufkin, p.65.
21. Ibid., p.66.
22. Hyslop, p.172.
23. Lufkin, p.56.
24. Hyslop, p.245.
25. Lufkin, p.53.
26. *Spokesman-Review*, Aug. 15, 1990, p.B2.
27. Lufkin, p.38.
28. Murray Morgan, *Skid Road*, Viking Press, N.Y., 1962, pp.151-158.
29. Lufkin, pp.39-45.
30. *Spokesman-Review*, July 6, 1925, Part Five, p.1.
31. *Spokane Daily Chronicle*, May 14, 1937.
32. George L. Lufkin, "American Theater," Spokane, Wash. *Marquee*, The Journal of the Theater Historical Society, Vol. 5-No.2, Second
   Quarter, 1973, pp.5,6, Vertical Files, Northwest Room, Spokane Public Library.
33. *Spokane Daily Chronicle*, Oct. 15, 1968, and other related articles, Cora and Robert Armstrong Scrapbooks, Courtesy of Beth Moore.
34. Lufkin, *Spokane Spectacle*, pp.57, 58.
35. Ibid., p.73.
36. Interview with Jim Wallrabenstein.
37. Hyslop, p.306.
38. Lufkin, p.54.

CHAPTER SIX. Radio and Radio Stations

1. (Compiled and edited by) Carl Partlow and Thorwald Jorgenson, *The Early Days of Spokane Broadcasting*, Privately published,
   Spokane, ca. 1981, p.91, Northwest Room, Spokane Public Library.
2. *Variety Radio Directory*, Vol. IV, 1940-41, p.731, Vertical Files, Northwest Room, Spokane Public Library.
3. Partlow and Jorgenson, p. 94.
4. Jim Kershner, "Radio Days," *Spokesman-Review*, Oct. 5, 1992, p.B1.
5. *Presenting Spokane's Pioneer Station*, KXLY, National Radio Personalities, Peoria, Ill., 1948, unpaginated, Vertical Files, Northwest
   Room, Spokane Public Library.
6. Robert B. Hyslop, *Spokane's Building Blocks*, Spokane, Standard Blueprint Co., 1983, p.291.
7. "Early Days of KFIO," D. Winsor Hunt, Parlow and Jorgenson, p.95.
8. *Presenting Spokane's Pioneer Station*, KXLY.
9. "'Inland Empire' Served by Voice of Station KHQ," *Christian Science Monitor*, Nov. 19, 1937.
10. *Variety Radio Directory*, Washington Stations, Vol. IV, 1940-41, p.732.
11. Dorothy Powers, "Montanan Remembers Davenport's Orchestra," *Spokane Daily Chronicle*, Jan. 27, 1987, p.A17.
12. Orville C. Pratt, *Story of Spokane*, Original unpublished manuscript, 1948, pp. 214, 217Northwest Room, Spokane Public Library.
13. "'Inland Empire' Served by Voice of Station KHQ," *Christian Science Monitor*, Nov. 19, 1937.
14. Washington Stations Listing, 1940-1941, Northwest Room, Spokane Public Library.
15. Pratt, p.275.
16. *Presenting Spokane's Pioneer Station*, KXLY.
17. Vertical Files, Northwest Room, Spokane Public Library.
18. *Presenting Spokane's Pioneer Station*, KXLY.
19. Washington Stations listing, 1940-41.
20. *Presenting Spokane's Pioneer Station*, KXLY,
21. Alex McNeil, *TOTAL TELEVISION*, A Comprehensive Guide to Programming from 1948 to the Present, Third Edition, Penguin Books,
   N.Y., pp.87, 88, 419, 477, 478.
22. *Presenting Spokane's Pioneer Station*, KXLY.

23. Washington Stations listing, 1940-41.
24. *Presenting Spokane's Pioneer Station, KXLY.*
25. Pratt, pp.259,260.
26. Ibid., p.260.
27. "Wasmer Making Million Dollar Building Plans," Gustav Pehrson Scrapbook, Northwest Room, Spokane Public Library.
28. "Radio Networks to Salute City," *Spokesman-Review*, Aug. 28, 1947, p.6.
29. "It's KNEW! it's for You!", *Spokesman-Review*, Sept. 1, 1947, p.5.

CHAPTER SEVEN. Ballrooms

1. Polk's Spokane City Directory, Spokane, R.L. Polk and Co., 1930 to 1949.
2. Gordon H. Coe, "Dance Halls Were Plentiful," *Spokane Daily Chronicle*, Feb. 19, 1973, p.5.
3. Ibid.
4. Robert B. Hyslop, *Spokane's Building Blocks*, Spokane, Privately published, Standard Blueprint Co., 1983, p.324.
5. Ibid., pp.113,114.
6. "Public Dancing Grading Better," *Spokesman-Review*, Jan. 9, 1936.
7. "Nation Watches Hi-Nite Club," *Spokesman-Review*, Aug. 13, 1943.
8. Ibid.
9. "Club Initiated by Swingsters," *Spokesman-Review*, Sept. 23, 1944.
10. "Hi-Nite Season Opens, With 500 There," *Spokesman-Review*, Sept. 11, 1948, p.6.
11. "Hi-Nite School Club to Reopen," *Spokesman-Review*, Sept. 1, 1947, p.6.

CHAPTER EIGHT. Street Railways

1. Robert B. Hyslop, *Spokane's Building Blocks*, Spokane, Standard Blueprint Co., 1983, Inside Cover.
2. *Motor Coach Age, Spokane United Railways*, XLI, 1989.
3. Ibid.
4. Chas. V. Mutschler, *Spokane's Street Railways*, Spokane, Inland Empire Railway Historical Society, 1987, p.123.
5. Jay J. Kalez, "Early Night Life Keyed to 'Owl' Trips," *Spokane Daily Chronicle*, April 29, 1967, p.13.
6. Larry Young, "Blaze of Glory," *Spokesman-Review*, Feb. 2, 1979, p.27.
7. Lois Valliant Ryker, *A Brief History of the Spokane United Railways*, 1981, p.2. Vertical Files, Northwest Room, Spokane Public Library.
8. Steve Blewett, *A History of the Washington Water Power Company, 1889-1999*, Spokane, The Washington Water Power Company, 1989, p.31.
9. Jay J. Kalez, "Early Night Life Keyed to 'Owl' Trips," *Spokane Daily Chronicle*, April 29, 1967, p.13.
10. "Bid Bye-bye to Street Car in City Today," *Spokane Daily Chronicle*, Aug. 31, 1936, p.1.
11. Larry Young, "Blaze of Glory," *Spokesman-Review*, Feb. 2, 1979, p.27.
12. Jay J. Kalez, "Early Night Life Keyed to 'Owl' Trips," *Spokane Daily Chronicle*, April 29, 1967, p.13.
13. *Spokesman-Review*, Sept. 2, 1936.
14. Larry Young, "Blaze of Glory," *Spokesman-Review*, Feb. 2, 1979, p.27.
15. Ibid.
16. "All Aboard! Railway society obtains old streetcar," *Spokesman-Review*, June 7, 1979, p.5.
17. Interview with Lee Tillotson.
18. Steve Blewett, *A History of the Washington Water Power Company, 1889-1999*, Spokane, The Washington Water Power Company, 1989, p.31.

CHAPTER NINE. Special Events and Celebrations

1. *Spokesman-Review*, Nov. 12, 1930, pp.1,2,7.
2. *The..Lincoln Memorial*, brochure, ca. 1930, Vertical Files, Northwest Room, Spokane Public Library.
3. "The Romance of Our Lincoln Memorial," Citizens' Emergency Committee for Spokane's Lincoln Memorial, Samuel P. Weaver, Chaiman, ca. 1924, Vertical Files, Northwest Room, Spokane Public Library.
4. "Lincoln Statue Imposing," Feb. 11, 1923, Vertical Files, Northwest Room, Spokane Public Library.
5. "The Romance of Our Lincoln Memorial."
6. *Program, Lincoln Memorial Statue Fund*, Benefit Performance—Dec. 15, 16, 17, 1927, American Theater, Spokane Players' Club, Vertical Files, Northwest Room, Spokane Public Library.
7. *Spokesman-Review*, Nov. 12, 1920, p.1.
8. Ibid.
9. *Spokesman-Review*, Oct. 19, 1967, p.1.
10. Ibid., Aug. 30, 1931, p.2.
11. Ibid., Sept. 4, 1931, p.1.
12. Ibid.
13. *Spokesman-Review*, Jan. 8, 1938, p.5.
14. Wilbur W. Hindley, "Fox Theater Is Last Word In Beauty and Efficiency," *Spokesman-Review*, Sept. 3, Special Section.
15. Ibid., Sept. 4, 1931, p.1.
16. Ibid., Sept. 3, Special Section.
17. Ibid.
18. *Spokesman-Review*, Sept. 6, 1931, p.1.
19. Ibid., Sept. 5, 1931, p.1.
20. Ibid., Sept. 6, 1931, p.1.

21. "1939 Is State's 50th Birthday," *Oroville Gazette*, Oroville, Washington, Jan. 6, 1939.
22. "Historic Sites Marked for Cavalcade," *Spokesman-Review*, July 9, 1939
23. Phil Alexander, Chairman of the Golden Jubilee Historical Spectacle, Spokane Chamber of Commerce, letter to prospective commitee members, Mar. 20, 1939, Vertical Files, Northwest Room, Spokane Public Library.
24. "1889—GOLDEN JUBILEE—1939, PAGEANT," Spokane Public Schools, Gonzaga Stadium, May 5...1:30 P.M., program, personal collection; pictures, Vertical Files, Northwest Room, Spokane Public Library.
25. *Spokane Daily Chronicle*, Feb. 23, 1939, p.5.
26. Grace Kirkpatrick, "Pageant in $25,000 Class With 1500 in Big Show," *Spokesman-Review*, July 30, 1939, Part Five, p.1.
27. *Spokesman-Review*, July 23, 1939, p.4
28. *Spokane Daily Chronicle*, July 6, 1939, p.1.
29. Ibid., July 17, 1939, p.1.
30. *Spokesman-Review*, July 8, 1939, p.6.
31. "Spokane Is Gay In Olden Garb," *Spokesman-Review*, July 17, 1939.
32. Ibid., July 18, 1939, p.6.
33. "Steptoe Battle Rehearsal Near," *Spokesman-Review*, July 21, 1939.
34. Ibid., Aug. 2, 1939, p.16.
35. Phil Alexander, letter, Mar. 20, 1939.
36. *Spokesman-Review*, Aug. 3, 1939, p.1.
37. Ibid.
38. Ibid.
39. *Spokesman-Review*, July 29, 1939, p.6.
40. Ibid., Aug. 1, 1939, pp.1,6; Ibid., Aug. 5, 1939, p.6.
41. *Spokane Daily Chronicle*, July 29, 1939, p.1.
42. Ibid., Aug. 4, 1939, p.1.
43. Ibid., Aug. 5, 1939, p.1.; Ibid., Aug. 7, 1939, p.1.
44. Ibid., Aug. 28, 1939, p.1.
45. "Young Victim Starts High School in September," Vertical Files, Northwest Room, Spokane Public Library.
46. *Spokane Daily Chronicle*, Aug. 4, 1939, p.1.
47. "Lilac Festival Dates May 17-24," *Spokane Daily Chronicle*, May 10, 1938.
48. Ibid.
49. "Spokane's First Annual Lilac Festival," *Spokane Daily Chronicle*, May 17, 1938, Vertical Files, Northwest Room, Spokane PublicLibrary.
50. *Spokane Lilac Festival, 1938-1994*, Spokane Lilac Festival Association, p.1.
51. Ibid.
52. "Freedom Train Plans Mapped," *Spokesman-Review*, Feb. 7, 1948, Vertical Files, Northwest Room, Spokane Public Library.
53. *Spokesman-Review*, April 14, 1948, p.1.
54. Ibid.
55. "Freedom Train Spokane Guest," *Spokesman-Review*, April 13, 1948, Vertical Files, Northwest Room, Spokane Public Library.
56. David W. Reid, "American Freedom Train begins 4-day Spokane stop," *Spokesman-Review*, Oct. 27, 1975, p.6.

CHAPTER TEN. World War II Years

1. *Spokesman-Review*, Dec. 9, 1941, p.1.
2. Ibid., Dec. 10, 1941, p.1.
3. Ibid.
4. Ibid., Dec. 12, 1941, p.6.
5. Ibid., p.1.
6. Ibid., June 19, 1942, pp.1,6; Ibid., July 31, 1942, p.1.
7. Ibid., May 17, 1942, p.A-6.
8. *Fairchild-Spokane, 1942-1992*, 92nd Wing History, 1991, p.13.
9. "Air View Shows Amazing Growth of Sunset Field Cantonment," Spokesman-Review, Mar. 6, 1941.
10. "Army Air Depot Story Thrills," Ibid., June 13, 1943.
11. "Chemical Warfare," Ibid., Aug. 3, 1941.
12. "Fort Projects Wide in Scope," Ibid., Dec. 17, 1944.
13. *Spokesman-Review*, Jan 3, 1943, p.1.
14. Florence B. Otto, *Wartime History, United States Naval Supply Depot*, Spokane, Washington, June 15, 1944, Appendix A.
15. Roger E. Glans, *United States Naval Training Station, Farragut, Idaho, 1942-1946*, Minneapolis, 1992, unpaginated.
16. *Spokesman-Review*, June 7, 1995, p.A-16
17. Glans, *Farragut*, 1992.
18. *Spokane Daily Chronicle*, May 18, 1943, p.1.
19. "USO Registers 645,000 in Year," *Spokesman-Review*, Dec. 28, 1943; "Service Men, Women, Enjoy USO Facilities," *Spokesman - Review*, Jan. 6, 1945.
20. Orville C. Pratt, *Story of Spokane*, Original unpublished manuscript, 1948. p.257, Northwest Room, Spokane Public Library.
21. "Dance Partners Plentiful Here," *Spokesman-Review*, July 5, 1944, *USO* Bulletins, Northwest Room, Spokane Public Library.
22. "Final Awards Given at USO," *Spokesman-Review*, June 30, 1947.
23. Staff Sergeant Coleman M'Campbell, "George Washington Carver U.S.O. Gay," *Spokesman-Review*, Dec. 26, 1943; "Carver Center to Have Beauty," *Spokesman-Review*, May 12, 1943.
24. "Service Men, Women, Enjoy USO Facilities," *Spokesman-Review*, Jan. 6, 1945.
25. "Center Director Presented Award," *Spokesman-Review*, Jan. 28, 1946.
26. Pratt, p.258; *Spokesman-Review*, Dec. 1, 1941, p.6.
27. *Fairchild-Spokane, 1942-1992*, 92nd Wing History, 1991, p.13.
28. Glans, *Farragut*, 1992.

29. "Air View Shows Amazing Growth of Sunset Field Cantonment," *Spokeman-Review*, Mar. 6, 1941.
30. Interview with Lou Farline, who worked as Assistant Superintendent of Construction at Trentwood and worked at both Mead and Trentwood plants from 1941 through the end of the war.
31. *Fairchild-Spokane, 1942-1992*, p.16.
32. Interview with Lou Farline.
33. Otto, *Wartime History, United States Naval Supply Depot*, p.O-12.
34. John A. Guthrie, *"Wartime Changes in Spokane's Labor Force,"* Bulletin No. 1, Pullman, Wa., The State College of Washington Bureau of Economic and Business Research, June, 1944, Vertical Files, Northwest Room, Spokane Public Library.
35. *Fairchild-Spokane, 1942-1992*, p.16.
36. Interview with Lou Farline.
37. Pratt, p.253
38. *Population 1880 to 1980*, Report No.10, City Plan Commission, Spokane, Sept. 1963, p.2.
39. W.W. Hindley, "Home Front Is Throughly Organized," *Spokesman-Review*, May 3, 1942, Special Section.
40. Margaret Bean, "Keeping Shop for Victory," *Spokesman-Review*, Feb. 14, 1943, Special Section.
41. Ibid., Aug. 7, 1945, p.1; "Keeping Shop for Victory," Ibid., Feb. 14, 1943, Special Section.
42. W.W. Hindley, "Home Front Is Throughly Organized," Ibid., May 3, 1942.
43. Ibid., Oct. 25, 1942, p.11.
44. W.W. Hindley, "Home Front Is Throughly Organized," Ibid., May 3, 1942.
45. Ibid.
46. Cheney Cowles Museum picture, Riverside-West-700-(Wall to Post) Cresent Interior
47. Ibid., 600 W. Riverside.
48. Ibid.
49. "War Memorial Uprooted by All-Vets' Council," *Spokesman-Review*, Oct. 29, 1952.
50. *Spokane Daily Chronicle*, May 23, 1942, p.5.
51. M.B., "They Have Pride in Their Work," *Spokesman-Review*, Feb. 1, 1948, Magazine Section, p.2.
52. Edward R. Murrow, Fred W. Friendly, "First Bulletin of Japanese Surrender," *I Can Hear It Now*, Columbia Masterworks Records, 1948, Side Ten.
53. *Spokesman-Review*, Aug. 15, 1945, pp.1,2.
54. Ibid., May 13, 1947, p.1
55. Ibid., April 18, 1947, p.6.
56. *Spokane Daily Chronicle*, Jan. 23, 1979, p.1.
57. "Slots Illegal, State's High Court Says; Rehearing Eyed," *Spokesman-Review*, Sept. 3, 1952.
58. "Eight Northtown Stores To Open," Dec. 8, 1954, Vertical Files, Northwest Room, Spokane Public Library.

BIBLIOGRAPHY:

Alexander, Phil, Chairman of the Golden Jubilee Historical Spectacle, Spokane Chamber of Commerce, letter to Prospective Committee Members, Golden Jubilee Celebration, March 20, 1939.

Blewett, Steve. *A History of the Washington Water Power Company, 1889-1989*. Spokane: Washington Water Power Company, 1989.

Brookes-Miller, Christopher S., *Davenport, Creation Damnation and Problems of Resurrection, 1890-1990*, Washington State University, 1990.

Campbell, Claude A., *The Old National Bank of Spokane*, Reprinted from *Research Studies of The State College of Washington*, Vol. XVII, 1949.

Compau, Nancy Gale, Oral History Interview, Dec. 1990, Canterbury Court, Northwest Room, Spokane Public Library.

Davenport Hotel, Spokane, U.S.A. C. W. Hill Printing Co. Spokane, Northwest Room, Spokane Public Library.

Davenport, Louis. "The Pride of an Empire," Spokane: Condensed from a book originally published by E.J. Boxer, 1915, Northwest Room, Spokane Public Library.

Fairchild-Spokane, 1942-1992, 92nd Wing History, 1991.

Glans, Roger E. *United States Naval Training Station, Farragut, Idaho: 1942-1946*. Minneapolis: Farragut Historical Booklet, 1992.

Guthrie, John A. *Wartime Changes In Spokane's Labor Force*, Bulletin No. 1, Pullman, Wa.: The State College of Washington, June, 1944.

Hines, Duncan. *Adventures in Good Eating*. New York, Duncan Hines, Inc., 1938, 1945, 1946, 1947, and 1950 editions.

Hyslop, Robert B. *Spokane's Building Blocks*. Spokane: Standard Blue Print Co., 1983.

Lackman, Ron, "Same Time...Same Station," NY: Facts on Files, Inc., 1996.

"Lincoln Memorial, The..," Brochure, ca. 1930, Vertical Files, Northwest Room, Spokane Public Library.

"Lincoln Memorial Statue Fund Program," Benefit Performance—Dec. 15, 16, 17, 1927, American Theater, Spokane Players' Club, Vertical Files, Northwest Room, Spokane Public Library.

Lufkin, George L., "American Theatre, Spokane, Wash.," Marquee, The Journal of the Theatre Historical Society, Vol. 5—No. 2, Second Quarter, 1973, Vertical Files, Northwest Room, Spokane Public Library.

Lufkin, George L. *Spokane Spectacle*. A Study of Spokane, Washington Theaters Between 1883 and 1983., Shelton, Wa.: Privately published, 1984.

MacDonald, J. Fred., "Don't Touch That Dial," Chicago: Nelson-Hall, Inc., 1979.

Matthews, Henry. "Wedding of Function and Fantasy", *Columbia*, V, 1991.

Matthews, Henry. "The Davenport Hotel, A Year of Hopes and Fears", *Arcade*, X, Feb./Mar., 1991.

McNeil, Alex, "TOTAL TELEVISION, A Comprehensive Guide to Programming from 1948 to the Present," Third Edition, Penguin Books, N.Y., 1980, revised 1984 and 1991.

Motor Coach Age, Spokane United Railways, West Trenton, New Jersey, Motor Bus Society, Inc., XLI, 1989.

Murrow, Edward R., Friendly, Fred W., "First Bulletin of Japanese Surrender," *I Can Hear It Now...*, Columbia Materworks Records, 1948.

Mutschler, Chas. *Spokane's Street Railways*, Spokane: Inland Empire Railway Historical Society, 1987.

Otto, Florence B. *Wartime History, United States Naval Supply Depot*, Spokane, Washington, 1944.

Pacific Northwesterner, The, Westerners, Spokane Corral, Vol. 35, No. 1, 1991,

Partlow, Carl, and Jorgenson, Thorwald, *The Early Days of Spokane Broadcasting*, Privately Published, Spokane, undated, Vertical Files, Northwest Room, Spokane Public Library.

Pehrson, Gustav A. Scrapbook, Northwest Room, Spokane Public Library.

Presenting Spokane's Pioneer Station, KXLY, National Radio Personalities, Peoria, Ill., 1948, Unpaginated, Vertical Files, Northwest Room, Spokane Public Library.

Polk's Spokane City Directory. Spokane: R.L. Polk and Co., 1892-1997.

Population 1880 to 1980, Report no. 10, City Plan Commission, Spokane, Sept. 1963, Vertical Files, Northwest Room, Spokane Public Library.

Pratt, Orville C. *Story of Spokane*. Original unpublished manuscript, 1948. Northwest Room, Spokane Public Library.

"Romance of Our Lincoln Memorial, The," Citizens' Emergency Committee for Spokane's Lincoln Memorial, Samuel P. Weaver, Chairman, ca. 1924, Vertical Files, Northwest Room, Spokane Public Library.

Ryker, Lois V. *Brief History of the Spokane United Railways*, April 13, 1981, Vertical Files, Northwest Room, Spokane Public Library.

Sanborn Maps of Spokane, Washington, Northwest Room, Spokane Public Library.

Schoenberg, S.J. *Gonzaga University, Seventy-five Years, 1887-1962*, Spokane: Gonzaga University, 1963.

Sons and Daughters of Pioneers Scrapbook. 1934-42, Northwest Room, Spokane Public Library.

Spokane Daily Chronicle, Spokane, Washington.

Spokane Lilac Festival, 1938-1994, Spokane Lilac Festival Association, 1994.

Spokane Telephone Directories, The Pacific Telephone and Telegraph Company, 1925-1955

Spokesman-Review, Spokane, Washington.

Stimson, William. *A View of the Falls, An Illustrated History of Spokane*. Northridge, CA.: Windsor Publications, 1985.

Travo Family Scrapbook, Courtesy of Della Travo.

Variety Radio Directory, Vol. IV, 1940-41, Vertical Files, Northwest Room, Spokane Public Library.

Brief History of Liquor Control in Washington State, Washington State Liquor Control Board.

Washington Stations Listing, 1940-1941, Vertical Files, Northwest Room, Spokane Public Library.